WHAT JESUS DID

365
Devotionals
From the Gospel of *John*

LEAFWOOD
PUBLISHERS

What Jesus Did
365 Devotionals from the Gospel of John
Published by Leafwood Publishers

Copyright 2006 by Phil Ware

ISBN 0-9767790-5-6
Printed in the United States of America
Cover design by Mark Decker, Moe Studio

Scripture quotations are from the Holy Bible: Easy-to-Read Version (Revised Edition)
copyright C 2005 by the World Bible Translation Center, Inc. and used by permission.
www.wbtc.org

For information:
Leafwood Publishers, Abilene, Texas
1-877-816-4455 toll free
Visit our website: www.leafwoodpublishers.com

06 07 08 09 10 / 7 6 5 4 3 2 1

FOR DONNA
my precious wife and partner in life, in love, and in ministry.

ACKNOWLEDGEMENTS

What Jesus Did! has been part of a decade long journey of sharing devotional thoughts on the web through www.heartlight.org. This journey would not have been possible without the patient understanding, sacrifices, and encouragement of my family. Thank you Donna, Megan, Zach and Mandy. The journey would not have begun without the clear call of God and my partnership with Paul Lee. Thank you Paul for the commitment to set sail on this wild adventure as we learned to trust the Father to make us more than what we really are. The journey would not have been funded without the loving support of thousands of readers and the encouragement of our friends and family at the Westover Hills Church in Austin, Texas, and the Southern Hills Church in Abilene. The journey would have been greatly diminished without the help of two incredibly precious proofreaders and friends, Ray Butts and Ed Holley. These two have generously donated their time and insight, without which the whole web enterprise would have been greatly diminished by my own inadequacies. My thanks to each and every one of you who have helped with the journey!

When we began this journey in 1996, the web was new and we were ignorant. God, faithful as He has been forever, was always faithful. He took two novices, called us to the wide-open range of the Internet and blessed us beyond our ability and our dreams. Without God's grace, these five loaves and two fishes would have remained a simple picnic. Why He chose to bless them is just another one of those mysteries of grace. What began as a few articles and letting folks read my daily devotionals over my shoulder has turned into a ministry reaching more than half a million users per month in more than 175 countries. They have shaped these devotionals through their questions, gentle criticisms, and consistent encouragement.

I have used the Easy to Read Version of the Bible prepared by the World Bible Translation Center of Fort Worth, Texas. The **ERV** was chosen because of its simple language which fits well with the format of daily devotional readings. We appreciate the cooperation of the World Bible Translation Center in this effort.

Finally, thanks to Leonard Allen and the folks at Leafwood Publishers for deciding to put this material into print. Many of us who spend so much time on the web still find our lives enriched by holding a book and pondering God's grace as we turn real pages that can be turned, dog-eared, and marked.

Phil Ware

INTRODUCTION

In the great Exodus story of deliverance, God came to Moses in the burning bush on the Great Mountain in the desert. He told Moses, "I have seen the troubles my people have suffered...And I have heard their cries...I know about their pain. Now I will go down and save my people...So now I am sending you..." (Exodus 3:7-8)

The Gospel of John picks up this same theme of God's compassionate concern and great deliverance. Only this time, when God says, "Now I will go down and save my people," he doesn't send Moses or a prophet or another kind of messenger. No, this time God comes himself. "We saw his glory!" says the follower that Jesus loved. "The only Son (Jesus) is God....And the Son has shown us what God is like," John declares. We live on the visited planet.

As we begin our daily journey through the remarkable Gospel of John, we can be sure of one thing: God has left footprints of heaven's grace in the soil of our wounded world. These are the footprints of Jesus of Nazareth, the one who we believe is the Son of God and our Savior.

The Gospel of John goes to great lengths to help us understand that Jesus is God living among us. The "follower that Jesus loved"—who is traditionally identified as John the Apostle—makes clear that God has walked among us in Jesus. Through the "I am" statements, Jesus claims to be the covenant God of Israel, living among God's people. Through Jesus' actions and words at the great Jewish festivals, God's Son fills up the meaning of God's great promises and Israel's great celebrations. Through his power to heal and raise the dead, the Son does the work of God on earth. Through the many different titles and names given Jesus, the Gospel of John makes clear that God has walked among us as Jesus of Nazareth, the Messiah and Son of God.

So, dear reader, my prayer is that as you daily come to John's well of blessing and grace, you will look for God's footprints and listen for your Shepherd's voice. If you do, I trust that you will not only find that God has left his footprints on our world, but also on your heart. And when he touches your heart, may you fall at Jesus' feet and proclaim, "My Lord and God."

By God's grace,

Phil Ware

Day: 1

THE MESSAGE THAT WAS THERE ALL ALONG

JOHN 1:1

*Before the world began, the Word was there. The Word was with God,
and the Word was God.*

REFLECTION:

What a strange way to begin a story: "God's message existed before anything else existed." But it's true, because that message is Jesus! When God wanted to tell human beings about himself, when he wanted to give them good news about salvation, when he wanted to give them a message about his love for them, he sent Jesus. Jesus is God's Message. And this Message was with God all along. In fact, he was by very nature God. Jesus is God come to us as Savior, in human flesh. He is God with us, the Messenger of all messengers and the Message of all messages.

PRAYER:

*Thank you, Father in heaven, for giving me a message that I can understand. Thank you
for giving me a message that I can see in action. Thank you for Jesus and all he is to me.
Thank you for your message of love, salvation, and grace.
In Jesus' name. Amen.*

CONTEXT: JOHN 1:1-18

RELATED REFERENCES: COLOSSIANS 1:15-17; TITUS 2:13-14; 1 JOHN 1:1

Day: 2
HE CREATED EVEN YOU AND ME!

JOHN 1:2-3
*He was there with God in the beginning. Everything was made through him,
and nothing was made without him.*

REFLECTION:
What you see in creation that is beautiful, what you find marvelous in nature,
and what astounds and bewilders you in our universe came into existence
through the one who allowed himself to be born as a human baby and placed
in a manger. His fingerprints are on all of creation. His power gave birth to the
universe and his ongoing word sustains it. Ponder that last phrase and then
realize both the enormity and the personal connection of it; the Word, Jesus,
God come in human flesh, made everything in the universe...including you and
me! He is great, awesome, beyond description and yet he made you and me! He
is powerful, yet cares enough for us to come to earth and die for us. The Creator
is also the one about whom we sing: "Jesus loves me this I know...."

PRAYER:
*Precious Jesus, thank you for knowing me and caring for me. You know my flaws, yet you
died to redeem me from them. I know you made me special to do specific things for your
Kingdom, so please help me to identify those things and fulfill your purposes for my life.
Father God, please accept my undying gratitude and praise for your plan and the love that
sent Jesus to earth for me. I offer these words of thanks in the name of Jesus,
heaven's message and my Creator. Amen.*

CONTEXT: JOHN 1:1-18

RELATED REFERENCES: 1 CORINTHIANS 8:6; HEBREWS 1:2; COLOSSIANS 3:10-11

Day: 3

LIFE THAT IS SHARED

JOHN 1:4

In him there was life, and that life was a light for the people of the world.

REFLECTION:

Often people want to sell us some formula, vitamin, exercise plan, marketing strategy, or business opportunity that will enhance our lives. Our email boxes are filled with spam about the newest, latest, and greatest ways to enrich our lives. The Bible offers one way to find life—not a few ways, just one way. This way to life is not a plan or a product; no, the only real way to life is a person—Jesus, God's living Word who took on human flesh! This Life, however, is not something we have to earn or pay someone else to receive. Instead, this Life was gladly willing to share everything that he has and is and will be. This Life gives light. It shares grace and glory for our gain. And the offer? Well, it's not to a select few, but is for everyone. So the real question for us today is pretty simple: "Have I found life in Jesus?" If we answer yes, then the second question is, "Am I sharing that life with others?"

PRAYER:

Father, thank you! You gave me your precious life through Jesus. As I receive the blessing of his light, help me to share that light and Life with others who do not know you or your Son. Bless me especially, O LORD, as I try to reach out to _____. Forgive me for those times when I have been timid or reluctant to share that grace with others.
In Jesus' name I pray. Amen.

CONTEXT: JOHN 1:1-18

RELATED REFERENCES: JOHN 14:6; JOHN 8:12; 1 JOHN 5:11

Day: 4

THIS LIGHT KEEPS SHINING

JOHN 1:5
The light shines in the darkness, and the darkness has not defeated it.

REFLECTION:

Lights go out! That's just part of Murphy's Law of lights. Sooner or later, and usually at the worst possible moment, our precious source of light will go out. That's true of all lights—except one! Jesus. He is the Light that keeps shining. Evil, Satan, and the forces of darkness can't snuff it out, hide its radiance, or fathom its power and grace. This Light keeps shining. Nothing can stop it. No one can put it out. No darkness can defeat it. So why not walk in this Light and find your life in the radiance of its glow?

PRAYER:

Father, forgive me for the times I strayed away from your will. I know that on each of those occasions I pushed Jesus and the light of his grace and truth away from me. Forgive me for not living my life in the light of Jesus, seeking his truth, and wanting his will to guide my steps. In Jesus' name I pray. Amen.

CONTEXT: JOHN 1:1-18

RELATED REFERENCES: 1 PETER 2:9; JOHN 3:18-21; MATTHEW 4:14-16

Day: 5
PREPARING THE WAY

JOHN 1:6-7
There was a man named John, who was sent by God. He came to tell people about the light. Through him all people could hear about the light and believe.

REFLECTION:
For most of us to hear the message of Christ, there had to be a John! Who was your John? Who prepared the soil of your heart to receive the Good News? Who taught you the truth of God and called you to repentance and excited expectation about what God would do in you through his Son Jesus and the powerful Holy Spirit? Why not take some time today to write that person a thank you note? Why not make a renewed commitment today to be "John" for someone else who needs to know the Savior?

PRAYER:
Father, thank you so much for the following people who helped prepare my heart to receive the message of Jesus:_____. Please bless my efforts at sharing this same message with others. In Jesus' name I thank you. Amen.

CONTEXT: JOHN 1:1-18

RELATED REFERENCES: MATTHEW 3:1-6; JOHN 5:31-33; MATTHEW 11:1

Day: 6

WITNESS TO THE LIGHT AND EXAMPLE TO ME

JOHN 1:8
John was not the light. But he came to tell people about the light.

REFLECTION:

John the Baptist was an incredible man. He was a prophet, inspired by God's Spirit. He spoke with an authority and authenticity that had been long silent among God's people. He courageously declared the truth to everyone no matter that person's rank and no matter his own personal cost.

However, John was only a witness to God's Light. As important as John may have been, his importance was as a servant to the Light—God's real Message and only Son. John freely testified to this. He knew his role. He refused to be a point of contention. He is a great example to us of what we can and should be to our loved ones and friends—a witness, someone who points others to the truth and light of Jesus.

PRAYER:

Thank you, Heavenly Father, for John the Baptist. Thank you for such a powerful example and such a wonderful person of integrity. Please use me to point those in my influence to the truth about Jesus as I seek to live with integrity before them.
In the name of the Lord Jesus I pray. Amen.

CONTEXT: JOHN 1:1-18

RELATED REFERENCES: JOHN 3:26-30; JOHN 1:29; MARK 1:1-4

Day: 7

LIGHT FOR EVERYONE

JOHN 1:9

The true light was coming into the world. This is the true light that gives light to all people.

REFLECTION:

John wasn't the Light. No, the True Light was going to come for everyone. He wasn't just sent to prepare Israel for the Messiah. He wasn't just going to set up his ministry in the desert and have people come to him. The True Light was coming into the world to save the entire world. He was going to shine for all people: men and women, slaves and free, Jew and Gentile (Gal. 3:26-29).

Since Jesus is the true Light, since he died for our sins and saved us, and since we are his followers, we need to ask ourselves one crucial question: "What are we—what am I—doing to make sure that everyone gets to know Jesus, God's true Light for everyone?" Let's be a part of letting the world know that God sent his Son to save them (John 3:16-17).

PRAYER:

O Father, give me a bigger heart for those whom I don't know. Use me to share Jesus with those outside my cultural comfort zone. Give me a greater sensitivity to those around me so that they can experience your love and welcoming grace because of the way I treat them. In Jesus' name I pray. Amen.

CONTEXT: JOHN 1:1-18

RELATED REFERENCES: JOHN 8:12; 1 PETER 2:9; 2 CORINTHIANS 4:4

Day: 8

REJECTED!

JOHN 1:10-11

The Word was already in the world. The world was made through him, but the world did not know him. He came to the world that was his own. And his own people did not accept him.

REFLECTION:

Jesus made everything in the universe, including the earth and all its peoples. Yet when Jesus came to his very own chosen people, they did not accept him. Think a minute about what that means for us when we feel alone, deserted, misunderstood, forgotten, or abused.

We DO have a Savior who knows how badly it hurts to be rejected by those we love. He's experienced it. He knows what it is like to be spurned by one we treasure. He felt it repeatedly. He knows what it is like to be despised by those for whom we have made major sacrifices. So when we have those overwhelming times of heartbreak, we can go to him knowing that a caring friend who has been there will hear us, minister to our needs, and listen to our cries.

PRAYER:

Father, I hate that Jesus had to bear the pain of being rejected by those he loved, by those who watched him grow up, and by those for whom he sacrificed so much. However, dear Father, it gives me great comfort to know that he has experienced those losses and empathizes with me when I feel down, forgotten, abandoned, and forsaken. I know I can come to you and receive grace to help me in my time of hurt and need. Thank you for being so intimately involved in this world. In Jesus' name I pray. Amen.

CONTEXT: JOHN 1:1-18

RELATED REFERENCES: MARK 3:20-22; LUKE 4:23-24, 29-30; JOHN 7:2-5

Day: 9
REBORN!

JOHN 1:12-13

But some people did accept him. They believed in him, and he gave them the right to become children of God. They became God's children, but not in the way babies are usually born. It was not because of any human desire or plan. They were born from God himself.

REFLECTION:

Not everyone rejected Jesus. In fact, everyone who believed in him and accepted him was given an incredible gift: they were made children of God! The blessing of this special gift is something that God alone could give us. It is not something we could achieve or accomplish. It is also something about which Jesus and John will have more to say.

Today, however, think about what it means to be God's child. Our Father painted the sunrise and will display his artistry once again at sunset. He set the boundaries of the universe, which we cannot begin to see. He is the greatest Father anyone could ever have, and he chose us to be his children!

Our adoption into the Father's family is something God did for us. We couldn't accomplish this any more than a baby can accomplish his or her own conception and birth. We are God's children because of his love, grace, and sacrifice. In fact, Jesus came as the Father's Message of sacrificial love and grace so that we can be children born of God!

PRAYER:

Expand my heart, O God, so that I can better show my love and appreciation to you for adopting me into your family. Open my mind, dear Father, so that I can understand more of your grace and mercy given to me through Jesus. I praise you and thank you for making me your child! In the name of my brother and Savior, Jesus Christ my Lord, I pray. Amen.

CONTEXT: JOHN 1:1-18

RELATED REFERENCES: JOHN 3:3-7; ACTS 16:30-33; 1 JOHN 5:1

Day: 10

JESUS IS GOD COME NEAR

JOHN 1:14

The Word became a man and lived among us. We saw his divine greatness—the greatness that belongs to the only Son of the Father. The Word was full of grace and truth.

REFLECTION:

God was not content to proclaim his Message. God wasn't satisfied that prophets could reveal his Message. God wasn't willing that his Message be confined to a book. No, God's message was found in Jesus—God came in human flesh to live as one of us. This made grace accessible, touchable, and available to human eyes. Yet even in human skin and burdened with human mortality, God's glory could not be hidden. Grace and truth are revealed in Jesus. God comes near. God becomes touchable. God's message becomes real. In Jesus, God leaves footprints of heaven's grace in our mortal soil.

PRAYER:

Holy and loving God, my Abba Father, thank you for the Scriptures, the prophets, the scribes, and the scholars. Thank you most of all for Jesus, who is your Word in human skin. Thank you for coming to my world and showing me how to live and how much you love me. As I journey daily through the Gospel of John, please make your presence and your will known to me as I get to know your Son better. In Jesus' name I offer my thanks and request this grace. Amen.

CONTEXT: JOHN 1:1-18

RELATED REFERENCES: HEBREWS 1:1-3; 2 TIMOTHY 3:14-15; 2 CORINTHIANS 1:20

Day: 11

JOHN'S ONE THING

JOHN 1:15

John told people about him. He said loudly, "This is the one I was talking about when I said, 'The one who is coming after me is greater than I am, because he was living before I was even born.'"

REFLECTION:

John was courageous. John was passionate. John was also just a "pointer." He knew that whatever he did or however important others may have viewed him, God had sent him to earth with one primary job: tell others about Jesus. It is clear that John did this with exuberance. What is your "one" thing you need to do most in life?

PRAYER:

Father, please help me find my role like John did. Please help me to identify what you made me to do and then to find great delight in doing it.
In Jesus' name I pray. Amen.

CONTEXT: JOHN 1:1-18

RELATED REFERENCES: COLOSSIANS 1:15-18; JOHN 8:57-59; JOHN 1:29-31

Day: 12

GRACE UPON GRACE

JOHN 1:16-17

Yes, the Word was full of grace and truth, and from him we all received one blessing after another. That is, the law was given to us through Moses, but grace and truth came through Jesus Christ.

REFLECTION:

Rich blessings, grace, mercy, unfailing kindness, and faithfulness ... the list could go on and on. God's blessings to us in Jesus are beyond our scope of imagining. As wonderful as the work of Moses had been for Israel, as defining as the Torah (the Law that Moses was given by God) was for humankind, Jesus is greater still. He brings grace and truth, love and faithfulness, and God's full salvation! Cherish the work of those great heroes of Scripture. Learn, memorize, and use the Scriptures to teach yourself God's will. But most of all, see Jesus as God's greatest message sent to teach and demonstrate to us God's grace, love, and faithfulness.

PRAYER:

Loving and Holy Father, thank you for your incomparable greatness and your incredible graciousness. Forgive my selfish and forgetful heart for not being full of joy and apprecia-tion for the blessings you lavish upon me daily. Most of all, dear Father, help me to see Jesus as the complete embodiment of your truth and grace.
In the name of Jesus, your Son, I pray. Amen.

CONTEXT: JOHN 1:1-18

RELATED REFERENCES: 2 JOHN 3; EPHESIANS 2:8-10; COLOSSIANS 1:19-20

Day: 13

GOD REVEALED!

JOHN 1:18

No one has ever seen God. The only Son is the one who has shown us what God is like. He is himself God and is very close to the Father.

REFLECTION:

God the Father is much too holy to be seen by human eyes. An encounter with the Holy God of Israel was beyond the scope of human capability. Jesus, however, was God come in human flesh, Immanuel, or God with us (Matthew 1:23). So Jesus did much more than tell us about God. He revealed God. Jesus is God revealed. In his touch of the leper, in his raising of Lazarus, in his healing of the blind, in his feeding of the 5,000, we see God at work and God in love with his human creation. Jesus is the great reminder that God wanted not only to know us, but he also wanted to be known by us. So as John finishes his beautiful prologue, please hear his invitation to come see what Jesus did and know this is God at work, God in ministry, and God offering us his love.

PRAYER:

Holy and righteous Father, thank you for wanting to make yourself known to me. Open the eyes of my heart Lord, and in Jesus' ministry help me fully see you, your love for me, and your call upon my life. I pray this in the name of Jesus, Immanuel. Amen.

CONTEXT: JOHN 1:1-18

RELATED REFERENCES: HEBREWS 1:3; JOHN 14:8-11; 1 JOHN 5:20

Day: 14
FLATLY DENIED

JOHN 1:19-21

The Jewish leaders in Jerusalem sent some priests and Levites to John to ask him, "Who are you?" He told them the truth. Without any hesitation he said openly and plainly, "I am not the Christ." They asked him, "Then who are you? Are you Elijah?" He answered, "No, I am not Elijah." They asked, "Are you the Prophet?" He answered, "No, I am not the Prophet."

REFLECTION:

Who are you? What would you do to be viewed as important and significant by others? How much does your acceptance by others matter? I don't know about you, but these are convicting questions for many people. Most of us are not happy just being the shadow of someone important. We want to be viewed as significant.

John the Baptist, however, lived a life of importance because he let God determine his role. He realized his value was based upon living out what God wanted him to do and not being valued by the world. That meant denying the rumors about himself. That meant pointing others away from following him. That meant sending his closest followers to someone else. It meant flatly denying that he was the star. It also meant that God was pleased. "Well done, good and faithful servant!" May this also be true of us!

PRAYER:

Almighty God, I ask that you make my role in your Kingdom clear. I want not only to be faithful, but I also want to be fruitful. Please show me where you want me to serve and empower me to serve with a heart of humility and grace. My prayer is that you will be glorified in my life and that I will be found faithful in your sight. In Jesus' name I humbly ask this. Amen.

CONTEXT: JOHN 1:19-34

RELATED REFERENCES: JOHN 7:18; JOHN 12:42-43; GALATIANS 1:10

Day: 15

POINTING THE WAY, CLEARING THE PATH

JOHN 1:22-23

Then they said, "Who are you? Tell us about yourself. Give us an answer to tell the people who sent us. What do you say about yourself?" John told them the words of the prophet Isaiah: "I am the voice of someone shouting in the desert: 'Make a straight road ready for the Lord.'"

REFLECTION:

John let the questioners know that his identity was not the issue; the one about whom he spoke was the important issue. Yes, John's coming was an answer to prophecy. Yes, John's ministry was powerful and touched many people. Yes, John's work changed untold number of lives. Yes, John's presence was a signal about God's coming Kingdom. John, however, always kept his role in perspective: "I'm here to point the way to the Messiah. My role is to clear the path for people to find the Lord."

No matter what our gifts may be, no matter what talents God has given to us, each of us in our own way is called to follow John's example. We have been put into a circle of friends, family, and acquaintances to point the way to the Messiah and clear a path for those we know to find the Lord.

PRAYER:

Precious and loving Father, King of the ages and LORD of my heart, please use me to bring others to know Jesus as their Savior and Lord. I especially ask that you will give me wisdom as I seek to be a faithful witness to your Son's grace with the following people: _____. In the mighty name of Jesus I pray. Amen.

CONTEXT: JOHN 1:19-34

RELATED REFERENCES: 1 PETER 3:15-17; 1 CORINTHIANS 3:5-9; ACTS 8:1-4

Day: 16
WHAT RIGHT?

JOHN 1:24-25
These Jews were sent from the Pharisees. They said to John,
"You say you are not the Christ. You say you are not Elijah or the Prophet.
Then why do you baptize people?"

REFLECTION:

What right do you have to do what you do? Good question for those of us who are blessed with freedom. We take our right to do what we do for granted. Behind this question, however, stands a powerful truth: we only have the right to do what we do because God in his grace has granted us that right.

John did what he did because God had called him to the task. John had the opportunities he had because God opened the doors for them. John had the effective ministry he had because he did what God wanted him to do. John's right to baptize, preach, teach, and prepare were given to him by God. More than just the right to do it, he had the authority of God to do it.

God has great plans for us. He calls us to his purposes. He has given us the right as his children to bring light to this dark world. Let's use those rights to our Father's glory!

PRAYER:

Father, thank you for giving me the right to be your child. Inspire me to bold and courageous living for the sake of the Kingdom and the cause of the Gospel. Please give me a heart as fearless and true as your great servant John the Baptist.
In Jesus' name I offer you my prayer. Amen.

CONTEXT: JOHN 1:19-34

RELATED REFERENCES: JOHN 1:12; 1 PETER 2:9-10; PSALM 139:16

Day: 17

REAL PLACES, REAL PEOPLE, REAL JESUS

JOHN 1:26-28

John answered, "I baptize people with water. But there is someone here with you that you don't know. He is the one who is coming later. I am not good enough to be the slave who unties the strings on his sandals." These things all happened at Bethany on the other side of the Jordan River. This is where John was baptizing people.

REFLECTION:

"Long ago in a galaxy far far away...." If we are not careful, we can find ourselves looking at the story of Jesus like we view an epic movie or a work of good fiction. John wants us to know that his story about Jesus is more than just a good tale. This is a story about real places, real people, and a real Savior.

There was real water for baptism. There was a real city around which John's ministry took place. There were real, everyday people who came to this place along the Jordan River to open their hearts to the Kingdom of God.

John reminds both them and us, that there will be a real Savior on the scene soon. God will walk among us in Jesus. He will get the dust of their streets on his feet. This One is so great that John declares "I am not good enough" to do the most menial work of a slave—kneel down, unlatch his sandals, and clean his feet. Look at John and you will see dirt, sweat, feet, sandals, rivers, people, cities, crowds...real people and real Jesus!

PRAYER:

O what wondrous love you've shown, O God, by sending your perfect Son to live in my imperfect world. O what wondrous grace you've given, dear Father, when you allowed yourself to be soiled by the dust of my existence so that I could live for the praise of your glory. I praise you, I thank you, and I love you in Jesus' name. Amen.

CONTEXT: JOHN 1:19-34

RELATED REFERENCES: JOHN 3:16-17; PHILIPPIANS 2:5-11; MATTHEW 3:13-14

Day: 18

LAMB OF GOD FOR THE WORLD

JOHN 1:29

*The next day John saw Jesus coming toward him and said, "Look,
the Lamb of God. He takes away the sins of the world!"*

REFLECTION:

Animal sacrifice seems so foreign, maybe even cruel, in our day. Yet it was God's way of helping people know that their sin was costly, injurious, and serious. Their sin didn't just impact them, but it touched all they influenced and damaged their relationship with God. Taking a lamb from their flock, which was precious to them and of great value, cost them, hurt them, and opened their eyes to the seriousness of their rebellion and failure.

However, when it came time for God to redeem us, to deal with our sin once and for all, he didn't ask us to offer something that cost us greatly. No, he furnished the sacrifice at great cost to himself. That Lamb of God and sacrifice for our sins is Jesus.

John's words remind us that from the beginning of his ministry, Jesus was God's Lamb. He came to save, redeem, and ransom us from sin. He is the Lamb of God. So at the beginning of Jesus' ministry, John the Baptist's words invite us to "Look!" and see the "Lamb of God. He takes away the sins of the world." If we watch, listen, and open our hearts, we will see that Lamb and rejoice that God in his grace would suffer the cost and endure the injury to deal with the seriousness of our sin.

PRAYER:

*Father, thank you for providing the sacrifice that paid for my sins. Give me a deeper sense
of sorrow for my sin and a deeper sense of wonder for your grace that provided such a
sacrifice. To you belongs all thanks, honor, and praise, now and forevermore,
in the name of Jesus. Amen.*

CONTEXT: JOHN 1:19-34

RELATED REFERENCES: 1 JOHN 2:1-2; 1 PETER 1:18-21; REVELATION 7:10

Day: 19
HE IS GREATER BY FAR

JOHN 1:30

"This is the one I was talking about when I said, 'There is a man coming after me who is greater than I am, because he was living even before I was born.'"

REFLECTION:

Sounds kind of like a broken record. But John the Baptist stays on message even though others continue to pelt him with questions. It's similar to the way the press hounds stars and politicians today, hoping they will make a mistake or reveal an ugly ego in reaction to their constant badgering.

John, however, will not falter or fail. He remains faithful and true to his task of pointing other genuine seekers to Jesus. He praises Jesus' greatness and trumpets the need of all people to repent. He tries to prepare hearts for the Kingdom of God. John shows us faithfulness over the long haul—faithfulness to God, faithfulness to the truth, faithfulness to his mission, and faithfulness to the Lord and his Kingdom. May such faithfulness be ours!

PRAYER:

Father, forgive me for my times of unfaithfulness. Renew a steadfast spirit in me and rekindle my resolve to live for Jesus faithfully throughout all of my days. In Jesus' name I ask this. Amen.

CONTEXT: JOHN 1:19-34

RELATED REFERENCES: 2 CORINTHIANS 4:5-7; LUKE 3:15-16; JOHN 1:15

Day: 20

HE IS THE ONE

JOHN 1:31-33

"Even I did not know who he was. But I came baptizing people with water so that Israel (the Jews) could know that Jesus is the Christ." Then John said, "I also did not know who the Christ was. But God sent me to baptize people with water. And God told me, 'You will see the Spirit come down and rest on a man. That man is the One who will baptize with the Holy Spirit.'" John said, "I have seen this happen. I saw the Spirit come down from heaven. The Spirit looked like a dove and sat on him (Jesus)."

REFLECTION:

Isn't it interesting how hard it is for us to see some things because we are too familiar with them? Jesus' brothers and sisters didn't recognize him as God's Son until after his resurrection. The people in his village didn't expect anything of importance from him. They missed who Jesus was!

Yet we are promised that if we seek him, we will find him. If we look at his teaching, we can determine if he comes from God. If we open the door to him, he will come in and share our life. If we obey him, he will come and make his home with us. If we receive him, we can be born into the Kingdom of God.

So the test for us is pretty simple: do I seek Jesus or am I seeking something else—a teaching, a doctrine, or a religion? If we seek the latter things, we can know a lot about Jesus, without really knowing HIM. So let's seek Jesus and his new way of life in the Spirit! As we daily journey through the Gospel of John together, let's always ask God to show us Jesus more clearly.

PRAYER:

Father, help me know Jesus more powerfully and more fully as I study his life and seek to reflect his character in my daily life. Please show yourself to me in Jesus, just as you promised. Open my eyes so that I can see your work more clearly in my life and praise you more fully with my heart. Jesus, please let me come to know you and not just know about you. In your precious name, my Lord and Christ, I pray. Amen.

CONTEXT: JOHN 1:19-34

RELATED REFERENCES: JOHN 7:1-5, 16-17; JOHN 1:10-13; JOHN 5:39-40

Day: 21
HE IS THE SON OF GOD

JOHN 1:34
"So this is what I tell people: 'He is the Son of God.'"

REFLECTION:

Our goal as we journey daily through the Gospel of John is to reach this same conviction! We want to know what Jesus did, so that when we reach the end of this journey we can confidently say, "So this is what I tell people: 'He (Jesus) is the Son of God.'"

When we truly realize that Jesus is a man, but more than a man—he is God with us, God's Son—then suddenly everything is different! We realize that the Creator of the universe values us. We realize that we are not a chance distillation of genetic code accidentally appearing after millions of years of random mutations. We are not an infinitesimally small speck of worthless dust in the great expanse of a random and meaningless universe. We are known and loved by God. He sent us his Son to be our brother, Messiah, friend, and Lord so that we can know that we are God's very own children. And when we truly know this, we too, like John, will tell people, "He is the Son of God."

PRAYER:

O God, my heavenly Father, help me better understand what it means for Jesus to be your Son. Strengthen my grip on this conviction and deepen my faith so that I can better tell others of the wonder and grace you have given me by sending your Son to be my Lord and friend. In Jesus' saving name I pray. Amen.

CONTEXT: JOHN 1:19-34

RELATED REFERENCES: MATTHEW 16:13-16; ROMANS 10:9-13; JOHN 3:36 & 20:30-31

Day: 22

THEY FOLLOWED!

JOHN 1:35-37

The next day John was there again and had two of his followers with him.
He saw Jesus walking by and said, "Look, the Lamb of God!"
The two followers heard him say this, so they followed Jesus.

REFLECTION:

John already talked about Jesus being the "Lamb of God. He takes away the sins of the world!" This time, however, his message provokes a response in two of his own followers. They followed Jesus. They shifted their allegiance from the human messenger to the glorious Message. As followers of Jesus, our goal is to resist preacher or teacher infatuation—our faith shouldn't be built on a preacher, a pastor, a teacher, an evangelist—and remember the goal of their ministry: to get people to follow the Son of God. Make sure your faith and hope are tied to Jesus and not to one of his messengers. The glory of any preacher's or teacher's message is Jesus, not that messenger's style or personality. Let's make sure we follow Jesus, for this is the Christian messenger's true glory.

PRAYER:

Father, thank you for those who have powerfully influenced my life toward faith. Your messengers who taught me about Jesus, stirred my heart to faith, and called me to righteousness are precious to me. However, dear Father, please guard me from so valuing your messengers that I forget your Message. By the power of your Holy Spirit, nudge me away from human dependency and help me to follow your Son wholeheartedly. In Jesus' name I live and pray. Amen.

CONTEXT: JOHN 1:35-51

RELATED REFERENCES: ACTS 14:11-15; 1 CORINTHIANS 3:5-9; 2 CORINTHIANS 4:5-7

Day: 23

WHERE ARE YOU STAYING?

JOHN 1:38-39

Jesus turned and saw the two men following him. He asked, "What do you want?" They said, "Rabbi, where are you staying?" ("Rabbi" means "Teacher.") He answered, "Come with me and you will see." So the two men went with him. They saw the place where he was staying, and they stayed there with him that day. It was about four o'clock.

REFLECTION:

"Where are you staying?" could be accurately translated by the slang phrase, "Where are you at, man?" The followers wanted to know where Jesus' heart was and what his life was all about. They wanted to know "what made him tick." They weren't looking to know about his room decor or the layout of his floor plan; they wanted to know if they should give up everything they had and follow him.

Jesus' invitation to these early followers is also an invitation to us. "Come with me and you will see!" Jesus says. "You want to know my heart? You want to know what is important to me? You want to know how I can bless you? Come and see!" Jesus invites us to meet him through the Gospel of John. If you are not sure about Jesus, don't just read books about him. Come read his own story in the Gospels, especially the Gospel of John. He asks us to come, stay awhile with him, and learn from him. He invites us to "come and see!"

PRAYER:

Father, I do want to know Jesus. I want to know his love for me and for all your human family. I want to know his deity and glory. I want to know why he did what he did and why he cares so much for me. Please reveal Jesus to me as I seek to know him better in this journey through the Gospel of John. In Jesus' name I pray. Amen.

CONTEXT: JOHN 1:35-51

RELATED REFERENCES: MARK 1:1; HEBREWS 1:1-3; LUKE 9:23-24 & 14:33

Day: 24

The First Thing!

John 1:40-41

These men followed Jesus after they had heard about him from John. One of them was Andrew, the brother of Simon Peter. The first thing Andrew did was to go and find his brother Simon. Andrew said to him, "We have found the Messiah." ("Messiah" means "Christ.")

Reflection:

Did you notice the first thing Andrew did after learning about Jesus? He searched, found his brother, and told him about finding the Messiah! When we see Andrew in the Gospel of John, he is always bringing others to Jesus. Shouldn't you be an Andrew, too? Who is someone with whom you would like to share Jesus? Why not begin to pray daily that the Lord will open his or her heart and help you see the opportunity to share your faith and Jesus' grace! Let this be the "first thing" you are committed to do in your relationship with this person.

Prayer:

Loving and righteous Father, please bless me as I seek to share Jesus with _____.
Give me wisdom to see your work in their lives, to know the right time for them to hear about Christ, and to have courage to share my faith and your grace with them.
In Jesus' name I pray. Amen.

Context: John 1:35-51

Related References: Matthew 28:18-20; John 6:5-9; John 12:20-23

Day: 25

ROCKY MEETS JESUS

JOHN 1:42

Then Andrew brought Simon to Jesus. Jesus looked at him and said, "You are Simon, the son of John. You will be called Cephas." ("Cephas" means "Peter.")

REFLECTION:

When a new child is born, godly parents stare lovingly at their gift from the Father and wonder, "What will this child grow up to be?" They name the child, usually taking great care not to give that child a name that will be a burden. They want their child to be blessed by God and to be a blessing to others. But they don't know and can't know what lies ahead.

Jesus changed Simon's name to Peter (Cephas), or the Rock. Jesus could look beyond Peter's blustering ego and upcoming horrible failures to the man who loved God and who could be used mightily for the Kingdom.

What does Jesus see in you? No matter where you have been or the road you have taken to this point, Jesus can give you a new life and a new name. He has great plans for you. Don't be dismayed. Don't let discouragement claim you. If he can change Simon into the Rock, he can change you and use you mightily, too!

PRAYER:

Father, please help me trust that you have great plans for me. Please help me catch a glimpse of what you can do with me and through me to bring you glory and bless those I love. In Jesus' name I pray. Amen.

CONTEXT: JOHN 1:35-51

RELATED REFERENCES: 2 CORINTHIANS 5:16-17; PSALM 139:13-16; LUKE 5:8-11

Day: 26

CHALLENGE TO PRACTICALITY

JOHN 1:43

The next day Jesus decided to go to Galilee. He met Philip and said to him, "Follow me."

REFLECTION:

Jesus finds Philip in Galilee. Philip, at his best, is a practical and sensible man. At his worst, Philip is earth-bound and without distinction. Yet Jesus saw something special in Philip. He was of eternal value, just like any other person. However, Jesus also felt Philip had something unique to offer to the work of the Kingdom. So led by God after a night of fervent prayer, (Luke 6:12-17) Jesus selected and designated Philip as one his 12 apostles. When Jesus called him to be his follower, Philip followed immediately.

Like he saw great things in Philip, Jesus obviously sees more in us than others see. He also gives us the opportunity to do the dangerous, awesome, and adventurous—to follow him and to be used by him in mighty ways. Are you ready for adventure? Then come follow Jesus!

PRAYER:

Gracious and Almighty God, forgive me for clinging to my habits, my earthbound forms of security, and my fears about surrendering everything to you. Please inspire me to greater courage to follow Jesus wholeheartedly. In the name of my Lord and Trailblazer I pray. Amen.

CONTEXT: JOHN 1:35-51

RELATED REFERENCES: LUKE 6:12-17; JOHN 6:5-7; HEBREWS 2:10

Day: 27
Anything Good?

John 1:44-46

Philip was from the town of Bethsaida, the same as Andrew and Peter. Philip found Nathanael and told him, "We have found the man that Moses wrote about in the law. The prophets wrote about him too. He is Jesus, the son of Joseph. He is from Nazareth." But Nathanael said to Philip, "Nazareth! Can anything good come from Nazareth?" Philip answered, "Come and see."

Reflection:

"Come and see!" What Christianity has to offer the world that no other religion has is two-fold: 1) a genuine relationship with Jesus, God who walked among us, and 2) grace that makes us acceptable to God rather than having to earn divine approval.

If you really want to decide about Christianity, or you have friends who are wrestling with a similar decision, don't get lost in all the religious debate. Instead, invite them to meet Jesus in the Gospel of John. Several times in the first chapter John calls us to "come and see" Jesus!

Meeting Jesus in John might not answer all of our questions, but it will point us to the only true answer—Jesus! So if you're doubting, if you're frustrated with the mess that organized religion often makes, or if you want to get past the religious hype into the life of God, then accept the invitation to "come and see" who Jesus really is. Begin your own search. See for yourself if "anything good can come from Nazareth"!

Prayer:

O Father, gloriously holy and mighty, thank you for becoming accessible to me through Jesus. I confess that I sometimes struggle with my faith because of all the imperfections in myself, in your people, and in our churches. However, I thank you for Jesus and his grace, which allow me to be your child and know your love even though I am a flawed person living in a flawed world. Please help me to see and know your Son more fully. In Jesus' name, I thank you. Amen.

Context: John 1:35-51

Related References: Matthew 7:7; John 7:17; John 3:16-21

Day: 28
I Could See You!

John 1:47-49

Jesus saw Nathanael coming toward him and said, "This man coming is a true Israelite, one you can trust." Nathanael asked, "How do you know me?" Jesus answered, "I saw you when you were under the fig tree, before Philip told you about me." Then Nathanael said, "Teacher, you are the Son of God. You are the King of Israel."

Reflection:

Jesus knows us. That's because he really knows what is inside our human hearts. That's because he walked among people just like us. That's because he made us and knows our inner being. And, if we are Christians, it's because he lives inside us now.

Jesus, however, doesn't want to know us to condemn us. No, he knows us to help bring about what is for our best, our holiest, and our most beneficial. He takes what is good and makes it better. He takes what is broken and mends it. He takes what is wrong and makes it right. He takes what is sinful and makes it holy.

So let's not hide from him. Instead, let's confess him as our Lord, Savior, Friend, and Teacher. Let's invite the Son of God into our lives to make us all that God wants us to be. After all, he left heaven's glory and suffered the indignities of the cross to redeem us even though he knew all about us—both the good and the bad!

Prayer:

O precious and righteous Father, forgive me for my sin. Search me and purify me from secret sin. Redeem my heart and purify my desires. I not only confess that Jesus is your Son; I also want him to transform my life. I make this request in his precious name. Amen.

Context: John 1:35-51

Related References: Psalm 139:1, 23-24; Hebrews 4:14-16; John 2:23-25

Day: 29
THE WINDOW TO HEAVEN

JOHN 1:50-51

Jesus said to him, "Do you believe this just because I said I saw you under the fig tree? You will see much greater things than that!" Then he said, "Believe me when I say that you will all see heaven open. You will see 'angels of God going up and coming down' on the Son of Man."

REFLECTION:

Jesus will fulfill and surpass many metaphors, images, and rituals from Israel's rich history. John will show us how Jesus is the great "I Am." He fulfills the meaning of many of the great Jewish feasts. Jesus is the Bread of Life, the true Vine, the Water of Life, the Good Shepherd—each image rich in emotion and meaning from Israel's past. Jesus is challenging Nathaniel to look beyond Jesus' power to know what was in his heart. Jesus wants to lead Nathaniel to see greater things. He wants Nathaniel to know that when he is around Jesus, he is looking through the window into heaven.

Jesus' invitation is not just limited to Nathanael. It is our invitation, too. If we believe in Jesus, we will see greater things. We will be able to look through heaven's window and see the very presence of God.

PRAYER:

Father, please help me see you, know you, and love you more perfectly as Jesus teaches me more about you. In your Son's name I pray. Amen.

CONTEXT: JOHN 1:35-51

RELATED REFERENCES: GENESIS 28:12-17; JOHN 1:14-15, 18; JOHN 2:19-22

Day: 30
GUESS WHO CAME TO THE WEDDING?

JOHN 2:1-2
Two days later there was a wedding in the town of Cana in Galilee, and Jesus' mother was there. Jesus and his followers were also invited.

REFLECTION:

While we often fail to realize it, God is always present. He joins us in our everyday lives and accompanies us on all of our daily wanderings. He is with us every step of the way.

Jesus reminds us of this truth in his ministry when he goes to fancy events at important times and when he meets the most forgotten people in the most out-of-the-way places.

John wants us to know that Jesus joins us in the highs and lows of all of life to get us to the ultimate high: to show us the glory of God and bring us home to our heavenly Father.

We shouldn't be surprised that Jesus and his followers joined in the celebration of a local wedding. Jesus entered all of life to enjoy it, to bless it, to help others catch a glimpse of God's glory. So let's not just look for the Lord's presence in the places we normally view as holy places; let's also seek his presence in the routine, the mundane, the forgettable, and the everyday events of life.

PRAYER:

Father, please help me see your presence in the things that I do—even in the boring, mundane, and routine activities of my life. Give others a glimpse of your glory as I seek to live the Christian life before all types of people in my world. I boldly trust, O God, that you are close by, even on those days when I cannot sense your nearness. I believe, dear Father, but help my faith remain strong that you walk with me each step I take.
In Jesus' name I ask this. Amen.

CONTEXT: JOHN 2:1-12

RELATED REFERENCES: PSALM 139:1-3, 7; MARK 9:23-24; JOHN 14:6-7

Day: 31

TIMING IS EVERYTHING

JOHN 2:3-4

At the wedding there was not enough wine, so Jesus' mother said to him, "They have no more wine." Jesus answered, "Dear woman, why are you telling me this? It is not yet time for me to begin my work."

REFLECTION:

For us, timing is everything. Deliver the punch line of a joke without enough pause, or too much pause, and the joke falls flat. Rush a proposal in marriage, and you may not be taken seriously. Apply for a job at the wrong time and you won't be hired.

Jesus also lived "on the clock." He lived by God's sense of timing, so he ordered his plans based on God's will and God's timing. He came to the world at just the right time. He went to the cross at just the right time. He was raised from the dead at the time he had promised.

While we may not ever know exactly what time it is in our world, we can base our lives on the will, work, and timing of God. To do otherwise would be to miss the redemptive moments in the lives of many people God wants us to influence or to place more pressure on ourselves than is proper. Let's humbly live our lives seeking God's will and God's timing to do what needs to be done.

PRAYER:

Father, I know I will never have the same sense of timing in my life that Jesus did for his, but please make me more alert to your timing in my life as I commit to make my heart more open to your will. In Jesus' name I pray. Amen.

CONTEXT: JOHN 2:1-12

RELATED REFERENCES: JOHN 7:6-8; GALATIANS 4:4-5; EPHESIANS 5:15-17

Day: 32

DO WHATEVER HE TELLS YOU!

JOHN 2:5-8

His mother said to the servants, "Do what he tells you." There were six large stone waterpots there that were used by the Jews in their washing ceremonies. Each one held about 20 or 30 gallons. Jesus said to the servants, "Fill the waterpots with water." So they filled them to the top. Then he said to them, "Now dip out some water and take it to the man in charge of the feast."

REFLECTION:

"Do what Jesus tells you to do," Mary commands the servants. Her voice rings out over the centuries. The servants' example of obedience transcends water turning to wine at an ancient wedding. When we do what Jesus tells us to do, even if we don't completely understand why he asks it, we get to see God's glory.

Sure this story is about a wedding and a hugely embarrassing wine shortage. Mainly, however, it's about Jesus doing greater things, better things, than we can do or even imagine. So let's do what he tells us. The words of Jesus that John will share with us will not just be good advice, but they will be "spirit and life." Let's not only listen with our ears; let's listen with our lives.

PRAYER:

Father, give me eyes to see and ears to hear what Jesus tells me to do. I want to be courageous enough to live up to what he asks of me. I want to be willing to do WHATEVER he tells me, even if I don't understand it completely. Empower me with your Spirit to that kind of faithful and courageous obedience.
In Jesus' name I pray. Amen.

CONTEXT: JOHN 2:1-12

RELATED REFERENCES: JAMES 1:21-22; MATTHEW 7:21; EPHESIANS 3:20-21

Day: 33

HIS FOLLOWERS SEE A GLIMPSE OF HIS GLORY

JOHN 2:9-11

So they did what he said. Then the man in charge tasted it, but the water had become wine. He did not know where the wine had come from, but the servants who brought the water knew. He called the bridegroom and said to him, "People always serve the best wine first. Later, when the guests are drunk, they serve the cheaper wine. But you have saved the best wine until now." This was the first of all the miraculous signs Jesus did. He did it in the town of Cana in Galilee. By this he showed his divine greatness, and his followers believed in him.

REFLECTION:

It wasn't the right time. It wasn't the right place. It was, however, the right Lord! So when Jesus asked, and people obeyed, his followers got to see a little of Jesus' awesome glory and their faith was stoked! The little ember of their faith in Jesus was set ablaze.

Let's not forget what John's story of Jesus is all about; John wants to stoke the flame of our faith until it gives us genuine and eternal life (John 20:30-31). Being a follower of Jesus is all about daily accompanying the Lord through the ordinary ups and downs of life, doing whatever he asks us to do, and looking for his glory to be revealed to us. We change, our lives are enriched, and our faith is set ablaze when we obediently journey with Jesus each day.

PRAYER:

Holy and righteous God, my loving Abba Father, give me today the bread I need for food and the grace I need to share with those around me. As I live my everyday life, please help me see Jesus' glory at work in ways that I never have seen it before. Father God, I don't ask this for my entertainment or for my selfish interest, but so that my faith may grow stronger and my Christian witness more powerful, to your glory. In the mighty name of Jesus I pray. Amen.

CONTEXT: JOHN 2:1-12

RELATED REFERENCES: JOHN 20:30-31; JOHN 6:24-29; JOHN 1:50-51

Day: 34
FAMILY TIME

JOHN 2:12

*Then Jesus went to the town of Capernaum. His mother and brothers and his followers
went with him. They all stayed there a few days.*

REFLECTION:

Ministry can be euphoric. Ministry can be discouraging. Ministry is always
dangerous. In fact, the euphoria can be more dangerous than the discouragement. Many of God's greatest servants faltered in times of victory and success.

Jesus, however, frequently gets away from the mayhem of the masses.
Regularly it is for time to be alone with God. Frequently it is to be with his
closest followers. Occasionally, it is simply for time with his family and friends.
Those of us who want so much to serve him must learn this vital lesson. We
need rest. We need nourishment. We need friendship. We need family.

Let's not let the euphoria of being used by Jesus lead us to an arrogant sense
of self-sufficiency that we don't need rest, time alone with God, and the
closeness of loved ones and friends.

PRAYER:

*Father, forgive me for trying to do so much and hoard my experience of you to myself.
Give me a better sense of balance, a holy sense of rest, and genuine sense of value in being
with people I need and who need me. In Jesus' name I pray. Amen.*

CONTEXT: JOHN 2:1-12

RELATED REFERENCES: LUKE 5:15-16; MARK 6:31; MARK 1:35-38

Day: 35

CONFLICT IN THE TEMPLE

JOHN 2:13-16

It was almost time for the Jewish Passover, so Jesus went to Jerusalem. There in the Temple area he saw men selling cattle, sheep, and doves. He saw others sitting at tables, exchanging and trading people's money. Jesus made a whip with some pieces of rope. Then he forced all these men and the sheep and cattle to leave the Temple area. He turned over the tables of the money traders and scattered their money. Then he said to those who were selling pigeons, "Take these things out of here! Don't make my Father's house a place for buying and selling!"

REFLECTION:

Jesus rarely displays his displeasure with such demonstrative action and fervent emotion. Passover was the celebration of God's deliverance of the Israelites from the Egyptian bondage. God's people came to the Temple in Jerusalem from all over the world to celebrate God's powerful grace and mighty deliverance. To turn this celebration into a time for scrounging money from Israelite visitors desecrated the Passover Feast and the Temple.

Jesus doesn't want us to turn God's meeting place into a market or to take advantage of our brothers and sisters. Instead, he wants the gathering to be a place of deliverance, grace, and prayer. We probably need to ask this question: What do we do in our gatherings that would so negatively stir Jesus' emotions and actions? What corrections do we need to make to please him with what we do?

PRAYER:

Holy and righteous God, please keep my heart set on glorifying you and encouraging my brothers and sisters in the faith when we assemble together. May the joyful remembrance of my deliverance through Jesus' sacrifice lead me to praise you and generously bless others. Help me to see anything in my worship that would disturb you, so that I can bring it into harmony with your holy will. In Jesus' name I ask this. Amen.

CONTEXT: JOHN 2:13-25

RELATED REFERENCES: HEBREWS 13:15-16; 2 CORINTHIANS 9:10-11; 2 PETER 2:1-3

Day: 36

PASSION FOR THE HOUSE OF GOD

JOHN 2:17-19

When this happened, his followers remembered what was written in the Scriptures: "My strong devotion to your Temple will destroy me." Some Jews said to Jesus, "Show us a miracle as a sign from God. Prove that you have the right to do these things." Jesus answered, "Destroy this temple and I will build it again in three days."

REFLECTION:

What can make you spiritually excited? What arouses your holy passion? Is your passion for the "House of God," God's holy Temple? (For us today, God's holy temple is Jesus' Body, the Church [1 Cor. 3:16-17; Eph. 2:20-21; 1 Peter 2:5]). God wants that to be one of our passions—a holy excitement so strong that we would be willing to give our life to support.

Jesus was ultimately condemned to be crucified partially based on this statement—defined as blaspheming the Temple (Matt. 26:61). So Jesus was in a sense "destroyed" because of his excitement and holy passion for God's things, God's business, and God's Temple.

So what is your passion? Life without holy excitement is flat and boring. Life with the wrong passions is dissipated on destructive pursuits. But when life is built around godly passions, it leaves a permanent impact. What's your holy passion?

PRAYER:

Father, give me a more fervent passion for your people, your work, and your Kingdom. Through your Holy Spirit, stoke the fires of my heart to live with a holy passion for your things. In Jesus' name. Amen.

CONTEXT: JOHN 2:13-25

RELATED REFERENCES: LUKE 2:41-50; 1 CORINTHIANS 3:16-17; EPHESIANS 2:19-22

WHAT RIGHT?

JOHN 2:18-21

Some Jews said to Jesus, "Show us a miracle as a sign from God. Prove that you have the right to do these things." Jesus answered, "Destroy this temple and I will build it again in three days." They answered, "People worked 46 years to build this Temple! Do you really believe you can build it again in three days?" But the temple Jesus meant was his own body.

REFLECTION:

My, oh my, can't you just feel the hostility in this exchange? But, it helps us get to the root of the whole issue of Jesus. "Prove that you have the right to do these things."

What right does Jesus have to speak to us about important things? What right does he have to correct our religious practices or change our religious traditions?

Every right! Jesus' death and resurrection make clear that he acts and speaks with God's authority. They may not have understood this principle when he spoke it, but we do. The crucified and risen Lord IS the Temple of God. He is the focus of worship. He is the authority on the will of God. He is the way to the Father. He proved *that* when they "destroyed" him and he rose again!

PRAYER:

Almighty God, you are holy and without your grace, I know I am unworthy to come into your presence. Thank you for the gift of Jesus—his loving sacrifice, his willingness to go into the unknown world of death, and his triumph over the grave. Forgive me for holding back part of my heart and part of my will, from his authoritative word. I want to live boldly, based on his authority by honoring your will as he has taught it. In the name of your Son and my Lord, Jesus Christ, I pray. Amen.

CONTEXT: JOHN 2:13-25

RELATED REFERENCES: MATTHEW 28:18-20; ROMANS 1:2-4; HEBREWS 3:1-7

Day: 38

RESURRECTION AFTERGLOW!

JOHN 2:22

After he was raised from death, his followers remembered that he had said this. So they believed the Scriptures, and they believed the words Jesus said.

REFLECTION:

We often feel that our faith would be greatly bolstered if we could have been there to see Jesus in action personally. However, John and other New Testament witnesses remind us that many of the truths about Jesus are hard to accept, understand, perceive, discern, and believe without the knowledge that God raised him from the dead.

Jesus' resurrection makes his sacrifice powerful in addition to being praiseworthy. He is not just a martyr but the Lord because he faced his cruel enemies, suffered a death of disgrace, was buried in a borrowed tomb, and rose. We don't follow the teachings of a wise, but now dead, leader. We have found truth because we follow a resurrected and living Lord.

PRAYER:

Open my eyes, Holy One, to the truth that you, God my Father, have given me a powerful and real Savior in the resurrection of Jesus from the dead. Open my heart, dear God, to your grace and truth displayed in Jesus as he ministered on earth and triumphed through death to give me eternal life. In the mighty name of Jesus I pray. Amen.

CONTEXT: JOHN 2:13-25

RELATED REFERENCES: JOHN 12:12-16; JOHN 20:3-9; 1 CORINTHIANS 15:1-7

Day: 39

HE KNEW WHAT PEOPLE WERE REALLY LIKE

JOHN 2:23-25

Jesus was in Jerusalem for the Passover festival. Many people believed in him because they saw the miraculous signs he did. But Jesus did not trust them, because he knew how all people think. He did not need anyone to tell him what a person was like. He already knew.

REFLECTION:

We often play for the acceptance of the crowd. We want others to notice us as significant. So many of us want our moment of fame. Jesus didn't operate in that fashion. He knew that those who cried "Hosanna" and welcomed him as their king one weekend could cry out, "Crucify him!" a week later. People who followed Jesus simply because he worked miracles were not trusted to be true followers.

So Jesus will do his ministry based on God's timing and his own obedient heart. He will submit to the Father and honor him at great personal cost. His miracles in John are signs that he came from the Father. He won't do them to show out or gain an audience. Why? Jesus wasn't trying to win the crowd's approval. Instead, he was willing to pay any price so the fickle masses could find a real Lord and not another power-hungry tinhorn false messiah.

PRAYER:

Thank you, O God, for your Son's faithfulness. Thank you, Lord Jesus, for your willingness to bear the crowd's scorn and not give in to the crowd's fickle approval. I know you did it to honor your Father and to provide for me, in your own body, the perfect sacrifice for my sin. How can I not praise you with all my heart? To you, and through your holy name, I offer my thanks and praise. Amen.

CONTEXT: JOHN 2:13-25

RELATED REFERENCES: JOHN 12:42-43; ROMANS 5:6-11; HEBREWS 2:14-18

Day: 40

A GOOD PLACE TO START

JOHN 3:1-2

There was a man named Nicodemus, one of the Pharisees. He was an important Jewish leader. One night he came to Jesus and said, "Teacher, we know that you are a teacher sent from God. No one can do these miraculous signs that you do unless they have God's help."

REFLECTION:

Some give Nicodemus a hard time for coming to Jesus at night. But John doesn't. In fact, if we listen to his story carefully, Nicodemus does exactly what Jesus says good people do—"the person that follows the true way comes to the light" out of the darkness (John 3:21). Nicodemus had taken a good first step. He recognized that what Jesus did showed his divine origin. So Nicodemus came to Jesus. That was a good place to start, but it was just the beginning point.

In the next few verses, Jesus will insist that Nicodemus has to be reborn by God's Spirit. Simply believing that Jesus was nice, good, and comes from God was not enough. Nicodemus' life would have to be re-made by heaven's power.

Jesus comes to us today, reminding us of the same truth. We cannot keep Jesus tame and nice by simply believing that he is someone special. Jesus is about to remind us that he must be Lord and that we must begin fresh through spiritual rebirth or else we stay in darkness. Are you ready to join Nicodemus in a life-changing spiritual journey toward the Light?

PRAYER:

Father, I confess that there are times when I want to tame Jesus and take some of the radical call of his Gospel out of my path. Yet I recognize that grace was costly to you and should not be trivialized by me. With all that I have, I surrender my heart to Jesus as Lord. Use your Spirit, O God, to open my heart to fully follow Jesus and to powerfully live as a witness to your transformational grace. In Jesus' name I pray. Amen.

CONTEXT: JOHN 3:1-21

RELATED REFERENCES: LUKE 9:23-24; MATTHEW 7:21-23; JOHN 3:17-22

Day: 41
MUST!

JOHN 3:3
Jesus answered, "I assure you, everyone must be born again. Anyone who is not born again cannot be in God's kingdom."

REFLECTION:

Jesus basically tells Nicodemus, a righteous and religious ruler and the very best of Israel, that he must start over spiritually if he is to take part in God's Kingdom. Not only that, he tells him he must have a fresh start that only God can bring about. Nicodemus cannot make this fresh start happen on his own. He must be reborn.

This is no longer a theological discussion, but a personal one: "Don't be surprised that I told you, 'You must be born again'" (John 3:7). But more than just being born "again," Jesus is telling Nicodemus that he must be born "from above" or "born of God's Spirit." Another human birth by human efforts and origins simply can't accomplish what is necessary for him to be a part of God's Kingdom (John 1:11-13). This new birth is something that even the best of the best on earth and in Israel—like Nicodemus—can't accomplish.

Good won't cut it. God is the standard and we cannot get there without his power and his Spirit. Only God can make this birth happen. Can we hear that? Oh yes, because in our heart of hearts, we all know we don't measure up. Deep down, we know that only God's grace and the power of the Holy Spirit can make us God's holy children.

PRAYER:
Father, thank you for not only providing the sacrifice for my sins in Jesus, but also for providing the birth that makes me your holy child. By grace and in the name of Jesus I pray. Amen.

CONTEXT: JOHN 3:1-21

RELATED REFERENCES: 2 CORINTHIANS 5:14-18; COLOSSIANS 3:10-11; TITUS 3:5

Day: 42

BORN OF WATER AND SPIRIT

JOHN 3:4-5

Nicodemus said, "How can a man who is already old be born again? Can he go back into his mother's womb and be born a second time?" Jesus answered, "Believe me when I say that everyone must be born from water and the Spirit. Anyone who is not born from water and the Spirit cannot enter God's kingdom."

REFLECTION:

Jesus wanted to move Nicodemus from philosophical discussion to a personal one. But Nicodemus tries to keep it philosophical: "But if a person is already old, how can he be born again? A person cannot enter his mother's body again!" Jesus reminds him that no one, not even a Ruling Council member, can enter the Kingdom without the water/Spirit birth.

Yes Nicodemus, clinging to your old righteousness by surpassing others in religious knowledge, practice, and effort won't cut it with God. Only a new birth will do—a birth from above. The very best that Israel had to offer couldn't enter the Kingdom without faith in Jesus and a new birth by the power of the Holy Spirit.

So where does that leave you and me? Have we tried to ensure our entry into God's Kingdom by our religious pedigree, hard work, and biblical knowledge? Or, have we realized that Kingdom life occurs only through the new birth by water and Spirit?

PRAYER:

O righteous Father, forgive me for trying to hang on to my earthbound righteousness and religious practice. I know that I cannot be a part of your Kingdom without being spiritually reborn. Thank you for providing the sacrifice that atones for my sin. Thank you for providing me the means to confess my faith in him and to share with him in his death, burial and resurrection through baptism. Please help me share this grace with others. In Jesus' name I pray. Amen.

CONTEXT: JOHN 3:1-21

RELATED REFERENCES: 1 CORINTHIANS 6:9-11; TITUS 3:3-7; 1 CORINTHIANS 12:13

Day: 43
HOLY AND WHOLLY NEW

JOHN 3:6-7

"The only life people get from their human parents is physical. But the new life that the Spirit gives a person is spiritual. Don't be surprised that I told you, 'You must be born again.'"

REFLECTION:

Not religious practice. Not religious accomplishment. Not religious titles. Not religious pedigree. Not the faith of parents. Not the recognition of community. There is no human means that can accomplish our new birth, our God-birth, our from-above-birth, our spiritual rebirth. Only the Holy Spirit can give us "spiritual life."

God's Kingdom is as revolutionary as it is eternal. Humans can't muster the righteousness or perfection or power to make it happen. But God can, and does, by the power of his Holy Spirit. That's why we call it being saved by grace! Only God can pull this off for us. Only the Holy Spirit of God can make us both holy and wholly new.

PRAYER:

Father God, thank you for your grace displayed in sending Jesus to be the sacrifice for my sins and for giving spiritual rebirth by the power of your Holy Spirit. May I never boast except in the Cross of Christ and your Holy Spirit's power. In the name of my Lord Jesus, I pray. Amen.

CONTEXT: JOHN 3:1-21

RELATED REFERENCES: JOHN 1:9-13; 2 CORINTHIANS 5:16-21; 1 PETER 1:23

Day: 44
THINGS ONLY JESUS CAN SHOW
JOHN 3:8-12

"The wind blows wherever it wants to. You hear it, but you don't know where it is coming from or where it is going. It is the same with everyone who is born from the Spirit." Nicodemus asked, "How is all this possible?" Jesus said, "You are an important teacher of Israel, and you still don't understand these things? The truth is, we talk about what we know. We tell about what we have seen. But you people don't accept what we tell you. I have told you about things here on earth, but you do not believe me. So I'm sure you will not believe me if I tell you about heavenly things!"

REFLECTION:

Jesus wants to drive home the essential point with Nicodemus. What is that point? Jesus is the authority on all things spiritual, especially spiritual rebirth.

If a respected teacher and leader like Nicodemus cannot understand the things of heaven, then who can explain them? Who can show the way? Only one—Jesus! He is "the one who comes from above" (John 3:13, 31). He knows the Father's will and came to reveal it to us. He knows the path to spiritual rebirth and has come to share it. He knows because he has been there and he has seen it.

Jesus is saying to Nicodemus, "Let me teach you, O teacher. Let me lead you, O leader!" He also comes to us and says the same thing: "Learn from me, dear child, I long to give you the things of heaven, the things no one else can give." This is Jesus' personal invitation to Nicodemus, and to us. Jesus calls us to follow his journey to the Cross and beyond. Will we follow?

PRAYER:

Create in me, O God, a searcher's heart. Make me hungry to know your will and your Son more completely. As I follow Jesus through his ministry, capture my heart, fire my imagination and conquer my will so that I can receive what only Jesus can give and so that I can understand what only Jesus can explain. It is in his name, the glorious Christ and Lord, that I pray. Amen.

CONTEXT: JOHN 3:1-21

RELATED REFERENCES: 1 CORINTHIANS 2:6-14; JAMES 1:5; EPHESIANS 1:15-18

ONLY JESUS

JOHN 3:13

*"The only one who has ever gone up to heaven is the one who came down
from heaven—the Son of Man."*

REFLECTION:

What is something that only you can do? Now think for a moment; is it really something only you can do? No one else in the world can do it? No one else but you has ever done it? For us mere mortals, there are not many things we can claim as "only" ours.

Jesus is different! Only Jesus was part of heaven and came to earth. Only Jesus is one with the Father. Only One was sent from the Father's side to return there in glory.

There are many reasons to believe and obey the words that Jesus says. Here, however, he reminds us of one very important reason. He has come from heaven to speak the words of God to us as the Word of God. He comes with heavenly authority and heavenly identity. Only he is the Son. Only he is truly from heaven. He alone is the one and only Jesus of Nazareth who is Christ and Lord!

PRAYER:

Father, in my frustrations, trials, disappointments, discouragements, and fears, please pull my heart back to Jesus. Holy God, in my failures, sins, rebellious moments, and weakness in the face of temptation, please bring me back to my Lord. I recognize that my hope, my future, my salvation, forgiveness, my identity, and my glory are found only in Jesus. Even now, dear Father, I am thankful that as I pray, he is at your side and makes my heart fully known before the throne of grace. So, dear Father, I offer this prayer in his name, Jesus. Amen.

CONTEXT: JOHN 3:1-21

RELATED REFERENCES: JOHN 14:6-11; JOHN 8:42; JOHN 13:1-5

Day: 46

LIFTED UP!

JOHN 3:14-15

"Moses lifted up the snake in the desert. It is the same with the Son of Man. He must be lifted up too. Then everyone who believes in him can have eternal life."

REFLECTION:

In the rest of the New Testament outside of John's Gospel, the word "lifted up" usually meant "to exalt." In a subtle way it also means that in John. However, when John used the term "lifted up" in his Gospel, he was always referring to Jesus' crucifixion. For Jesus to be exalted to the highest place meant that he submitted himself to being lifted up to the worst of places, the Cross of Golgotha.

Why would Jesus submit to such a thing? The answer will be clear again and again as we journey through the Gospel: Jesus is determined to follow the will of God. He is committed to set an example and to be the sacrifice for us. He will let himself be "lifted up" to draw all people to himself. He will lay his life down and let his body be "lifted up" to bring redemption and eternal life to us.

The Cross was both a despicable place of cruelty and humiliation as well as a place of salvation and glory. We exalt Jesus because he was "lifted up" on the Cross for us. And, in a powerful way, Nicodemus is moved to reveal his love for and faith in Jesus when Jesus was "lifted up" (John 19:38-42).

PRAYER:

Father, thank you for your grace demonstrated in Jesus. Thank you, dear Savior, for going to the Cross and enduring its horrors and shame so that I can be saved. I exalt you, Lord Jesus, for your grace and mercy. I exalt you, O God, for raising Jesus from the dead. I look to the Cross and the sacrifice made there and trust that Jesus was lifted up for me. Thank you. In the name of Jesus I lift up my prayer and praise. Amen.

CONTEXT: JOHN 3:1-21

RELATED REFERENCES: JOHN 12:23-33; JOHN 8:28; ACTS 2:32-36

Day: 47
GOD GAVE TO GIVE US LIFE

JOHN 3:16

"Yes, God loved the world so much that he gave his only Son, so that everyone who believes in him would not be lost but have eternal life."

REFLECTION:

God loves us! That is the triumphant message of the Bible. That is the greatest message we will ever hear. Thankfully, however, this is not just a message in words. God wanted us to know his love for us, so he demonstrated that love at great personal cost.

God loves us! We know that because he gave his Son for us.

God loves us! He didn't want the power of "perish" to claim us, so he gave us the power of his sacrificial love.

God loves us! He sacrificed so we could have life that begins now and is without end.

God loves us! Don't ever doubt it. Don't let the evil one rob you of this life-giving truth.

God loves you and wants to give you life!

PRAYER:

Father, I believe that you gave Jesus to save me from my sins. I confess that I cannot fully understand that love, but I thank you and praise you with all of my heart. Please forgive me when my life does not reflect your loving estimation of my worth. Give me strength to believe what you say about me. I place my full trust in your love to continue its transformational work of redemption in me. Thank you that you are making me better than I am right now. Thank you even more for ransoming me from my sin and giving me life with you. In Jesus' name I thank you. Amen.

CONTEXT: JOHN 3:1-21

RELATED REFERENCES: JOHN 10:10-11; JOHN 20:30-31; 1 JOHN 3:16-20

Day: 48

GOD SENT HIS SON!

JOHN 3:17

"God sent his Son into the world. He did not send him to judge the world guilty, but to save the world through him."

REFLECTION:

The world stands under the shadow of destruction. Were it not for God's love for us in Jesus, we would face that same end. God, however, is the Creator, the Life-giver, and the Joy-bringer. The goal of his holiness is not destruction, but redemption. The goal of his righteousness is not anger, but salvation.

Jesus came to our world, a world literally hell-bent and headed for destruction, and placed God's stamp of grace upon it. He came to reverse the powers of decay, death, and destruction and put in their place permanence, life, and salvation. Jesus is God's great reminder to us that he not only loves us, but that he also has only good and glorious intentions for us—both in this life and the life to come.

PRAYER:

O God, redeem my view of you and your intentions for me, just as you have redeemed my heart and soul from sin. I confess that my view of you is so limited and earthbound. Through your Holy Spirit, fill my heart with a more accurate, glorious, and gracious understanding of your intentions for my life. In Jesus' name I pray. Amen.

CONTEXT: JOHN 3:1-21

RELATED REFERENCES: ROMANS 5:8-11; ROMANS 8:31-34; 1 JOHN 4:9-10

Day: 49

A WATERSHED DECISION

JOHN 3:18

"People who believe in God's Son are not judged guilty. But people who do not believe are already judged, because they have not believed in God's only Son."

REFLECTION:

We don't fear judgment because we live trusting in God's great love for us. That love casts out all fear. (1 John 4:18) We know we don't face judgment, only life. However, this glorious future is not based upon our confidence in ourselves, but upon our trust in Jesus' sacrifice to save us. When people reject Jesus, their lives are caught in the world of impending destruction. They have judged themselves by rejecting Jesus and refusing to trust in him. They have rejected the only source of lasting life in our bent and battered world of destruction. The gift of Jesus is the watershed grace. Our acceptance or rejection of Jesus as our Savior and Lord means everything.

PRAYER:

Glorious and righteous God, my Heavenly Father, thank you for the promise of a glorious future with you. Thank you that I do not have to fear that future. As I expectantly wait for that future to unfold, please use me to influence others to trust in Jesus. Never let my life be a stumbling block to someone seeking the answers that only Jesus can give him or her. In the name of Jesus, my Lord, I pray. Amen.

CONTEXT: JOHN 3:1-21

RELATED REFERENCES: JOHN 5:24; EPHESIANS 2:1-6; 1 JOHN 4:16-18

Day: 50
LOVERS OF DARKNESS

JOHN 3:19

"They are judged by this fact: The light has come into the world. But they did not want light. They wanted darkness, because they were doing evil things."

REFLECTION:

Some folks don't just reject Jesus; they hate God, Christianity, religion, Christians, and anything that smacks of wholesome living. Evil is real and controls the lives of those who give it safe harbor.

Evil recoils from truth. Too often, people not fully controlled by evil end up rejecting the truth of God for a simple reason; they love how they are living and don't want to give it up. They are well on their way to being lovers of darkness.

Don't let the opposition that comes from what is evil and the Evil One dull your spiritual senses to God's gracious and liberating truth. If you find yourself flirting with sin and evil, use the Joseph solution—get up and flee! (Gen. 39:1-18). When evil is allowed a place to grow, it will ultimately push us to flee the light like cockroaches scurrying for cover when we turn on the light.

PRAYER:

Holy and righteous Father, keep my heart tuned to your Son's grace, love, and righteousness. Make me hunger and thirst for your righteousness. Kindle my desire to seek first your Kingdom and your holy character. Give me a holy passion to live in your light and to seek your Son as the Light of my life. In Jesus' holy and mighty name I pray. Amen.

CONTEXT: JOHN 3:1-21

RELATED REFERENCES: COLOSSIANS 1:19-23; EPHESIANS 2:1-2; EPHESIANS 6:12

Day: 51
Doing What God Wants?

John 3:20-21

"Everyone who does evil hates the light. They will not come to the light, because the light will show all the bad things they have done. But anyone who follows the true way comes to the light. Then the light will show that whatever they have done was done through God."

Reflection:

A life dedicated to God comes to the Light. A person living this kind of life doesn't fear judgment or rejection or truth. Falsehood, dishonesty, sinfulness, greed ... all can be addressed through the lens of grace when we come to the Light. So the question we face each day is very simple: Do I gladly come to the Light to let God show me his grace in ways that allow me to see my sinfulness, shallowness, and selfishness, and be transformed?

My desire to open my life to the Light of God's truth reveals my desire to do what is right. My reluctance reveals how the power of sin has edged its way into my heart. Let's open ourselves to God and freely admit the things we are ashamed for him to know about our thoughts, words, and actions. Many of us struggle with the shame of secret sin, yet hold a place for it in the dark crevices in our hearts. An old adage proves itself true in this regard: "You can't get rid of the cobwebs in the corner until you get rid of the spider." Let's bring our spiders to the light so that the Lord can share his mercy, the Spirit can cleanse us and empower us, and God can do great things in us.

Prayer:

Almighty Father, God of holiness and grace, search me and try me and convict me of my sin. I want to be holy and blameless, not just by your gift of grace, but also through the power of your Spirit at work to transform me to be more like Jesus. Finally, dear Father, do your will in me so that everyone who meets me can see that the good deeds I do and the life that I live are done through you. In the holy name of Jesus, my Light, I pray. Amen.

Context: John 3:1-21

Related References: 1 John 1:5-7; Colossians 1:13; 1 Peter 2:8-10

Day: 52
JESUS, JOHN, FOLLOWERS AND BAPTIZING
JOHN 3:22-24

After this, Jesus and his followers went into the area of Judea. There he stayed with his followers and baptized people. John was also baptizing people in Aenon, a place near Salim with plenty of water. People were going there to be baptized. This was before John was put in prison.

REFLECTION:

Jesus' followers and John the Baptist practiced baptism—immersion of repentant folks who were preparing themselves for God's coming Kingdom. Two things about this are particularly interesting. First, until the ministries of John and Jesus, most of the "baptisms" in Judaism were self-administered washings. Second, baptism like John practiced was in use, but primarily for Gentiles who were becoming Jewish proselytes. Imagine the attention and furor—Jews being baptized like Gentiles!

Matthew, Mark, Luke, and John all reveal this attention to baptism in their stories of John the Baptist and Jesus. Many people realized God was doing something special in his people. To prepare themselves for this work of God, many were willing to do whatever God asked of them even if it meant being brutally honest about their need for changing their lives.

Maybe the most important question for each of us to ask is this: "Am I willing to do anything God asks of me to follow Jesus?" I hope our answer is, "Yes." So now let's ask God to show us what that "anything" truly is.

PRAYER:

Almighty God, please remove any stumbling block in my heart that would keep me from loving you with all my heart, soul, mind, and strength. I confess that this prayer makes me a bit afraid because I often do not recognize my blind spots, areas of unresolved sinfulness, and latent immaturity. So I ask, dear Father, that you humble me gently and take control of my heart. I want to follow your Son wholeheartedly and do your will without reluctance. In Jesus' name I pray. Amen.

CONTEXT: JOHN 3:22-36

RELATED REFERENCES: MATTHEW 28:18-20; MATTHEW 3:1-6; JOHN 4:1-2

Day: 53

REMEMBER WHO IS BOSS!

JOHN 3:25-27

Some of John's followers had an argument with another Jew about religious washing.
Then they came to John and said, "Teacher, remember the man who was with you on the
other side of the Jordan River? He is the one you were telling everyone about. He is also
baptizing people, and many are going to him."
John answered, "A person can receive only what God gives."

REFLECTION:

One of the most important questions you will ever answer is this: For whom do
I work? No matter what your job or vocation might be, this is the vital question.

Do you work to please yourself? Do you work to please your boss? Do you
work to impress your peers or your superiors? Do you work for God?

John the Baptist knew his job and his boss. He also knew his job description:
please God who sent him by preparing the way for Jesus. So when Jesus'
ministry began to take off, John was not his rival, but his biggest supporter.

So much of our angst and frustration in life comes back to not recognizing
this one crucial point: if we are Christians, we work for God. If we do the work
he assigns to us, we don't have to be bitter or jealous about someone else getting
the attention or the accolades. If God is pleased, each of us is a success. So let's
ask God to reveal his job for us, and then let's go do it with joy and passion as we
live out lives for him at home, at church, and especially in the marketplace.

PRAYER:

Father, give me a heart like John the Baptist. I want to find joy and satisfaction in doing
your work for my life. Give me a heart that is satisfied with pleasing you. Give me a heart
that is freed from envy and jealousy because someone else gets more attention for what
they do or even if they get the praise for what you do through me. When my life is over,
dear Father, please help me live in such a way that I can hear your words,
"Well done good and faithful servant." In the name of Jesus I pray. Amen.

CONTEXT: JOHN 3:22-36

RELATED REFERENCES: JOHN 21:17-22; LUKE 22:24-27; LUKE 7:28

Day: 54
THE FRIEND OF THE BRIDEGROOM
JOHN 3:28-29

"You yourselves heard me say, 'I am not the Christ. I am only the one God sent to prepare the way for him.' The bride always belongs to the bridegroom. The friend who helps the bridegroom just waits and listens. He is happy just to hear the bridegroom talk. That's how I feel now. I am so happy that he is here."

REFLECTION:

What a beautiful image! The friend of the bridegroom finds his joy in seeing the bride come to her groom. This attitude seems so simple to understand in the context of a wedding. Why is it so hard in the rest of life?

Imagine if we all lived with the same commitment that John had. What amazing power would be unleashed among God's people if we all lived to prepare the way for Jesus! So why don't we? Why not start right now and commit to giving the rest of your life to prepare the way for others to know Jesus?

Prayerfully begin each day asking God to open your eyes to someone who is looking for the love and mercy of Jesus. Keep a list of four or five folks to whom you are carefully listening, waiting in anticipation for the door of their hearts to open for you to share God's grace. Rejoice with those who become Christians by dropping them a note of joyous thanks for their salvation. Find a way to put a good word in for Jesus in a surprising place each day. Give thanks each evening for the Lord using you to touch the lives of others with his grace.

PRAYER:

Loving Father, please use my words, my influence, and the rest of my life to help others come to know Jesus and his love. Open my eyes to the opportunities around me to touch others with your grace. Open my ears to hear the cries of those hungry for your Living Bread. Please give me the joy of the friend of the bridegroom! In Jesus' name I ask this. Amen.

CONTEXT: JOHN 3:22-36
RELATED REFERENCES: JOHN 1:19-26; JOHN 1:35-37; PHILIPPIANS 1:15-18

Day: 55

OUR PATH TO GREATNESS

JOHN 3:30

"He must become more and more important, and I must become less important."

REFLECTION:

Want to be great? Want to do something great? Then live so that others will see more and know more of Jesus and less of you. There is not a lot more that needs to be said about the path to true greatness!

PRAYER:

Father, I know that you have shown the path to true greatness. Please give me the courage to live it with passion. Please conform me more fully to the character and nature of your Son. When people have been with me, may they know something more of your love for them in Jesus, my Savior, in whose name I pray. Amen.

CONTEXT: JOHN 3:22-36

RELATED REFERENCES: MATTHEW 17:27-30; 2 CORINTHIANS 4:5-7; 1 CORINTHIANS 4:1

Day: 56

DISCOVER THAT GOD IS TRUE

JOHN 3:31-33

"The one who comes from above is greater than all others. The one who is from the earth belongs to the earth. He talks about things that are on the earth. But the one who comes from heaven is greater than all others. He tells what he has seen and heard, but people don't accept what he says. Whoever accepts what he says has given proof that God speaks the truth."

REFLECTION:

John the Baptist is consistent in his ministry. He points us to Jesus' greatness and reminds us of our human limitations and frailties. Because Jesus comes from heaven, he can share with us the message of heaven—he has seen the glories of heaven and heard the Father's message. John also reminds us that even though many will never listen to that message, those who do will discover that God speaks the truth. Their lives will resonate with that truth and they will find life in that truth.

If we hear what is being said, we understand what will be said more explicitly in other places. Jesus has come and he alone can truly reveal the will of God. Because he has come from heaven, he is the only one that can fully reveal the way to God. But, this will and this way are no mystery: Jesus does the will of the Father and he speaks only what the Father wants said. So, if we want to know the Father's will, we need to listen and watch Jesus.

PRAYER:

O LORD, God of Israel and Father of all grace, please show yourself to me as I seek to know you more fully in Jesus, in whose name I pray. Amen.

CONTEXT: JOHN 3:22-36

RELATED REFERENCES: JOHN 3:10-13; MATTHEW 7:21-23; JOHN 6:38

Day: 57

AUTHORITY OVER EVERYTHING

JOHN 3:34-35

"God sent him, and he tells people what God says. God gives him the Spirit fully.
The Father loves the Son and has given him power over everything."

REFLECTION:

Jesus is THE authority! Jesus has authority over life, death, and the truth about God. Jesus has authority over religion, faith, and spiritual experience. Jesus has authority over our lives and our destinies. Why? He was sent by God. He has the Spirit of God without any limit. He is loved by God as God's Son. And, as we will see at the end of his earthly ministry, God has validated his authority through the resurrection.

So to whom have you given the control of your life? Is it the folks that sell ads in the media? Do your peers and their acceptance control your life? Are your fears in control? Do your possessions possess and control you? Only One truly has true authority and can speak for God. His name is Jesus. Are you listening to him?

PRAYER:

Father, please help Jesus' words to cling more powerfully to my heart. Give me a deeper hunger to know what he has said. Help me yearn to be more like him in what I do, think, and say. Make my heart confident when among my peers and yielding when I read the words of Jesus. I ask this in the name of your Son, Jesus. Amen.

CONTEXT: JOHN 3:22-36

RELATED REFERENCES: MATTHEW 8:5-13; JOHN 12:49; JOHN 13:3

Day: 58

SAVED FROM WRATH

JOHN 3:36

"Whoever believes in the Son has eternal life. But those who do not obey the Son will never have that life. They cannot get away from God's anger."

REFLECTION:

God sent Jesus to save us. Faith in God's Son is our doorway to life. However, John reminds us that faith is not just what we THINK. True faith always leads us to obedient ACTION. So when we don't believe (when we don't obey), we shut ourselves off from life.

Jesus not only has all authority (as we learned yesterday), but he also longs to give us life. Let's respond to him with obedient faith and enjoy the blessings of God's life. Let's also remember that faith is more than what we believe in the gray matter of our heads; it is what we de do and why we do it as we trust in Jesus and submit to him as Lord in our daily lives. This kind of life is a forever life—lived in the mercy and grace of God. But what about the person who does not obey the Son's message? They will never have the life God longs to give them.

PRAYER:

Glorious Father, thank you for sending Jesus to give me life. I do believe that your Son, Jesus, came to be my Savior by dying for my sin on the Cross. I believe you raised him from the dead to ensure my future. I believe that he poured out the Holy Spirit. And, dear Father, I believe he is returning in glory to bring the redeemed home to be with you. So bless me as I try to live obediently to Jesus, my Lord, in whose name I pray. Amen.

CONTEXT: JOHN 3:22-36

RELATED REFERENCES: EPHESIANS 2:1-10; JOHN 3:16-17; GALATIANS 3:26-28

Day: 59
AVOIDING CONFLICT AND CONFUSION

JOHN 4:1-3

Jesus learned that the Pharisees had heard the report that he was making and baptizing more followers than John. (But really, Jesus himself did not baptize anyone; his followers baptized people for him.) So he left Judea and went back to Galilee.

REFLECTION:

Jesus' ministry with his followers involved baptizing. However, because of John the Baptist's association with baptism, Jesus carefully avoided conflict and confusion. While he highly regarded John's ministry, and John personally, he did not want to be confused with John. John was not the Messiah. Jesus was. John was not the Son of God. Jesus was. John was not the Savior of the world. Jesus was. John was not the King of Israel. Jesus was. In fact, Jesus still is Messiah, Son, Savior, and King. But to avoid confusion and conflict and to follow God's timetable and not the world's expectations, Jesus went back to Galilee, his home. Jesus would not allow his enemies to cause discord and trouble between his followers and the followers of John.

Unfortunately one of the greatest tools used by Satan is jealously and rivalry between ministers and ministries. The care with which both John the Baptist and Jesus carried out their ministries in proximity to each other must be an example to us. We must not let personality conflicts and petty jealousies derail the greater work of God.

PRAYER:

Father, I know there are all sorts of conflicts that go on today between religious leaders and their followers. Please help me to value those who have given their lives to sharing the truth of Jesus. At the same time, dear Father, please protect me from infatuation with these messengers and keep my heart focused on your Message, Jesus, in whose name I pray. Amen.

CONTEXT: JOHN 4:1-26

RELATED REFERENCES: MATTHEW 16:13-16; ACTS 4:8-12; JOHN 14:6-7

Day: 60
A WEARY SAVIOR!

JOHN 4:4-6

On the way to Galilee he had to go through the country of Samaria. In Samaria Jesus came to the town called Sychar, which is near the field that Jacob gave to his son Joseph. Jacob's well was there. Jesus was tired from his long trip, so he sat down beside the well. It was about noon.

REFLECTION:

Jesus took the "short cut" between Judea in the south and Galilee in the north. He went through Samaria. He was tired from his journey. He rested by the historic site of Jacob's well. So much history and promise come together in this moment and at this place.

We are right to expect something grand to happen. Jesus has come to the well dug by Father Israel. (Jacob's name was changed to Israel.) What great word do we hear? What triumphant deed does Jesus do?

None. At least not at first. Jesus' primary action was simply to sit down. He was a weary Savior. Sounds almost bizarre as our hearts exalt and hold Jesus in the highest of places. At the same time, something wondrous is once again revealed to us. Jesus became flesh. Human flesh. Wearying flesh.

Jesus knows us not only in his position as God, but as one of us whose feet got dirty, whose legs grew tired, and whose stomach growled when it was empty. Jesus is a Savior who knows us; he knows us because he has lived in our world, sharing our burdens and feeling our weariness. So Jesus can speak to us the truth of heaven because he has been there. Jesus also can speak to us the truth of heaven on earth because he has lived here as one of us.

PRAYER:

Father, how can I thank you for making yourself so accessible to me through Jesus? Jesus, thank you for becoming mortal for me. Your sacrifice has given even greater confidence that I can come to the throne room of heaven and receive grace to help me in my time of need. Thank you Lord Jesus. I praise you most holy and gracious God, in your Son's name. Amen.

CONTEXT: JOHN 4:1-26

RELATED REFERENCES: JOHN 19:28; JOHN 1:14; HEBREWS 2:11-18

Day: 61

A Barrier Breaker

John 4:7-9

A Samaritan woman came to the well to get some water, and Jesus said to her, "Please give me a drink." This happened while his followers were in town buying some food. The woman answered, "I am surprised that you ask me for a drink! You are a Jew and I am a Samaritan woman!" (Jews have nothing to do with Samaritans.)

Reflection:

Asking for a drink doesn't seem like a big deal. In this case, however, it is a huge deal! Jesus is a Jew. Jews considered Samaritans unworthy and unclean cousins. Simple fellowship with a Samaritan would defile a righteous Jew. Jesus is a Rabbi, a male teacher of Israel. A "real" Rabbi didn't talk publicly with women in Jesus' day. But this woman was seeking. This woman was alone. This woman was thirsty for living water. This woman needed Jesus. Jesus let nothing stand in his way of reaching her.

Jesus is always a barrier breaker. He doesn't let time, space, race, or culture keep people from God's grace.

We must ask ourselves; "Are we barrier breakers?" The concern is not that we use the latest iteration of politically correct speech; rather it is that we actively and intentionally reach across cultural, social, racial, and economic lines and to engage others and work for their redemption in daily life. As Jesus shows us here, this involves getting out of comfort zones, getting involved in conversation with others, and sharing with them in their lives—the good, the bad, the hard, and the spiritual.

Prayer:

O Father, give me a heart to treat people as Jesus did. Fill me with your Spirit. Open my heart to your concerns. Use me to break through barriers and establish connections so that others can come to know Jesus, find his living water, and share that gift with others. I ask this in the name of the Jesus. Amen.

Context: John 4:1-26

Related References: Ephesians 2:11-18; Galatians 3:26-29; Matthew 28:18-20

Day: 62

IF YOU ONLY KNEW

JOHN 4:10

Jesus answered, "You don't know what God can give you. And you don't know who I am, the one who asked you for a drink. If you knew, you would have asked me, and I would have given you living water."

REFLECTION:

But we do know, don't we? We do know who stands before the woman at the well! We do know that he is the gift of God! So why don't we ask that the Lord Jesus slake our thirst with living water.

PRAYER:

Lord Jesus, please make me alive to your living water welling up within me. Slake my thirst. Nurture my soul. Fill me with your grace. Uphold me in your presence. Most of all, energize me through your Spirit to the glory of your name and to the praise of our Father in heaven. Amen.

CONTEXT: JOHN 4:1-26

RELATED REFERENCES: JOHN 7:37-39; REVELATION 3:15-21; JOHN 14:12-14

Day: 63
YOU CAN'T DO THIS ... CAN YOU?

JOHN 4:11-12

The woman said, "Sir, where will you get that living water? The well is very deep, and you have nothing to get water with. Are you greater than our ancestor Jacob? He is the one who gave us this well. He drank from it himself, and his sons and all his animals drank from it too."

REFLECTION:

When life is not going well, when our dreams lie shattered at our feet, we long for someone who is bigger than our experience and larger than our hope to come and ransom us from our lifeless drudgery. Yet when we are given the opportunity to escape the monotonous drudgery, we often find it too good to be true and our cynicism swallows our hope.

We are not surprised when the woman tells Jesus, "You can't get me water; you don't have anything to put it in much less a rope that will reach down into the well and draw out water!" Behind her doubt, however, is an inkling of hope. She's looking. She's longing. Her hope hasn't been encased in desperation so long that it has died.

We know who Jesus really is. We know the answer to woman's question about greatness. Our hearts want to cry out to her, "Yes, the one you talk to, dear lady, is greater than your ancestor Jacob—much greater. And he doesn't need a rope or a pot. In fact, he doesn't need a well. You are about to have your flickering hope revived and your parched soul refreshed. Just keep seeking. Just keep asking. Living water is already starting to flow."

PRAYER:

O precious Father, I have several people on my heart today whose hope is nearly gone. They can't seem to find their way to Jesus. Please keep their flickering hope alive. Please use me to help them find Jesus to slake their thirsty souls. Use the people around them to keep them asking and looking and longing for something, for Someone, to do what no one else can do for them. I pray this earnestly for those I love, in the name of Jesus. Amen.

CONTEXT: JOHN 4:1-26
RELATED REFERENCES: MATTHEW 5:13; JOHN 6:33-35; MARK 9:17-24

Day: 64
A DEEPER DRINK

JOHN 4:13-14

Jesus answered, "Everyone who drinks this water will be thirsty again. But anyone who drinks the water I give will never be thirsty again. The water I give people will be like a spring flowing inside them. It will bring them eternal life."

REFLECTION:

So often, we settle for what is shadow and not what is substance. All too frequently, we take the shortcut and miss the destination. We are willing to settle for what is shallow rather than seek what is deep and sustaining. Only Jesus can supply the water that our thirsty souls desire. Only he can fill the emptiness and the ache in our hearts. Anything and everyone else are simply shadows, shortcuts, and shallow.

The amazing promise of Jesus' gift flowing water is that it is lasting. This water that Jesus gives is a spring of water, not a cistern. It is living, not stagnant. This water gives life and this life provides more water. Later in his ministry, Jesus' makes clear this water is the Holy Spirit (John 7:37-39). God comes to live in us through the Holy Spirit. God fills us with his life through the Holy Spirit. God cleanses and transforms us by his Spirit. God quenches our thirst with the Holy Spirit Jesus gives and living water springs up within us giving us life that is forever.

PRAYER:

O God, I'm not sure why the spiritually dry periods come. I find, at times, that my soul needs to be filled, my thirst needs to be quenched, and my hunger needs to be satiated. I gladly confess, however, that these times make my desire to experience Jesus' living water more intense. I have tasted your goodness. I have drunk from your fountain of grace. Please, dear Father, keep your life-giving water flowing in me. In Jesus' name I pray. Amen.

CONTEXT: JOHN 4:1-26

RELATED REFERENCES: JOHN 7:37-39; JOHN 3:5-6; LUKE 11:9-13

HAVE YOU ASKED?

JOHN 4:15

The woman said to Jesus, "Sir, give me this water. Then I will never be thirsty again and won't have to come back here to get more water."

REFLECTION:

Even when we aren't sure what to ask, we need to come to Jesus and ask! We're thirsty. We're tired. Our resources are limited. Our strength is on the wane. We realize that we cannot do it alone. So let's ask, trusting that even if we are not sure what we should request, we can ask for the water that quenches our thirst. The Lord will know what we need! "Sir ... Lord ... Jesus, please give me this water so I will never be thirsty again!"

PRAYER:

Holy God, I come to you in Jesus' name and ask that you fill that hole in my soul that I cannot quite identify. Quench my thirst and fill me with your living water. Amen.

CONTEXT: JOHN 4:1-26

RELATED REFERENCES: MATTHEW 7:7-11; ROMANS 8:26-27; 1 JOHN 5:14-15

Day: 66

GETTING TO THE HEART OF THE MATTER

JOHN 4:16-18

*Jesus told her, "Go get your husband and come back." The woman answered,
"But I have no husband." Jesus said to her, "You are right to say you have no husband.
That's because, although you have had five husbands, the man you live with now is not
your husband. That much was the truth."*

REFLECTION:

While the conversation had focused upon water and remained a bit
confusing to the woman, Jesus now is going to get to the heart of the matter. It's
not about coming to a well for water; it's about parched souls broken by life
finding truth and refreshment in Jesus.

Some portray this woman as a woman of questionable morals. However, we
must remember that Samaritan women, just like their Jewish counterparts, did
not have the right to divorce their husbands. This is a woman who had been
rejected by five men and now lived with a man who would not legitimize their
relationship. She came to the well in the middle of the day because she was
shunned. This woman was discarded and alone. Jesus wanted to get to the heart
of the issue so he could bring his "living water" to the barren and parched
recesses of her soul. He longs to do the same for us today. What question would
Jesus ask to get to your hurt and get you to share your heart with him?
Remember, he's asking it so you will ask him to help you address it. Don't go
another day, parched and dry in soul. Bring Jesus your hurt and ask him to
restore and renew you.

PRAYER:

*Father, forgive me for my sins. Even more, Father, please give me the strength to quit hiding
my brokenness, weakness, and sin from you and myself. Please bring Jesus'
living water to the parched and broken areas of my soul.
I pray this, in the name of your Son. Amen.*

CONTEXT: JOHN 4:1-26

RELATED REFERENCES: MATTHEW 7:1-5; MATTHEW 19:3-12; JOHN 7:24

Day: 67

CONFLICT OVER PLACE

JOHN 4:19-20

*The woman said, "Sir, I can see that you are a prophet. Our fathers
worshiped on this mountain. But you Jews say that Jerusalem is the place
where people must worship."*

REFLECTION:

So much of the conflict found in Christian groups resolves around what we
see as the central issues of worship—the place, content, and method. Isn't it
interesting that God has provided us with some very needed insight for our
world and our time through a rejected Samaritan woman at an old Jewish well?

We could dismiss this woman's question about the importance and place of
worship as a dodge of Jesus' probing of her soul. Jesus doesn't do that. He takes
her question seriously. His answers to her are words that we, too, must carefully
consider. And we will do that tomorrow.

Today, however, let's notice something about many of the people we label as
not interested in Jesus, yet who are actually seeking God in their lives. This is a
woman broken by life. She is an outcast in her own community. Yet she has
deep yearnings to know the truth of God. Who is like that in your world? Who
have you missed because you didn't think they had any serious questions about
the Lord since they didn't seem very religious to you? What do you think Jesus
would have to say about that? How would Jesus have approached them?

PRAYER:

*Holy God, speak to my heart and teach me about true worship as I listen to Jesus' words
to this woman. I too come to you thirsty and longing to draw near and find my life's joy in
you. And Father, please open my heart wide to others, especially those whom I think have
little interest in your truth because their lives are such a mess. Give me the compassion of
Jesus to enter their world with personal attention and heavenly grace.
In Jesus' name I pray. Amen.*

CONTEXT: JOHN 4:1-26

RELATED REFERENCES: EPHESIANS 2:14-18; ACTS 7:48-50; MATTHEW 16:13-16

Day: 68

BEYOND PLACE, THROUGH THE JEWS

JOHN 4:21-22

Jesus said, "Believe me, woman! The time is coming when you will not have to be in Jerusalem or on this mountain to worship the Father. You Samaritans worship something you don't understand. We Jews understand what we worship, since salvation comes from the Jews."

REFLECTION:

True worship is not centered on a place, but upon the Father—God, who has been revealed to us by Jesus as our ever close, always holy, Abba Father. The truth about God has been revealed to us through God's work among the Jewish people. God began to reveal his plan of salvation for all peoples with his promises to Abraham. The Holy One of Israel kept those promises through the difficult years of Israel's history and brought them to fulfillment in Jesus.

Jesus becomes the new Temple. He institutes a whole new approach to worship and to God. The time is here! Let's worship as Jesus teaches us to worship. His first point: God is our Father, and the focus of our worship is on him, our relationship to him as our Father, and the salvation he brings to us.

PRAYER:

Holy One of Israel, the Almighty God who is faithful to his promises, I praise you for your majesty and might. I come to you as my Abba Father, the giver of salvation in Jesus. I am humbled at your incredible work through history in your people Israel. I praise you for the salvation that you have brought to me in Jesus. Keep my heart centered on you as I worship you in deed and truth. In Jesus' name I pray. Amen.

CONTEXT: JOHN 4:1-26

RELATED REFERENCES: JOHN 2; 1 CORINTHIANS 6:19-20; EPHESIANS 1:3

Day: 69

GOD IS LOOKING FOR US

JOHN 4:23

"But the time is coming when the true worshipers will worship the Father in spirit and truth. In fact, that time is now here. And these are the kind of people the Father wants to be his worshipers."

REFLECTION:

Remember playing hide and seek as a child? Part of the fun in playing was being found. Jesus tells us that the heart of worship is honoring God as our Father for the salvation he brings to us in Jesus.

Today, however, Jesus reminds us that God is seeking us as we worship him. When we approach God to worship him, we should understand that God is rushing to meet us and welcome us into his holy presence. God seeks us. This is truly an incredible thought. But then, isn't that the image we have of him coming to meet with Adam and Eve in the cool of the garden? God longs to not only receive our worship, but to also run to meet with us when we worship. What incredible grace!

PRAYER:

Father, I confess that I cannot adequately understand your majesty and holiness. Your greatness humbles me. To know, dear Father, that you run to meet me in worship totally overwhelms me. Thank you for loving me so completely. May the words of my mouth and the meditations of my heart and the works of my hands all be pleasing in your sight. Please accept my praise in Jesus' holy name. Amen.

CONTEXT: JOHN 4:1-26

RELATED REFERENCES: ACTS 17:22-31; LUKE 15:20; GENESIS 3:8-9

GOD IS SPIRIT!

JOHN 4:24

"God is spirit. So the people who worship him must worship in spirit and truth."

REFLECTION:

One of the truly remarkable truths that Jesus teaches us is that worship is Spirit to Spirit. God is Spirit and we are given his Spirit when we are born from above (John 3:3-7). We worship Spirit to Spirit—our spirit, sanctified by the Holy Spirit within us, offering worship to God, who is Spirit. We have access to God through the Holy Spirit. So as we come to God authentically, seeking him in truth, the Spirit of God enables us to worship God fully, truthfully, and acceptably.

PRAYER:

Holy Father, I come to you knowing that I can approach you with boldness through the Holy Spirit. Thank you for providing this gift of access through the Spirit so that I can come to you in holiness and truth. In Jesus' name I praise you. Amen.

CONTEXT: JOHN 4:1-26

RELATED REFERENCES: EPHESIANS 5:15-22; 1 CORINTHIANS 2:9-13; EPHESIANS 2:18

Day: 71

CHRIST WILL EXPLAIN EVERYTHING

JOHN 4:25

The woman said, "I know that the Messiah is coming." (Messiah is the one called Christ.)
"When he comes, he will explain everything to us."

REFLECTION:

For the second time in the Gospel of John, a woman seeking to meet an everyday problem tells us the truth about Jesus and our relationship to him. The first was Mary at the wedding: "Do what Jesus tells you to do." This time, it is the woman at the well: "The Christ ... will explain everything to us." Do you hear what these two women are telling us?

Do you want to know about life ... truth ... holiness ... relationships ... family matters ... problems ... worship? Then listen to Jesus. As the woman is about to learn, Jesus is the Messiah, the Christ of God. He does explain everything to us. Will we listen? Will we follow? Will we obey? Will we respond to Jesus as this woman did?

PRAYER:

Father, give me the confidence to trust that Jesus does explain everything I need to know.
Please give me the boldness to obey—to respond to Jesus as fully and openly as this
woman does. His words are life. His truth is sustenance to my soul. I confess that Jesus is
the Christ, the promised Messiah sent to Israel and the nations to lead us to you,
O God. I praise you for sending your Son for my salvation. I commit to
follow him as my Lord and obey what he commands.
Accept my thanks in the name of Christ Jesus, my Lord. Amen.

CONTEXT: JOHN 4:1-26

RELATED REFERENCES: MATTHEW 7:24-29; JOHN 6:63 & 68-69; 2 TIMOTHY 3:14-17

Day: 72

I AM THE MESSIAH

JOHN 4:26
Then Jesus said, "He is talking to you now—I'm the Messiah."

REFLECTION:

Jesus is the Messiah! Jesus is the Christ of God! Jesus is the long awaited Savior promised to Israel, and in this woman's case, to the Samaritans who also awaited the Messiah like unto Moses. Jesus came in fulfillment of all that God promised Abraham and David. He came as the fulfillment of all the prophets. He is God's answer. He is our Lord. Let's not only listen to him; let's live each day for him.

PRAYER:

Holy God, I believe that Jesus is the Christ. I ask that he will always be vibrantly present in my heart as I offer myself again to be his follower and to live for him. Forgive me for those times in the past when my loyalty has been tainted and my influence diluted by my weakness and sin. Strengthen me so that I may follow with unwavering devotion. In the name of Jesus Christ I pray. Amen.

CONTEXT: JOHN 4:1-26

RELATED REFERENCES: JOHN 10:30-38; JOHN 17:1-5; MATTHEW 23:63-66

Day: 73

A CONFUSING CHRIST?

JOHN 4:27

Just then Jesus' followers came back from town. They were surprised because they saw Jesus talking with a woman. But none of them asked, "What do you want?" or "Why are you talking with her?"

REFLECTION:

The followers return and find themselves confused and astonished. Jesus was doing the unthinkable—he was visiting with a woman from Samaria. During their journey with Jesus through his years of ministry, they will find themselves confused again and again.

Jesus came to reach the lost, to save the sinner, to mend the broken, to raise the dead, and to heal sick. He reached out to touch the untouchables and welcome the outcasts. Such behavior was confusing to the religious culture of Jesus' day. He broke their religious "rules of engagement," breaching every prejudice and plowing through every barrier to reach the seeking heart.

We may not know how to cross social, racial, and ethnic barriers as well as Jesus did, but we know we must try. This was not just the Lord's example; it was also his final command to us in the Great Commission (Matthew 28:18-20).

So Jesus is not really the confusing Christ; he is the Christ on a mission to reach the world. He is only confusing when we choose to keep his grace to ourselves or limit it to those who seem socially and religiously worthy to us. But let's join him. Let's not let any false barrier keep others from the grace of God in Jesus our Lord.

PRAYER:

Father, please give me a heart for people who are seeking to find your truth. Give me wisdom to see the opportunities to touch these seekers that you have placed in my path. Let my love for the lost astonish others to your glory and to further the ministry of Jesus, in whose name I pray. Amen.

CONTEXT: JOHN 4:27-44

RELATED REFERENCES: LUKE 19:1-10; JOHN 3:16-17; MARK 9:30-32

Day: 74
LEAVING THE WATER JAR BEHIND

JOHN 4:28-29

*Then the woman left her water jar and went back to town. She told
the people there, "A man told me everything I have ever done.
Come see him. Maybe he is the Christ."*

REFLECTION:

Can you imagine coming to the city well by yourself in shame and returning to the village, your water jar left at the well, proclaiming the Gospel to the people who rejected you.

This lady had found it! She had received a drink of living water. Her life, her influence, her world was suddenly changed ... redeemed ... and made significant.

Have you been blessed by the Christ? Have you received a drink from the Messiah? Then why not join this unnamed woman and invite those in your world to come meet Jesus so they can find the Messiah, too!

PRAYER:

*Holy and righteous Father, please give me a powerful sense of your mission for my life.
Use me to influence others to come to Jesus. In Jesus' name and for his glory I pray. Amen.*

CONTEXT: JOHN 4:27-44

RELATED REFERENCES: JOHN 20:30-31; 1 PETER 3:15-16; ACTS 1:8

Day: 75

REVERSAL OF INFLUENCE

JOHN 4:30
So the people left the town and went to see Jesus.

REFLECTION:

How does this happen? How does a spurned woman who came to the well in isolation and shame lead a whole village of people to come discover their Messiah? The answer is simple: Jesus has the power to change people. That change is noticeable. That change is influential.

We are left with three questions from today's short verse. First, have you been changed by Jesus? Second, who have you influenced to come meet Jesus? Third, who have you not told about Jesus because you weren't sure they would change?

PRAYER:

Father of mercies, God of infinite love, Almighty Yahweh of transformation, please help me lead others to Jesus so their lives can be changed by his grace. Jesus, thank you for changing me; and thank you for interceding for me at the Father's right hand when I don't live like I've been changed. All praise and glory to the Father who sits on the throne and to the Lord Jesus, my redeemer and transformer. Amen.

CONTEXT: JOHN 4:27-44

RELATED REFERENCES: 2 CORINTHIANS 5:16-17; MARK 5:1-17; ACTS 9:17-21

Day: 76
FOOD YOU DON'T KNOW ABOUT

JOHN 4:31-33

*While the woman was in town, Jesus' followers were begging him,
"Teacher, eat something!" But Jesus answered, "I have food to eat that you
know nothing about." So the followers asked themselves, "Did someone
already bring him some food?"*

REFLECTION:

Jesus had real food—food that sustained his soul and not just his body.
While food is greatly valued by Jesus and his followers, we must always
remember that Jesus is trying to open our eyes so we can see the real food God
longs to provide us. The same power that sustained Jesus can sustain us. Let's
find that food!

PRAYER:

*Open my eyes, dear Lord, and help me see what is important. Turn my heart to your will,
your Word, and your Spirit for I know that only these can truly nourish me and sustain me.
In Jesus' name I pray. Amen.*

CONTEXT: JOHN 4:27-44

RELATED REFERENCES: JOHN 6:24-29; PHILIPPIANS 3:17-20; HEBREWS 12:16-17

Day: 77
The Nourishment to Continue

John 4:34
Jesus said, "My food is to do what the one who sent me wants me to do. My food is to finish the work that he gave me to do."

Reflection:

Where do you find the strength to continue your service to the Father? Clearly, some things in which we invest our time prove futile. Still others are worse than futile; they are depleting as well as useless. However, consciously doing what we do to honor the Father, to follow his will, enables us to experience his empowering presence (John 14:19-23). Rather then leaving us depleted, we find a new strength and vitality. Accomplishing the will of God and doing the work he created us to do (Eph. 2:10) blesses us as we bless others. That's why Jesus reprimanded the devil with the truth that God's word nourishes more than bread (Matthew 4:2-4). So we need to ask ourselves today, "What do I need to obey? What will help me live in God's will for my life today?" and then do it. As we consciously seek to live in the Father's will each day, we too can rejoice in the nourishing presence and power of heaven.

Prayer:

Majestic and awesome God, mighty in power and gracious in mercy, please give me the eyes to see what I most need to do each day to live in your will and do the work you have prepared for me to do.
In Jesus' name I pray. Amen.

Context: John 4:27-44

Related References: Matthew 4:1-4; John 19:25-30; John 6:53-58

Day: 78

THE SURPRISE HARVEST

JOHN 4:35

When you plant, you always say, 'Four more months to wait before we gather the grain.' But I tell you, open your eyes, and look at the fields. They are ready for harvesting now."

REFLECTION:

For the discerning heart and the listening ear, God reveals that we don't have to wait for the harvest. He has already called some of us to sow, others to be used by him to nourish the seed, and some of us to be his instruments of harvest.

Let's pray for hands willing to sow, for hearts willing to cultivate the growing plant, and for eyes that can see the fields that are already ripe harvest. Let's pray for God to send out more workers into his harvest fields. Most of all, let's pray for the people that God places in our paths each day by name, asking our Father to know whether it is planting, cultivating, or harvesting time in their lives.

PRAYER:

Loving Father, please give me a farmer's eyes and your Son's heart so that I can see those you have placed in my life for me to touch with your grace. Guide my words so they are appropriate. Protect my influence where evil would like to stain it. Most of all, use me to do your work in the lives you have given me to touch. In the name of the Savior of all people, I pray. Amen.

CONTEXT: JOHN 4:27-44

RELATED REFERENCES: JOHN 12:20-26; MATTHEW 23:18-23; LUKE 10:1-2

Day: 79

What Joy at the Harvest

John 4:36-38

"Even now, the people who harvest the crop are being paid. They are gathering crops for eternal life. So now the people who plant can be happy together with those who harvest. It is true when we say, 'One person plants, but another person harvests the crop.' I sent you to harvest a crop that you did not work for. Others did the work, and you get the profit from their work."

Reflection:

When people come to Christ, when they repent and turn their lives from sin, there is great joy. This is the joy of God's harvest. For the vineyard owner, it is the fresh taste of ripe grapes, it is the sweet juice running down his chin, and it is the joy of a full harvest. For the planter, it is the dusty smell of grain as it runs through his fingers, the heaviness of bags of freshly milled flour, and the smell of baking bread. For the gardener, it is the sweet taste of fresh vegetables bursting with flavor. For those of us in the Kingdom, it is the wet embrace of one newly baptized, it is the cry of "Hallelujah!" from each friend who has prayed for this moment, and it is the celebration of angels as the lost have been brought home to God. The harvest is about joy! Let's anticipate, pray, and work for the great harvest of God!

Prayer:

O dear Father, God of heaven and earth, please let me experience the joy of your harvest in my day like in the days written about in the book of Acts. Make this time the day of salvation and make me one of your instruments of the harvest. In the name of the Lord of the harvest, Jesus the Redeemer, I pray. Amen.

Context: John 4:27-44

Related References: Luke 15:3-8; Matthew 28:18-20; Matthew 20:1-16

Day: 80

He Has Told Me Everything!

John 4:39

Many of the Samaritan people in that town believed in Jesus. They believed because of what the woman had told them about him. She had told them, "He told me everything I have ever done."

Reflection:

What has the Lord Jesus taught you? How has the Savior shown you God's grace? When did you realize that Jesus could look inside your heart and know you completely ... and still love you with an everlasting love?

You see, when Jesus comes into our lives, we have every bit as much to share with others as this woman did and we have far fewer reasons to fear their reaction to us than she did. So let's follow her example; let's share with others what Jesus has done in our lives.

Prayer:

Loving Father in heaven, you are holy and righteous. Only because of your grace and the intercession of the Holy Spirit do I have the boldness to come into your presence in prayer. Please give me that same boldness, touched with gentleness and respect, to share with my friends the wonderful things you have done in my life. In the name of Jesus, your consummate gift of grace, I pray. Amen.

Context: John 4:27-44

Related References: Matthew 15:21-28; Luke 10:30-37; 1 Peter 3:15-16

Day: 81

PLEASE STAY!

JOHN 4:40-41

The Samaritans went to Jesus. They begged him to stay with them. So he stayed there two days. Many more people became believers because of the things he said.

REFLECTION:

Some people who saw the powerful work of Jesus in the lives of those they knew asked him to leave. Others tried to take that power and use it selfishly for themselves. Some, like the people in this village, asked him to stay longer so they could know him more completely.

God's messengers often find each of these same basic reactions to their message about Jesus—fearful rejection, selfish misappropriation, or a yearning for more of Jesus. Which is your reaction? Do you want Jesus to draw closer to you? Do you push him away because you want to keep him at arm's length? Do you sometimes wonder about what and why you believe?

Basically, none of us is ever really going to know about Jesus fully until we ask him to come "stay with us." There is something about inviting Jesus to come stay in our lives that enables us to hear him more clearly and believe in him more passionately. He stands at the door and knocks. Will you invite him in to stay with you so that you may learn more from him? (Rev. 3:20).

PRAYER:

LORD God, the Almighty of Israel, please come live in my heart through faith and help me believe in you more passionately. Please abide in me, O God, for without your presence I would surely fail. In Jesus' name I pray. Amen.

CONTEXT: JOHN 4:27-44

RELATED REFERENCES: MARK 5:9-17; MATTHEW 10:11-15; ACTS 8:4-8, 14-17, 25

Day: 82

EVERYWHERE BUT HOME

JOHN 4:42-44

The people said to the woman, "First we believed in Jesus because of what you told us. But now we believe because we heard him ourselves. We know now that he really is the one who will save the world." Two days later Jesus left and went to Galilee. (Jesus had said before that a prophet is not respected in his own country.)

REFLECTION:

One of the most crushing heartbreaks occurs when we can reach strangers with the gospel of Jesus while those we know and love most don't share our faith. Lest we think we are alone in this heartbreak, we need to remember that Jesus suffered this same rejection. He knows the weight of this specific sorrow (John 1:11; 7:1-5). We can share our similar personal grief with him. It took his resurrection to change many of them.

That's probably why Peter reminds us that to influence our family members, "they will be persuaded" through the changes they see in our lives because of Jesus (1 Peter 3:1-2). In our frustration and heartbreak because of unbelieving loved ones, let's go to God our Savior and ask for his comfort. Let's pray that his power will transform us so that our loved ones will come to see Jesus as Lord and Savior through the character and quality of our lives.

PRAYER:

Holy and mighty God, Father of compassion and grace, my heart is broken because of several in my family who do not know your Son as their Savior and Lord. Transform me by the power of your Holy Sprit to be more like Jesus. Give me wisdom to know when and what to say. Give me discernment to know when to be silent and to simply demonstrate the character and compassion of Jesus. In the name of your Son, I pray. Amen.

CONTEXT: JOHN 4:27-44

RELATED REFERENCES: LUKE 6:16-24; LUKE 10:13-15; MARK 3:20-21, 30-31

Day: 83

MORE THAN A PASSING INTEREST IN A MIRACLE MAN

JOHN 4:45-47

When he arrived in Galilee, the people there welcomed him. They had been at the Passover festival in Jerusalem and had seen everything he did there. Jesus went to visit Cana in Galilee again. Cana is where he had changed the water into wine. One of the king's important officials lived in the city of Capernaum. This man's son was sick. The man heard that Jesus had come from Judea and was now in Galilee. So he went to Jesus and begged him to come to Capernaum and heal his son, who was almost dead.

REFLECTION:

There were many reasons for people to seek out Jesus. Some were enthralled with him as a great teacher. Others were just fascinated by him as a miracle worker. Some wanted to find out what all the fuss was about.

Some, however, found themselves in situations too big and too grave to master by themselves. They knew they needed a Savior. We read about a powerful government official in these verses. But he was powerless when it came to what mattered most. He came to Jesus for help that only Jesus could provide. He wasn't ashamed to beg. He wasn't hesitant about inviting Jesus into his home. Only Jesus could help and he knew it. What about you? Do you find yourself in a situation too big for you to master? Then why not call on Jesus to return and be your Master?

PRAYER:

Father, I confess that I sometimes remove myself from dependency upon your power and grace. I often get so caught up in all the things that I think that I can do on my own that I quit depending upon you to sustain me. Now in this moment, I openly confess that I cannot control the things that matter most in my life. I ask for your mercy, help, and grace. I ask that Jesus will come into my life and mend what is broken, strengthen what is weak, and pick up what is fallen. Without your grace and the Savior's powerful presence I will surely fail. In the mighty name of Jesus I ask for this grace. Amen.

CONTEXT: JOHN 4:45-54

RELATED REFERENCES: HEBREWS 4:14-16; REVELATION 3:20-22; AMOS 5:4-8

WHAT MUST HE DO?

JOHN 4:48

*Jesus said to him, "You people must see miraculous signs
and wonders before you will believe in me."*

REFLECTION:

I have often heard people of today remark that if they could just have seen Jesus do one of his amazing miracles then they would find it easier to fully trust him. There are two problems with this point of view. The first is that Jesus is often doing miracles in our lives and in the lives of those around us every day; we just don't notice them. Second, many who saw Jesus do a miracle kept wanting him to do more or they would quit believing—they had to have booster shot miracles or their shaky believing would fizzle. This is not real faith. This is wanting a no-demand, sideshow Jesus who keeps us entertained and fascinated by his wonderful world of wonders.

What must Jesus do before you will really believe? I'm not talking about making a decision in your mind that what the Bible says about Jesus is true. I'm talking about faith the way most New Testament writers talk about it; do you trust enough to live your life governed by the truth of Jesus? This kind of trust leads us to lifestyle changes, a shift in our ethics, and radical changes in the way we view people and face the future. What must Jesus do to help you believe? Hasn't he already done it?

PRAYER:

Father, forgive me for not letting my head faith transform my lifestyle faith. I want to trust Jesus as my Lord in every area of my life. Empower me by the power of your Holy Spirit and convict me as I read your Word so that my life may directly show that I believe in Jesus and that my heart belongs to you. In Jesus' name. Amen.

CONTEXT: JOHN 4:45-54

RELATED REFERENCES: JOHN 6:26-30; MARK 9:20-24; JOHN 12:42

Day: 85

SOMETIMES OUR KIDS DRIVE US TO JESUS

JOHN 4:49-50

The king's official said, "Sir, come before my little son dies."
Jesus answered, "Go. Your son will live."
The man believed what Jesus told him and went home.

REFLECTION:

Sometimes the circumstances with our children drive us to Jesus for help.
Deep inside our souls, we already know that we should seek Jesus with all of
our heart daily. Unfortunately, everyday "busy-ness" and routine distractions
choke out our apparent hunger to be in his presence. Then the crisis comes and
we realize again how much we need him.

The real question for us is whether we will come to Jesus for help in our time
of need. If your concern for children or grandchildren is heavy on your heart,
please turn to Jesus for a listening ear, a sensitive heart, and the power to act. If
you aren't at the point of crisis, now is the best time to bring your children and
grandchildren to the Lord in prayer and spend time with them talking about
the Lord.

PRAYER:

Father, give me the courage to seek you in my crises and trust Jesus to act in my family to
provide those I love the opportunity to change. Give me the discipline and the will to bring
my family to you before crises come and lives are damaged. Make my house a house in
which your name is praised and your love is shared. In Jesus' name I pray. Amen.

CONTEXT: JOHN 4:45-54

RELATED REFERENCES: MATTHEW 8:5-10; MARK 10:13-16; JOSHUA 24:14-15

FAITH CONFIRMED

JOHN 4:51-54

On the way home the man's servants came and met him. They said, "Your son is well." The man asked, "What time did my son begin to get well?" They answered, "It was about one o'clock yesterday when the fever left him." The father knew that one o'clock was the same time that Jesus had said, "Your son will live." So the man and everyone in his house believed in Jesus. That was the second miraculous sign that Jesus did after coming from Judea to Galilee.

REFLECTION:

Sometimes we are blessed with the special grace of having our faith confirmed through obvious answers to our prayerful requests. These blessed moments not only enrich us, but they also give us something to share with our families and our friends. They inspire and strengthen the faith of those who know the story. With whom have you shared the story of God's work in your life? Who in your circle of family and friends needs to know the stories of God's faithfulness and grace in your life?

PRAYER:

Thank you, dear Father, for the many ways you have confirmed my faith in you. While I have gone through seasons of doubt and struggle, you have also blessed me with obvious answers to my prayers and your leading in my life has been clear. Bless me as I try to share this story with those who are closest to me. In Jesus' name. Amen.

CONTEXT: JOHN 4:45-54

RELATED REFERENCES: 1 PETER 3:15-16; MARK 5:18-20; ACTS 16:29-34

Day: 87

GOD MAKES HIMSELF AVAILABLE IN JESUS

JOHN 5:1-4

*Later, Jesus went to Jerusalem for a special Jewish festival. In Jerusalem there is a pool
with five covered porches. In Aramaic it is called Bethzatha. This pool is near the Sheep
Gate. Many sick people were lying on the porches beside the pool. Some of them were
blind, some were crippled, and some were paralyzed.*

REFLECTION:

One of John's recurring themes is that Jesus comes to Jerusalem during
important feasts to make God's love and grace available to the people. Like he
so often does, Jesus puts himself in a place that makes him accessible to
everyday people. This group of people had serious health problems and had
come to a place that legend had made a place of healing.

John, however, will remind us once again that Jesus catches up all the legend,
tradition, and meaning of his Jewish heritage and makes it all come alive in
himself. He is the great healer—not legend, not tradition, and not the feasts.
This healer makes God available to common everyday folks. No matter where
we go for physical, emotional, and physical healing, we must always remember
that true healing is ultimately found in Jesus. He chose to enter our world to
draw near to our hurt and show God's love for us in problems. No wonder that
Christians today sometimes refer to Jesus as the Great Physician.

PRAYER:

*Thank you, Father, for walking among everyday folks like me. Thank you for revealing
your glory in Jesus. I believe he is my Savior, Messiah, Redeemer, Healer, Teacher, Lord,
and Friend. I believe you sent him so that I could better understand your heart. Conform
my life to his example and his will. I pray this in his name, Jesus my Lord. Amen.*

CONTEXT: JOHN 5:1-15

RELATED REFERENCES: JOHN 1:14-18; LUKE 7:11-17; MATTHEW 1:20-23

Day: 88
WOULD YOU LIKE TO GET WELL?

JOHN 5:5-7

One of the men lying there had been sick for 38 years. Jesus saw him lying there and knew that he had been sick for a very long time. So he asked him, "Do you want to be well?" The sick man answered, "Sir, there is no one to help me get into the water when it starts moving. I try to be the first one into the water. But when I try, someone else always goes in before I can."

REFLECTION:

"Do you want to be well?" Sometimes our biggest disease isn't what appears in our body. Instead, the disease hides in our hearts. Our first hint of this man's real problem is found in his first reply: "There is no person to help me."

"Do you want to be well?" That's a much harder question to answer than meets the eye. I might have to change if I were well. I might have to give up my excuses if I were to be healed. I might have to take some responsibility for my own condition if my illness were removed.

Yes, many are sick and ill because of awful diseases, unfortunate genetics, or horrible accidents. However, many of us allow our illnesses to become our identity. Jesus asked the man this question because, in his case, his unwillingness to take responsibility was the real disease. As the man shows by the end of the story, he wasn't ready to take responsibility for anything—not his disease, not his healing, and not giving thanks. What about us? Do we really want to get well? Then we must come to Christ and be ready for the Holy Spirit to change us, and we must take responsibility for who we are whether we are sick or well!

PRAYER:

Father, I do want to be made well. I want to be saved through and through—body, soul, mind, and spirit. Even if you choose not to heal me, I commit to not let my disease or problems define me. I want my relationship with you to be the basis of my identity and my praise. I pray in Jesus' name, Amen.

CONTEXT: JOHN 5:1-15

RELATED REFERENCES: JAMES 5:14-15; COLOSSIANS 1:28-29; ACTS 2:36-42

Day: 89
Doesn't Fit My Religious Agenda

John 5:8-9
Then Jesus said, "Stand up! Pick up your mat and walk."
Immediately the man was well. He picked up his mat and started walking.
The day all this happened was a Sabbath day.

Reflection:

God created the Sabbath to be a day of blessing, rest, and reverence. Isn't it sad how religion can ruin the intended blessing of God with its own rules? Because Jesus did something the religious leaders classified as unlawful on the Sabbath (rather than looking at God's intent of establishing the Sabbath), they discounted the miracle, ignored the joy of the one healed, and criticized the one who provided the blessing.

How often do we do that in other areas in our religious lives? Hmm ... better move on; that's too convicting. Bottom line: let's make sure our traditions and rules don't keep out God's blessings simply because they don't fit into our religious agenda. As we journey through John, let's ask God to show us his heart, his will, and his intent for our lives through Jesus as he calls us to be holy children.

Prayer:

God forgive us for turning your blessings into hardships, your joy into drudgery, and your grace into a set of rules. Forgive me for not rejoicing more with those who rejoice and for not comforting those who have been wounded. Help me find the balance that Jesus demonstrated—knowing your will about worship while responding to the needs of those around him. In Jesus' name I pray. Amen.

Context: John 5:1-15

Related References: Matthew 12:9-14; 7:21-24; Mark 2:27-28

Day: 90
YOU GOTTA BE KIDDIN' ME

JOHN 5:10-13

*So some Jews said to the man who had been healed, "Today is the Sabbath.
It is against our law for you to carry your mat on the Sabbath day." But he answered,
"The man who made me well told me, 'Pick up your mat and walk.'" They asked him,
"Who is the man who told you to pick up your mat and walk?" But the man who had been
healed did not know who it was. There were many people there, and Jesus had left.*

REFLECTION:

You don't know who healed you? You've been trying to get into the pool all
these years and now that you are healed you don't know the name of the person
who did it? Didn't you ask? Didn't you hear everyone talking about him?

Yes, Jesus did slip away in the crowd, but how did this man let that happen
without finding out who he was? Here is a man who doesn't want to take
responsibility for anyone or anything. Here is a man with potentially a far
greater testimony than the woman at the well (John 4). Yet instead of sharing
his story with others, he's still trying to dodge responsibility.

And when the man does finally learn the name of his healer, instead of
saying "Thank you!" he turns Jesus in to the authorities. How sad! Which brings
to mind one crucial question for us: Do we want Jesus to be our "Mr. Fixit," but
fail to stand up for him in a hostile crowd or live by his values in an immoral
world? Sadly, this makes us like the man in John 5, doesn't it!

PRAYER:

*Cleanse my heart, O God, and teach me to love what you love and despise what you
despise. Give me a heart to tell your story of grace in my life so others can know that Jesus
is the one who has healed me through and through. Forgive me for those times when I
wanted only the Mr. Fixit Jesus instead of a daily Lord.
I pray in his mighty name. Amen.*

CONTEXT: JOHN 5:1-15

RELATED REFERENCES: EXODUS 31:12-17; DEUTERONOMY 5:12-15; LUKE 14:1-6

Day: 91

STOP!

JOHN 5:14-15

Later, Jesus found the man at the Temple and said to him, "See, you are well now. But stop sinning or something worse may happen to you!" Then the man left and went back to the Jews who questioned him. He told them that Jesus was the one who made him well.

REFLECTION:

"Stop sinning ...!" Interesting, isn't it, that while all the fury and fuss were about Jesus' supposed sin on the Sabbath, the real sinner was the man who was healed. He didn't want to take responsibility for anything. He wouldn't go out on the limb to honor Jesus and follow him. Jesus warns him, but the man ignores it. He goes and immediately betrays Jesus into the hands of those who would do him harm.

When we become ashamed to share the testimony of what Jesus is doing in our lives, the sad reality is, we are easily conscripted to do holy-sounding things that actually do the Kingdom great harm. Jesus says to us, "Stop sinning!" Let's heed his warning today.

PRAYER:

Father, stop me and confront me when I am being led astray. Stop me, I pray, especially when I am led astray by things that sound pious and religious, but which are really sinful and unfaithful actions. Give me a clearer and more holy understanding of your will in my life and a more powerful and holy influence upon my friends.
In Jesus' name I earnestly ask this. Amen.

CONTEXT: JOHN 5:1-15

RELATED REFERENCES: JOHN 8:4-11; JOHN 13:2, 27-29; MATTHEW 26:23-25

Day: 22
My Father Never Stops Working

John 5:16-17

Jesus was doing all this on the Sabbath day. So these Jews began trying to make him stop. But he said to them, "My Father never stops working, and so I work too."

Reflection:

For centuries, God heard prayers, created babies, healed diseases, and upheld the universe on the Sabbath. Why? So his children, his human creations, could be blessed by his rest and honor him. To turn the Sabbath rest into a legalistic debate, forgetting the very people for whom he created it, was a sham and a shame.

Jesus places his actions on the level of God's actions. He emphasizes that as long as his Father is working on the Sabbath to do things that bless others, he will too. Jesus' statement is both bold and daring. He is claiming the right to do what is good on the Sabbath, not just because God wants goodness to be a part of the Sabbath rest; Jesus, like God who is his Father, will not rest nor abandon his human children in their misery on any day!

Prayer:

Father, I do thank you that when I sleep, you do not. Thank you for working on my concerns, answering my prayers, sustaining my world, and doing your work while I sleep. I cannot comprehend it, but I am truly thankful that you are the God who does not tire or grow weary in doing what is good and what is a blessing. I recognize that all the good things that I have in my life have come because of your blessing. I praise you for your mercy and grace that sustain me. I thank you in Jesus' name. Amen.

Context: John 5:16-30

RELATED REFERENCES: PSALM 19:1-4; HEBREWS 1:1-4; DEUTERONOMY 5:14

Day: 93

EQUAL WITH GOD

JOHN 5:18

This made them try harder to kill him. They said, "First this man was breaking the law about the Sabbath day. Then he said that God is his Father! He is making himself equal with God!" Jesus has God's Authority

REFLECTION:

John's Gospel confronts us with a crucial decision: is Jesus really the Son of God, God with us in human flesh? He paints the story of Jesus so that we will see his claims to be God. One way he does this is through Jesus' "I AM" statements that tie Jesus to the revelation of Israel's God in Exodus 3. Jesus does only what the Father wants him to do. Jesus and the Father are one. If we have seen Jesus, we have seen the Father.

While we may not fully grasp what the incredible statement "God is my Father" means, Jesus' opponents in his own day did. They knew he was making himself equal with God by claiming to be Son of God. Their reaction is appropriate because when Jesus identifies himself as God's Son, he is either a blasphemer who must be stopped, a delusional power-grabbing religious rebel who must be thwarted, or he is God with us, Immanuel, the Son of God. He isn't just a servant, a messenger, or a prophet sent from God. He is God among us!

PRAYER:

Father in heaven, thank you for being God come in human flesh. Jesus shows me so much of who you are and how you care about me. Forgive me for the times I have not held you in appropriate reverence. Also forgive me, dear Father, for the times that I have robbed your incarnation in Jesus of its grit and mortality. I confess that I cannot fully comprehend how this all works, but I do know this, dear Father: I believe that Jesus Christ is your Son and my great God and Lord. In Jesus name I pray and offer you my thanks. Amen.

CONTEXT: JOHN 5:16-30

RELATED REFERENCES: JOHN 1:1-2, 14, 18; JOHN 14:6-11; TITUS 2:11-14

Day: 94
FATHER, SON, AND GREATER THINGS!

JOHN 5:19-20

But Jesus answered, "I assure you that the Son can do nothing alone. He does only what he sees his Father doing. The Son does the same things that the Father does. The Father loves the Son and shows him everything he does. This man was healed. But the Father will show the Son greater things than this to do. Then you will all be amazed."

REFLECTION:

Amazed? Yes, that is the word for it. Jesus will do many more miracles in his ministry, he will touch many more people, and he will teach many other awe-inspiring truths. The people haven't begun to see all that God will reveal through his Son.

The greatest of these astonishing revelations, however, will bring the people to full amazement; God will raise his Son from the dead and bring him back to life in their presence.

They will be amazed. Then his followers will begin to do great works in his name and the work of Jesus will continue to amaze millions as he works through his followers through the centuries and right down to today. Jesus' work is amazing! And, if we will look closely, some of that amazing work is being done in us!

PRAYER:

Righteous and Almighty God, your power is incredible and your holiness is unapproachable. Thank you for bringing this amazing set of characteristics together in Jesus and then sharing Jesus with us as our Savior. Give me eyes to see his amazing work, not just as I read the stories of his life, but also as I live for him and he does his work through me. In Jesus' mighty name I pray. Amen.

CONTEXT: JOHN 5:16-30

RELATED REFERENCES: JOHN 1:45-51; JOHN 20:24-28; JOHN 14:19-24

Day: 95

He Will Raise the Dead!

John 5:21

The Father raises the dead and gives them life. In the same way,
the Son gives life to those he wants to."

Reflection:

Death was inevitable for us. We could not escape it. We could not get around it. We could not see beyond it. Then God sent his Son Jesus.

Jesus conquered death. Jesus destroyed it as our most dreaded foe. As Lord, he showed us what is on the other side of death. Just as surely as the Father raised Jesus from the dead, Jesus will also raise from the dead those who love him and live for him. He has promised it. He has demonstrated it. He now longs to do it. He will one day raise the dead. Then, as God's children, we will experience his glory firsthand.

Prayer:

Father, thank you for not letting death have the final word. Thank you for demonstrating
your power over our death through Jesus' resurrection. Give me the courage to live with
conviction and faithfulness, knowing that my life will not be claimed by my death. I know,
dear Father, that real life has already begun for me with Jesus. However, I do look forward
to the day my Savior returns to take me home to you and I will live and reign with him in
glory. In his name, Jesus Christ my Lord, I pray. Amen.

Context: John 5:16-30

Related References: 1 Thessalonians 4:14-17; 1 Corinthians 15:25-28, 52-57;
Matthew 11:2-6

Day: 96

HONOR THE SON!

JOHN 5:22-23

"Also, the Father judges no one. He has given the Son power to do all the judging. God did this so that all people will respect the Son the same as they respect the Father. Anyone who does not respect the Son does not respect the Father.
He is the one who sent the Son."

REFLECTION:

"Show respect to the people you should respect. And show honor to the people you should honor" (Romans 13:7). I can't think of any human more worthy of honor than the Son of God. He left the glory of heaven and became human. He lived among ordinary people and was killed by common hands and thereby became a sacrifice for human sins. He was raised from the dead as God's powerful Son and has now ascended to God's right hand in glory. He will return in the clouds with unlimited and unveiled glory for every eye to behold. He will take all those who have loved him and lived for him home to glory.

How can we not honor him and the Father who sent him? How can we not long for his coming in glory? All praise to Christ the Lord, our King, Savior, Brother, and Friend.

PRAYER:

Convict me and empower me this day, dear LORD, and each day that follows so that my life brings honor to Jesus. Christ Jesus, please receive my praise as a gift of my love for all that you have done and all that you are and all that you will do. You are worthy of all praise. I exalt you and proclaim that you, Jesus Christ, are Lord! Amen.

CONTEXT: JOHN 5:16-30

RELATED REFERENCES: PHILIPPIANS 2:5-11; PSALM 96:1-13; JOHN 1:14

Day: 97

PASSED INTO LIFE!

JOHN 5:24

"I assure you, anyone who hears what I say and believes in the one who sent me has eternal life. They will not be judged guilty. They have already left death and have entered into life."

REFLECTION:

Every great once-in-a-while, I awaken after the sun is up and the glory of the day has begun. Without my fully realizing it, night has already passed into day and darkness into light. Without my awareness or wakefulness, dawn has broken and day is here.

In much the same way, as I come to know Christ and the salvation he brings, the more fully I realize that my life has begun again in a new, fresh, and exciting way. I have passed from death to life. Even though my body will ultimately fail me, my Lord Jesus will not. While death and decay will claim my physical existence, the eternal part of me is joined to Jesus and will never die. My future is tied to Christ. My sin is gone and eternal life has already dawned to be experienced more fully later in glorious day!

PRAYER:

Author of life, thank you for giving me a new life in Jesus. I know that I have passed from death to life. The life I live, I now commit to live for Jesus. Bless me as I seek to live wholeheartedly and vibrantly for you so that when my physical life is over, my real life is ready to fully share with you in glory. In Jesus' name I pray. Amen.

CONTEXT: JOHN 5:16-30

RELATED REFERENCES: JOHN 20:30-31; 1 JOHN 5:11-13; JOHN 3:16-21, 34-36

HEAR MY VOICE!

JOHN 5:25-27

"Believe me, an important time is coming. That time is already here. People who are dead will hear the voice of the Son of God. And those who listen will live. Life comes from the Father himself. So the Father has also allowed the Son to give life. And the Father has given him the power to judge all people because he is the Son of Man."

REFLECTION:

I have a friend who has been deaf for most of his life. His greatest anticipation is of the day he will hear again. He tells everybody that he knows the very first words he will hear are these: "Lloyd, this is Jesus. It's time to rise up and come home to be with me in glory!" All of us who have lived for the Lord will hear him call us from our graves. What an awesome thought: even though I live thousands of years after Jesus' death, resurrection and ascension, I will get to hear his voice and share in glory and grace.

PRAYER:

Almighty God, Father of all life and sustainer of the universe, you spoke into existence the things in my world. You spoke your Word through the prophets and the inspired writers of Scripture. I trust that you will one day have Jesus also call my name and I will rise up and come home to you. Please accept my thanks and praise until that day is fully realized! In Jesus' name I humbly thank you. Amen.

CONTEXT: JOHN 5:16-30

RELATED REFERENCES: JOHN 1:1-5; JOHN 6:35-40; JOHN 4:10-14

Day: 99

THEY WILL HEAR AND RISE AGAIN

JOHN 5:28-29

"Don't be surprised at this. A time is coming when all people who are dead and in their graves will hear his voice. Then they will come out of their graves. Those who did good in this life will rise and have eternal life. But those who did evil will rise to be judged guilty."

REFLECTION:

Do you remember the voice of your mother or father calling you to come home? I do. Of course my perception of that voice was greatly influenced by what I was doing and whether that was pleasing to my mother and father when they called!

For those of us who have lived for Christ, hearing the voice of our Savior and being raised from the dead will be glorious! His voice will be powerful, majestic, and thrilling. However, for those who have not lived for Jesus, who have done what is evil and not come to him for grace and salvation, his voice will be startling and terrifying. Let's make sure our love for the Lord ensures that whether we are alive or dead, when he comes, the sound of his voice will thrill us with the anticipation of our eternal glory!

PRAYER:

Father, shape my life into the character of your Son. Empower me toward holiness by your Holy Spirit as I seek to honor you with both my heart and my behavior. Forgive me for not being more passionate about living for your glory. Fill me with expectation as I await the sound of my Savior's voice at his glorious return. I ask this in Jesus' name. Amen.

CONTEXT: JOHN 5:16-30

RELATED REFERENCES: JOHN 11:23-27, 33-40; MARK 5:36-43; LUKE 7:11-15

Day: 100

THE GRAND CONSULTANT

JOHN 5:30

"I can do nothing alone. I judge only the way I am told. And my judgment is right, because I am not trying to please myself. I want only to please the one who sent me."

REFLECTION:

When businesses or key business leaders get in a bind or try to decide about strategic opportunities, they sometimes hire a consultant. They use a consultant to help them sort through the issues, avoid making careless mistakes, and make the best decisions.

Jesus consistently used this same strategy in his ministry. However, Jesus used only one consultant—the Grand Consultant, his Father. Incredibly, Jesus taught us to use this same Consultant as well. So as you face tough decisions or questions about what you need to do, why not follow the example of your Savior? Spend time consistently with the Grand Consultant! Make your decisions with one ultimate criteria: what will please the Father?

PRAYER:

Father, the all-wise and all-knowing Creator, please give me wisdom. I face decisions and I need your help. I have opportunities placed before me and I need your guidance. I have blind spots in my perception and need your truth. Help me know the way I am to go and the things I need to do to live victoriously and to fully honor you. Please reveal to me the places my life must go to please you. In Jesus' name I pray. Amen.

CONTEXT: JOHN 5:16-30

RELATED REFERENCES: JOHN 12:44-50; LUKE 5:16; JAMES 1:5-8

Day: 101

THE TESTIMONY OF SOMEONE ELSE

JOHN 5:31-32

*"If I tell people about myself, they cannot be sure that what I say is true.
But there is someone else who tells people about me, and I know
that what he says about me is true."*

REFLECTION:

Jesus didn't claim his authority as Son of God on his own. John the Baptist gave his life to testify that Jesus came from God. Using the principles of Jewish Law, Jesus will also add other witnesses to show he is from God—his miracles and the testimony of his own Father.

What John had to say about Jesus was all true; some of it even more true than John himself could realize when he said it. Jesus is the Light of the World, the Lamb who takes away the sin of the world, and the Living One who was alive before Abraham was born. He is greater than John the Baptist and he did exist before John was born. He is Jesus the Son of God. Now what we do with John's testimony, that eternal truth about Jesus, will determine our destiny!

PRAYER:

Father, I do believe you sent your Son into the world to be my Savior and Lord. Thank you for his sacrifice for my sins. Thank you, Lord Jesus, for all you did to save me. I believe that you are the Son of God, the Lord who conquered death, the Lamb sacrificed for my sins, and the Savior of the world who will come when the Father says the time has come. I praise you for your obedience to the Father and for your redeeming love for people like me. All praise belongs to you, Lord Jesus, the Son of God. Amen.

CONTEXT: JOHN 5:31-47

RELATED REFERENCES: JOHN 1:6-9; JOHN 1:19-23; 1 JOHN 5:6-10

Day: 102

A GREATER TESTIMONY

JOHN 5:32-34

"But there is someone else who tells people about me, and I know that what he says about me is true. You sent men to John, and he told you what is true. I don't need anyone to tell people about me, but I remind you of what John said so that you can be saved."

REFLECTION:

John the Baptist told the truth. John died for telling the truth. John gave his life to prepare the way for the truth. We could search through all of history and, except for Jesus, we could not find a more credible and authentic witness to integrity and truth than John the Baptist. John helped thousands find their way to Jesus and salvation.

However, as great a witness as John was, Jesus had a greater witness. God himself chose to offer his testimony about Jesus. He is the "someone else who tells people about me" Jesus mentioned. He had given his witness through the prophecies about Jesus' coming. He revealed himself in the words and actions of Jesus, which had the authentic ring of God's own words and actions. He validated Jesus through the miracles he performed and the resurrection that showed him to be God's powerful Son. How has God helped validate the truth about Jesus to you? How has the Father's testimony helped you to see Jesus as your Lord?

PRAYER:

Father, thank you for your word spoken through the prophets and shared with your people through the Scriptures across the centuries. Thank you for confirming Jesus' identity through his miracles and his resurrection. Thank you for showing your resurrection power in Jesus through the Church. Help me find ways to help my lost friends find your testimony to Jesus and come to him and be saved. I pray in your Son's name, Jesus my Lord. Amen.

CONTEXT: JOHN 5:31-47

RELATED REFERENCES: JOHN 1:-34; LUKE 3:21-22; MARK 9:2-8

Day: 103

BELIEVE MY WORDS AND DEEDS

JOHN 5:35-36

"John was like a lamp that burned and gave light, and you were happy to enjoy his light for a while. But I have a proof about myself that is greater than anything John said. The things I do are my proof. These are what my Father gave me to do. They show that the Father sent me."

REFLECTION:

How do you decide about Jesus? Is he just a good guy? Is he anything more than a great teacher?

Jesus asks us to make our decision based on the proof about him—especially his words and deeds. He asks us to listen to him. He invites us to examine his miracles. Then he challenges us to decide about him. Is he a blasphemer? Is he self-deluded? Or is he God's Son, the Messiah, and Savior of the world?

Many of us feel like we made that decision long ago. Does that mean we should take that decision for granted? Of course not. Nothing builds our faith quite like spending time with Jesus in the Gospels. So why not dedicate some time in the near future to reading through Matthew, Mark, Luke, and John and look to Jesus' greater witnesses, his teachings and miracles, to build your faith. Our journey through John is a good start, but it will be so much more powerful if you listen to all the witnesses to Jesus!

PRAYER:

Father, thank you for leaving a powerful testimony to Jesus in the Gospels. Thank you for the unique way each of these Gospels presents the story of Jesus. Build my faith and strengthen my commitment as I seek to get to know Jesus even better by studying his words and his mighty deeds. I pray this confidently in his name. Amen.

CONTEXT: JOHN 5:31-47

RELATED REFERENCES: JOHN 20:30-31; 10:22-30, 36-38; JOHN 15:23-25

Day: 104

YOU DON'T BELIEVE THE ONE HE SENT

JOHN 5:37-38

"And the Father who sent me has given proof about me himself. But you have never heard his voice. You have never seen what he looks like. The Father's teaching does not live in you, because you don't believe in the one the Father sent."

REFLECTION:

God sent Jesus to touch our hearts and call us back to himself. He sent his Son with a message of grace and with deeds of kindness. He sent Jesus to proclaim the coming of the Kingdom and to call us to live by Kingdom values. Incredibly, many religious people reject him either through blatant disregard or through hostile unbelief. They want God or religion or religious experience, but they don't want to believe that God came to earth in the Son.

Jesus, however, makes a powerful statement: "If you are choosing God, then you must choose me. If you reject me, you reject God who sent me." Crucial? Absolutely! Challenging? Yes indeed. Exclusive? Yes!

Jesus calls us to decide about him because he claims to be THE way to the Father. The issue isn't what we think about those claims, but whether or not Jesus is who he claims to be. If he is, then everything for us hinges on our decision about him. The issue isn't whether it is politically correct for Jesus to claim to be the one way to the Father, but whether or not he is eternally correct and if we align our lives to his will!

PRAYER:

Father, thank you for sending your Son to reveal your will and to save me. I truly believe that Jesus is your Son and that he died to save me from my sins. Help me to share my faith in Jesus with those who I love and to do it with gentleness and respect so that they, too, can come to see Jesus for who he is. I pray this in his precious and holy name. Amen.

CONTEXT: JOHN 5:31-47

RELATED REFERENCES: JOHN 14:6-11; ACTS 4:8-12; JOHN 1:9-14

Day: 105

THE CENTER OF SCRIPTURE

JOHN 5:39-40

"You carefully study the Scriptures. You think that they give you eternal life. These same Scriptures tell about me! But you refuse to come to me to have that life."

REFLECTION:

As important as the Scriptures are, Jesus is very much more important. He is the message to whom all Scripture points. He is the key to unlock the message of God in the Bible. He is the reason the "Amen" can be spoken when Scripture is read.

Jesus is the crucial, central, essential message around which all Scripture turns. Why? Because he is God's greatest word (Hebrews 1:1-3). He is God with us, Immanuel (Matthew 1:23). He is God's message (John 1:1). He gives life.

PRAYER:

Thank you, O LORD God of Israel, for speaking through nature, through Scripture, and through experience. Thank you, most of all, for speaking so clearly and definitively in Jesus. Please open my heart and my mind to the message you want me to hear from your Son. In Jesus' name I ask this. Amen.

CONTEXT: JOHN 5:31-47

RELATED REFERENCES: 2 TIMOTHY 3:14-17; 2 CORINTHIANS 1:18-20; JOHN 1:1-3

Day: 106

LISTENING TO THE WRONG FOLKS

JOHN 5:41-44

"I don't want praise from you or any other human. But I know you—I know that you have no love for God. I have come from my Father and speak for him, but you don't accept me. But when other people come speaking only for themselves, you accept them. You like to have praise from each other. But you never try to get the praise that comes from the only God. So how can you believe?"

REFLECTION:

Whose approval are you trying to receive? Peer pressure is powerful in the lives of teens, but if we are really honest, adults are even more susceptible to peer pressure. Look at designer fashions, the latest hot car on the market, the newest house styles, the most recent popular movies, the top ten books on the market, and a host of other areas where fads and peer pressure carry the day.

Can we stand up to the ridicule of others to stand with Jesus, or do we cave in, hide out, or give up our faith when it's unpopular? Sometimes our churches are stained glass museums filled with spiritually impoverished people afraid to speak up for Jesus because they're too concerned about what others think and say. Let's pray that we may be both bold and respectful with our faith in Jesus (Acts 4:31 & 1 Peter 3:15-16).

PRAYER:

Glorious Father, please give me courage to stand up for Jesus as much in the marketplace as I do when I am around other believers. Help my witness to be genuinely consistent as well as sensitive to those around me. Forgive me when I have worried more about what others think about me than I have about honoring Jesus as my Lord. In the name of your Son and my Savior I pray. Amen.

CONTEXT: JOHN 5:31-47

RELATED REFERENCES: JOHN 12:37-43; 1 CORINTHIANS 15:33; ROMANS 12:1-2

Day: 107
BELIEVE MOSES!

JOHN 5:45-47

"Don't think that I will be the one to stand before the Father and accuse you. Moses is the one to accuse you. And he is the one you hoped would save you. If you really believed Moses, you would believe me, because he wrote about me. But you don't believe what he wrote, so you can't believe what I say."

REFLECTION:

Jesus is that great prophet like Moses that God had promised would come. Except he is greater than Moses, and the covenant he brings is greater than Moses' covenant. At the same time, Jesus fulfills the Law of Moses. Jesus teaches the heart of God that lies underneath the Law of Moses. So we look to the Law as a way to bring us to a deeper appreciation of God's grace given us in Jesus (Galatians 3:26-4:4). Our appreciation and admiration go to Moses, but we set our hopes on Jesus, God's Son!

PRAYER:

Father, thank you for the Old Testament which so powerfully reveals your holiness, power, mercy, deliverance, and care. Thank you that your old Covenant looked toward the coming of a New Covenant when your will and words would be written on people's hearts. May I live the holy character that your Law reveals, yet may I live it out of appreciation for your overwhelming grace in Jesus and by the power of the Spirit he sent to me as a gift. In Jesus' name I pray. Amen.

CONTEXT: JOHN 5:31-47

RELATED REFERENCES: DEUTERONOMY 18:15-19; LUKE 16:19-31; HEBREWS 3:3-8

Day: 108

ATTRACTING A CROWD

JOHN 6:1-2

Later, Jesus went across Lake Galilee (also known as Lake Tiberias).
A great crowd of people followed him because they saw the miraculous signs
he did in healing the sick.

REFLECTION:

Folks follow the show, especially if they can get something for free. This chapter begins with a huge crowd who was seeking to commandeer Jesus' ministry for their own reasons. It ends with most of them turning away. We also get to see what makes up the heart of a true follower who does not turn away from Jesus when things grow tough.

However, the point we might want to make here is that when we do acts of kindness, service, and genuine compassion in the name of Jesus, people can't help but be attracted. Yes, some will turn away when hard times or difficult truths confront them, but others will come to Jesus and be saved and blessed. They will find life in him because they have seen it demonstrated through us. So let's serve and bless and let Jesus take care of the rest!

PRAYER:

LORD God, Father of mercy and God of all compassion, use me to serve others in the
name of Jesus. Give me courage not to compromise his truth, but also give me compassion
to serve others as he did. In Jesus' name I pray. Amen.

CONTEXT: JOHN 6:1-21

RELATED REFERENCES: MATTHEW 4:23-5:; MARK 3:7-12; JOHN 2:23-25

Day: 109

TIME TOGETHER

JOHN 6:3-4

Jesus went up on the side of the hill and sat there with his followers.
It was almost the time for the Jewish Passover festival.

REFLECTION:

If God's people live with a proper sense of urgency and passion before the lost world, they are going to grow weary. They will grow weary physically. They will grow weary spiritually. They grow weary of all the demands placed upon them.

Jesus frequently got away from the crowds—or at least tried to get away from them for a time—to spend time with his followers and his Father. Some of that time was for rest. Some of that time was for teaching. Some of that time was for prayer.

We must realize that we all need some "into the hills" time where we can be in Jesus' presence, learn from him, rest in his grace, and speak with him without being in a hurry and without the urgency of pressing demands. How are you doing with your "into the hills" time? A short email or online devotional fits our harried lifestyle and can sustain us for a time, but we all have to have some "into the hills" time. Set aside some time each day to be in the Father's presence and go "into the hills" with Jesus! Build into your busy schedule intentional "into the hills" time with your closest friends, your family, and your Father.

PRAYER:

O my, dear Father, I often lose track of how busy I let myself get. It seems that I try to cram my time with you into the few quiet moments I can find. Please open up some time for me in my schedule to spend some unhurried and concentrated time with you. Tug my heart so that I yearn for that time. Give me the conviction to not let other things deter or distract me. I confess that I cannot make it without your presence and power in my life. Draw me close, O LORD. In Jesus' name I ask this. Amen.

CONTEXT: JOHN 6:1-21

RELATED REFERENCES: MATTHEW 4:23-5:1; MARK 6:30-32; LUKE 5:13-16

Day: 110

A GREAT CROWD OF PEOPLE

JOHN 6:5-7

Jesus looked up and saw a crowd of people coming toward him. He said to Philip, "Where can we buy enough bread for all these people to eat?" He asked Philip this question to test him. Jesus already knew what he planned to do. Philip answered, "We would all have to work a month to buy enough bread for each person here to have only a little piece!"

REFLECTION:

"Be careful what you pray for, you may get it!" My experience with major church outreach efforts have been mixed. Some of them have gone bust—much prayer, planning, and effort with not much visible result. Others have seen such overwhelming and unanticipated response that we were left scrambling to handle all the "opportunities" that God placed upon us.

Let's confess something about our plans to do great things for God: God already knows what he is going to do. The issue isn't God; it's our faithfulness. God can and will make us more than we are for special times of ministry and mission. That's not only his promise to us; it's his track record through the centuries. So when presented with great opportunities, let's not resort to the greatest killer of all: "We can't." Instead, let's go to God and pray fervently for his guidance, our faith, and our willingness to work for his glory.

PRAYER:

Father, you are the God who is able to do far more than I can even dream. However, I confess that my abilities to execute challenging plans and see beyond my own limitations can make me hesitant to seize the great opportunities you place before me. Give me a clearer and broader vision of your will, your work, and your power. Give me a more willing heart to work hard and to dream larger dreams. Do your work through me and surprise me with the results. In Jesus' name I pray with anticipation and praise. Amen.

CONTEXT: JOHN 6:1-21

RELATED REFERENCES: JOHN 14:12-14; EPHESIANS 3:14-21; JOHN 5:20

Day: 111
WHAT GOOD IS THIS?

JOHN 6:8-9
*Another follower there was Andrew, the brother of Simon Peter. Andrew said,
"Here is a boy with five loaves of barley bread and two little fish.
But that is not enough for so many people."*

REFLECTION:
Our resources are limited. God's aren't. Our wisdom is limited. God's isn't.
Our power is limited. God's isn't. What we offer, in the face of such great need,
is small ... until it is brought to God through Jesus, and then it is multiplied,
empowered, enhanced, broadened, increased, and more than sufficient. This is
not just our hope; it is God's track record throughout his time with his people.

Let's bring Jesus what we have now and not wait until we think we have the
plan, the power, and the resources lined up to do what only he can do. Let's
quit waiting and wandering and wondering and bring him what we have and
see what he does with it and with us.

PRAYER:
*Lord God Almighty, God of Israel and God of the nations, I come offering you who I am
and what I have to be used for your work in the world. I know that may not go very far in
the view of a world so much in need, but I bring it to you because you are the mighty God
and it is what I have. I believe that you can do more with it than I can imagine.
I offer this in Jesus' name. Amen.*

CONTEXT: JOHN 6:1-21

RELATED REFERENCES: 1 SAMUEL 17:38-47; JUDGES 6:13-16; ISAIAH 60:22

Day: 112

WHAT DO YOU NOTICE HERE?

JOHN 6:10-11

Jesus said, "Tell everyone to sit down." This was a place with a lot of grass, and about 5000 men sat down there. Jesus took the loaves of bread and gave thanks for them. Then he gave them to the people who were waiting to eat. He did the same with the fish. He gave them as much as they wanted.

REFLECTION:

What do you notice here? The organization? The number of people? The bread and the fish? The blessing? The full bellies?

Take a moment and look at the impossible. This kind of thing just doesn't happen. It's ludicrous. It's simplistic. Yet the impossible occurs when our limited resources are brought to Jesus. Jesus and the impossible go together. The question is not whether Jesus can and will do the impossible, but whether or not we'll choose to participate with him in the impossible. Notice that with Jesus, the impossible is suddenly within reach, even in the most difficult of circumstances and with only the most basic of resources.

PRAYER:

Father, thank you for inviting me to share in the impossible through the work and presence of Jesus, in whose name I pray. Amen.

CONTEXT: JOHN 6:1-21

RELATED REFERENCES: MARK 9:17-24; MARK 10:24-27; LUKE 1:34-37

LEFTOVERS!

JOHN 6:12-13

They all had plenty to eat. When they finished, Jesus said to his followers, "Gather the pieces of fish and bread that were not eaten. Don't waste anything." So they gathered up the pieces that were left. The people had started eating with only five loaves of barley bread. But the followers filled twelve large baskets with the pieces of food that were left.

REFLECTION:

Some leftovers I love. Others I can do without. These leftovers are marvelous. I especially love the fact that there are 12 baskets of leftovers, one for each of the apostles!

I really don't think Jesus' main concern was cleaning up a mess. No, I believe he wanted to leave an indelible memory on 12 men. These men would be faced with impossible challenges and situations that they couldn't begin to handle when he left. This one memory would remind them again and again that their power was from Jesus, not from them. They had picked up the scraps with their own hands. They had carried the baskets. They had seen the picnic lunch shared by the boy that had fed the thundering hoard. Those leftovers were the tangible grace of Jesus left for them to touch. Nothing could be a more powerful reminder that their meager resources, touched with prayer and the blessing of Jesus, could meet the needs of others and much much more.

PRAYER:

Father, let me experience the leftovers of your mighty work after having stepped out in faith. I believe you can move mountains, heal diseases, and perform works that I neither can comprehend nor imagine. But, dear Father, I am always happy to pick up the leftovers from such an event! Show me the leftovers. In Jesus name I pray. Amen.

CONTEXT: JOHN 6:1-21

RELATED REFERENCES: LUKE 6:38; 2 CORINTHIANS 6:6-15; 2 CORINTHIANS 4:5-7

Day: 114

SURELY!

JOHN 6:14

*The people saw this miraculous sign that Jesus did and said,
"He must be the Prophet who is coming into the world."*

REFLECTION:

The people were "wowed"! They recognized something incredible had happened. Their reaction didn't last long. At least when they saw it the first time, they were convinced that something great was going on. Unfortunately, this was the "miracle on demand" crowd. They let their praises die down and their desire to see another "miracle show" rev up. In the following verses, they will get mad because Jesus won't continue the "miracle on demand" show.

God still does mighty things among us today. When he does them, let's praise him. Even when we endure a season where he doesn't appear to be working, let's remember that he is still at work even if he remains unseen. Let's be drawn closer to him—not to see another mighty deed, but to give him our hearts. The mighty deeds will come in God's time, not ours. So instead of our expectations, let's focus on God's incredible work among us!

PRAYER:

Father, thank you for your mighty deeds throughout history. Thank you for your mighty deeds in my life as well. I can only see an incredibly small glimpse of all that you have done, and yet I am awe-struck and I praise you. In the name of Jesus thank you. Amen.

CONTEXT: JOHN 6:1-21

RELATED REFERENCES: MARK 15:33-39; LUKE 7:11-16; MATTHEW 16:13-16

Day: 115

A DIFFERENT KIND OF KING

JOHN 6:15

Jesus knew that the people planned to come get him and make him their king.
So he left and went into the hills alone.

REFLECTION:

While tucked away in the middle of a busy couple of days in Jesus' ministry, this insight is the crucial one of the whole chapter. Jesus was being tempted with fame and power. It was a shortcut to glory that didn't entail the Cross. But, Jesus refused to be pushed and pressed into the crowds' mold (Romans 12:2). Instead, Jesus followed God's plan, not his own—and certainly not the crowd's self-serving plan. The Son is going to do God's work and will not be distracted by shortcuts or easy ways around the necessary.

How did he stay on his course? How did he not succumb to the adulation of the crowd? He spent time with the Father, alone. He shut out the voices of the crowd and listened to the tug of his Father's will on his heart.

How are we going to stay on course in our walk with God? We're going to have to follow the example of Jesus. We're going to have to say "No!" to the shortcuts and then go spend time in the Father's presence letting him tune our hearts to his song of grace. If Jesus occasionally "left and went into the hills alone" to be with the Father, then so must we!

PRAYER:

Give me patience, O LORD, to wait on you and your timing. I confess that I sometimes take things into my own hands and forget to spend time with you discerning your will. Give me the courage and patience to do your will, at your time, no matter what those around me want me to do. In Jesus' name I pray. Amen.

CONTEXT: JOHN 6:1-21

RELATED REFERENCES: MATTHEW 2:1-12; JOHN 19:13-20; JOHN 12:12-13

Day: 116

I Am; Do Not Fear!

John 6:16-20

That evening Jesus' followers went down to the lake. It was dark now, and Jesus had not yet come back to them. They got into a boat and started going across the lake to Capernaum. The wind was blowing very hard. The waves on the lake were becoming bigger. They rowed the boat about three or four miles. Then they saw Jesus. He was walking on the water, coming to the boat. They were afraid. But he said to them, "Don't be afraid. It's me."

Reflection:

Jesus' words to his terrified followers were powerful: "Don't be afraid. It's me." These words could literally be translated, "I Am; do not fear!"

Built on the purpose of his "I Am" statements throughout the Gospel of John, this one shouldn't be underestimated. Jesus' words build upon the twin concepts of the God of Israel who revealed himself as the great "I Am" in Exodus and the God who rescues from the ocean deep in the Psalms. "I am God with you; you don't need to be afraid! I can still the storm. I can preserve and protect."

Jesus comes to us in the middle of our storms and says the same to us. Storms are inevitable. But rather than taking cover and remaining a safe distance from the storms of our lives, Jesus comes and meets us in the middle of them so that we don't have to be alone! "I Am," he says to us. "Do not fear!"

Prayer:

Give me faith, O God, to believe that in the worst of my life's storms, I can trust that you are there and that you will ransom me home. Thank you for the assurance that you will never leave me or forsake me. In Jesus' name I thank you. Amen.

Context: John 6:1-21

Related References: Exodus 3:7-14; Romans 8:31-39; Hebrews 13:5-6

Day: 117

EAGER FOR HIS PRESENCE

JOHN 6:21

When he said this, they were glad to take him into the boat. And then the boat reached the shore at the place they wanted to go.

REFLECTION:

Sometimes we get so caught up in where we are going that we forget to take Jesus along with us. We try to do it ourselves rather than depending upon him. Bottom line, if we don't welcome Jesus eagerly into the middle of our lives, especially in times of difficulty and struggle, we're not going to make it to the place we want to go. With him, our journey is faster, safer, and more assured.

PRAYER:

Please forgive me, dear Father, when I try to do things by myself and do not depend upon your grace, the Son's presence, and the Spirit's power. I recognize that I will not accomplish what I want to accomplish without your grace, the Spirit's power, and Jesus' presence. I pray in his name, Jesus my Lord. Amen.

CONTEXT: JOHN 6:1-21

RELATED REFERENCES: 2 SAMUEL 24:1-10; JOHN 15:4-5; MATTHEW 28:18-20

Day: 118

WANTING JESUS FOR THE WRONG REASONS

JOHN 6:22-26

The next day came. Some people had stayed on the other side of the lake. They knew that Jesus did not go with his followers in the boat. They knew that the followers had left in the boat alone. And they knew it was the only boat that was there. But then some boats from Tiberias came and landed near the place where the people had eaten the day before. This was where they had eaten the bread after the Lord gave thanks. The people saw that Jesus and his followers were not there now. So they got into the boats and went to Capernaum to find Jesus. The people found Jesus on the other side of the lake. They asked him, "Teacher, when did you come here?" He answered, "Why are you looking for me? Is it because you saw miraculous signs? The truth is, you are looking for me because you ate the bread and were satisfied."

REFLECTION:

There are many reasons to follow Jesus. Often these can be selfish reasons. People who grow disillusioned with their walk with Christ may say that it wasn't "working for them." What they mean is that being a follower is harder than they thought and they aren't getting the obvious "payoff." We don't follow Jesus because of what we get out of him, but because of who he is and what he did for us. Sometimes we have to follow him in spite of the circumstances. If we follow only when we get what we want, then when hardship comes and the evil one attacks us, we're going to give up on God. Jesus' blessings remind us who he is and where he is from. They point us to God and our home with him. Let's live for him no matter what our temporary circumstances may be.

PRAYER:

Purify my heart, O LORD God Almighty. I want to follow Jesus because he is Lord and worthy of my obedience, not for self-serving motives. Please remove from my heart anything that is selfish and manipulative in my relationship with him so I can follow him with wholehearted joy! In Jesus' name I pray. Amen.

CONTEXT: JOHN 6:22-40

RELATED REFERENCES: HEBREWS 11:8-10, 13-16; JOHN 20:30-31; PHILIPPIANS 3:17-21

Day: 119
SEEK THE IMPERISHABLE

JOHN 6:27

"But earthly food spoils and ruins. So don't work to get that kind of food.
But work to get the food that stays good and gives you eternal life.
The Son of Man will give you that food. He is the only one qualified
by God the Father to give it to you."

REFLECTION:

Think about how hard we work and how much money we spend for things that are perishable. Most of what we purchase is subject to decay and destruction. Think of all the effort and energy we put into gaining fame and fortune even while knowing that those things are fleeting, but that faith and family endure.

Life—real life, authentic life, eternal life—is found in Jesus; he is its source, purpose, and destination. We must not forget that. Most other things eventually deplete our lives. Only Jesus gives us meaningful and enduring life that lasts.

PRAYER:

God, please give me wisdom to know what is important and what isn't. Help me use my
time and my influence wisely. Give me courage to choose the right thing over the acceptable
thing. Give me passion to invest myself in what is most important to you.
In Jesus' name I pray. Amen.

CONTEXT: JOHN 6:22-40

RELATED REFERENCES: 1 CORINTHIANS 15:50-57; 2 CORINTHIANS 5:1-9;
MATTHEW 6:19-21

THE ONE THING

JOHN 6:28-29

The people asked Jesus, "What does God want us to do?" Jesus answered,
"The work God wants you to do is this: to believe in the one he sent."

REFLECTION:

What does God want us to do? What is the work that endures to eternal life?
What matters most in the scope of all other things? Believe that God sent Jesus
to be your Lord.

PRAYER:

O Father, I do believe in Jesus. I believe you sent him to save us and bring us to yourself.
Thank you for this incredible gift. In Jesus' name I praise and thank you. Amen.

CONTEXT: JOHN 6:22-40

RELATED REFERENCES: 1 JOHN 5:11-13; PHILIPPIANS 3:4-9; ACTS 20:24

Day: 121
PROVE IT ONCE AGAIN!

JOHN 6:30-31

So the people asked, "What miraculous sign will you do for us? If we can see you do a miracle, then we will believe you. What will you do? Our ancestors were given manna to eat in the desert. As the Scriptures say, 'He gave them bread from heaven to eat.'"

REFLECTION:

Come on folks who lived in Jesus' day, get real! How many times does he have to do something spectacular? He gave you bread the day before. He got to where you are standing mysteriously and miraculously. You've heard about his great healing miracles elsewhere. What will it take to prove to you he is from God?

Oops, all I need to do is change the century and the story is the same for our day. Jesus has done so many things to bless us today. How many more will he have to do before we truly believe he came from God and he gives us life?

PRAYER:

Father, forgive me when I discount the wonderful things you have done for me through your Son Jesus. Forgive me for not giving thanks for your blessings in my life. Forgive me for not seeing Jesus' work of shaping me and changing me. I don't need another miracle or mighty deed to believe. I truly believe that your Son Jesus gives life. Thank you. I ask this in Jesus' name. Amen.

CONTEXT: JOHN 6:22-40

RELATED REFERENCES: JOHN 20:24-29; COLOSSIANS 4:2; LUKE 17:11-19

Day: 122

TRUE BREAD GIVES ITS LIFE

JOHN 6:32-33

Jesus said, "I can assure you that Moses was not the one who gave your people bread from heaven. But my Father gives you the true bread from heaven. God's bread is the one who comes down from heaven and gives life to the world."

REFLECTION:

Bread is the "staff of life" in many countries. But physical bread can only sustain the physical body for a short time. Only God's heavenly bread can sustain long term. It gives genuine life. Why? Because it has come from heaven!

As incredible a leader as Moses was for God's people, he couldn't give or bring the heavenly bread to God's people. Only God could send that bread. This was true when God sent them manna—his bread from heaven to sustain his people in the wilderness during the time of Moses (Exodus 16). Now, however, the Father has sent Jesus, the true bread that has come down from heaven. He alone can sustain life forever. When our life is joined to his, his glory and his life become our own.

Jesus didn't come down from heaven to keep this promise of life just for us—for religious insiders and people who already know him. He also came down from heaven to give life to everyone. As John reminds us elsewhere, Jesus was for the whole world (1 John 2:1-2). So let's not only enjoy this true heavenly bread, let's also share him with those who do not know about him!

PRAYER:

Thank you, dear Heavenly Father, for giving me true bread. Only your Son, Jesus, can feed the hunger I feel in my soul. I come to you to be sustained and fed. As I find my life and joy in him, dear Father, I also commit to share his grace with others. In the name of Jesus, the Bread of Life I pray. Amen.

CONTEXT: JOHN 6:22-40

RELATED REFERENCES: PSALM 63:1, 3-5; LUKE 22:19; COLOSSIANS 3:1-4

Day: 123

GIVE US DAILY BREAD

JOHN 6:34
The people said, "Sir, from now on give us bread like that."

REFLECTION:

The request is a valid one. Jesus even taught us to pray this prayer in the Lord's Prayer—"Give us today our daily bread" (Matt. 6:11). The problem is that this request for "daily bread" is substituted for a relationship with Christ, God's true Bread.

"Daily bread" only sustains for a day. The Bread God longs to give us sustains forever. What have you set your sights upon, "daily bread" or "eternal Bread"? Our goal must be to pursue the "eternal Bread," depending upon God to give us our "daily bread" as he has promised! Pursue God's eternal Bread and you get both. Pursue daily bread and you are left with eternal hunger.

PRAYER:

O LORD God, my Father in heaven, please fill my heart with passion for the right Bread. Please give me the true Bread of Life to sustain, nourish, and fill me. I believe that Jesus not only has the words of life, but that he is the true Bread that has come from you to give me life. Give me a holy passion to know him and to be filled by him.
I pray this in Jesus' name. Amen.

CONTEXT: JOHN 6:22-40

RELATED REFERENCES: MATTHEW 6:9-13; 1 TIMOTHY 6:6-8; MATTHEW 6:25-34

Day: 124

NOT HUNGRY?

JOHN 6:35

Then Jesus said, "I am the bread that gives life. No one who comes to me will ever be hungry. No one who believes in me will ever be thirsty."

REFLECTION:

Hunger is a powerful motivator. When human beings get hungry enough, they will do almost anything to acquire food.

What if we were that hungry for God? What if we were that hungry for God's Bread, his Son Jesus? While we have learned to recognize our physical hunger, so many today cannot identify that empty spot in their souls and the ache in their hearts as a hunger for God. Only God, through his Son Jesus, can truly fill this hungry spot. Jesus is the one who quenches our spiritual thirst and satisfies our spiritual hunger. Come to him. Listen to him. Let his words and his love give you life!

PRAYER:

Quench my thirsty soul, O God, and satisfy my spiritual hunger. I have tried to fill the void with diversions and trifles that do not satisfy. Father, I know that only Jesus can fill this empty spot in my soul. Only your Son can sustain me through the challenging days I face. I believe in you, Lord Jesus. Please come in and fill my hungry soul. I praise you and thank you for taking this prayer to the Father. In your name and by your I grace I pray. Amen.

CONTEXT: JOHN 6:22-40

RELATED REFERENCES: ISAIAH 49:8-12; PROVERBS 18:4; REVELATION 22:17

Day: 125

I WILL NOT REJECT THEM

JOHN 6:36-39

"I told you before that you have seen me, and still you don't believe. The Father gives me my people. Every one of them will come to me. I will always accept them. I came down from heaven to do what God wants, not what I want. I must not lose anyone God has given me. But I must raise them up on the last day. This is what the one who sent me wants me to do."

REFLECTION:

Imagine being in a relationship where you could be sure you would never be rejected. You are absolutely certain you would never wake up one morning and hear, "I'm sorry, but I've grown tired of you." You don't fear ever hearing the words, "I'm sorry, but I've grown apart from you." You never have to worry about hearing, "I never really loved you." Jesus came to seek us out and bring us home to the Father. When our heart is his, his love and his home are ours. Our guarantee is the Cross and our assurance is the empty tomb. He will not abandon us. He will not forget us. He will not forsake us. He will never leave us. He will not lose us. He will raise us up and take us home to be with the Father because that is what the Father sent him to do.

PRAYER:

Father, help me live with confidence today, knowing that I am your child and that nothing can separate me from your love as I depend upon Christ. Thank you that my future is bound up in you and not in my own spiritual strength or the capricious will of some religious tyrant. In Jesus' name I pray. Amen.

CONTEXT: JOHN 6:22-40

RELATED REFERENCES: ROMANS 8:31-39; COLOSSIANS 3:1-4; 1 JOHN 3:1-3

Day: 126

THE FATHER'S WILL: ETERNAL LIFE!

JOHN 6:40

"Everyone who sees the Son and believes in him has eternal life. I will raise them up on the last day. This is what my Father wants."

REFLECTION:

So often, people picture God as a surly old man looking for someone who messes up so he can punish that person. God's will, however, is that all come to salvation. He doesn't want any person to perish (2 Peter 3:9). He wants all to know Jesus and find salvation in him. This is what the Father wants!

Jesus is the way to God. Jesus is the door to a new and lasting life—not a temporary or imaginary one. Jesus is the focus, the hope, and the life behind God's plan. Learning to believe in Jesus is everything! Learning to see Jesus as God's Son is the doorway to forever! God wants us to receive a life that outlasts history. He wants us to know the assurance that nothing can ever conquer us once we belong to Jesus! He wants us confident that he will raise us up in victory and give us eternal life (1 John 5:13). So have you accepted God's invitation to find life in his Son?

PRAYER:

Thank you, God Almighty, the God of the Ages. You are the Alpha and the Omega and you have given me forever in Jesus. Please fan the fires of faith and keep them vibrant. Help me focus my eyes upon Jesus and trust him to lead me home. Give me wisdom to see through the doubts that Satan sometimes places in my heart. Help me experience the eternal life that begins now and that will never end. In Jesus name I pray and offer my sincerest praise. Amen.

CONTEXT: JOHN 6:22-40

RELATED REFERENCES: JOHN 3:16-17; JOHN 5:24-30; 1 CORINTHIANS 15:51-58

Day: 127

TOO CLOSE TO HOME?

JOHN 6:41-42

Some Jews began to complain about Jesus because he said, "I am the bread that comes down from heaven." They said, "This is Jesus. We know his father and mother. He is only Joseph's son. How can he say, 'I came down from heaven'?"

REFLECTION:

"I have come down from the Father!" That is the claim of Jesus' life and ministry in the Gospel of John. Either he is the Son of God, come from the Father, or he is not. Believing that has never been easy. However, let's not dismiss the claim too quickly or too easily simply because it doesn't fit into our oversimplified and greatly prejudicial boxes of human judgment. Let's not accept it so quickly that we fail to see the wonder of God's plan—to come to earth as a real person at a real time in history and live among real people and face the struggles of real life so we could know his deep love for us.

Some correctly looked at Jesus and saw a Savior that had come from God. Others simply saw a boy who grew up in Joseph's carpenter's shop in Nazareth. What you and I decide about that boy matters eternally ... and we must decide.

PRAYER:

Father, thank you for sending Jesus. Thank you for having him enter our world as one of us. I am comforted to know that he faced the challenges of my world and still triumphed over sin and death. Through your Spirit, keep my passion and interest in your Son aroused. Don't let me outlive my faith or ever take Jesus for granted. In the name of my Lord and Christ I pray. Amen.

CONTEXT: JOHN 6:41-59

RELATED REFERENCES: MARK 6:1-6; JOHN 1:43-46; JOHN 19:16-22

Day: 128

GOD'S WORK ON PEOPLE'S HEARTS

JOHN 6:43-44

But Jesus said, "Stop complaining to each other. The Father is the one who sent me, and he is the one who brings people to me. I will raise them up on the last day. Anyone the Father does not bring to me cannot come to me."

REFLECTION:

One of the reasons we pray so fervently for the lost is that it is God's work to open their hearts and bring people to Jesus (Acts 16:14). We can't make that happen. We can live as an example of Jesus' character, courage, and compassion before them. We can share the story of Jesus with them. But ultimately, only God can bring people to his Son and help open the door of their hearts to Jesus.

So, who are you praying for God to draw closer to Jesus? Or maybe a better question is, "Who do you know that needs Jesus, and are you praying for God to open your heart to him?"

PRAYER:

Gracious Father and Almighty God, I ask that you be at work in the following people's lives, bringing them to Christ and opening their hearts to the Gospel ...
In Jesus name I pray. Amen.

CONTEXT: JOHN 6:41-59

RELATED REFERENCES: JOHN 12:26-33; ACTS 14:27; ACTS 16:13-15

Day: 129

THOSE WHO KNOW GOD, KNOW ME!

JOHN 6:45-46

"It is written in the prophets: 'God will teach them all.' People listen to the Father and learn from him. They are the ones who come to me. I don't mean that there is anyone who has seen the Father. The only one who has ever seen the Father is the one who came from God. He has seen the Father."

REFLECTION:

Sometimes we miss the exclusive claims of Jesus because we've heard them so often. This claim is bold: "If you have listened to God and learned the truth from him, then you are going to come to me!"

Jesus not only claims to be the only way to the Father and the only one who has seen the Father, but he also claims that anyone who really knows God recognizes that he has come from God. Jesus comes to lay claim over your heart as a God-seeker. If your heart is tuned to God, you will find that Jesus is God's Son and your Savior. Don't let other false saviors and other religious claims cloud this one central decision: Jesus is everything or he is a false teacher and pretender.

PRAYER:

Father God, you are awesome in might, righteousness, and faithfulness. No one is comparable to you. Please bless me, dear Father, as I seek for you in the Scriptures. Please reveal yourself to me and reconfirm the identity and uniqueness of your Son as I study your Word and I am guided by your Spirit. In Jesus' name I pray. Amen.

CONTEXT: JOHN 6:41-59

RELATED REFERENCES: JOHN 1:14-18; 1 THESSALONIANS 4:9-10; ISAIAH 54:13-15

ETERNAL LIFE NOW

JOHN 6:47
"I can assure you that anyone who believes has eternal life."

REFLECTION:

John repeatedly reminds us that deciding about Jesus is THE watershed event in our lives. When we believe and obey Jesus, we pass from death to life—this is not a delayed transaction awaiting us in the "sweet by and by," but something that happens now.

When we place our full trust in Jesus, we no longer stand under judgment, but share in eternal life. While that life is not all that it will be when Christ returns, it is a quality of life, a character of life, and fullness of life that begins now! Don't settle for anything less than eternal life today!

PRAYER:

Holy God, please give me the courage and the confidence to live the life you have given me to its fullest. In Jesus' name, and by his power and grace, I pray. Amen.

CONTEXT: JOHN 6:41-59

RELATED REFERENCES: JOHN 5:19-24; JOHN 11:20-26; 1 JOHN 5:11-12

Day: 131

BREAD FROM HEAVEN

JOHN 6:48-50

I am the bread that gives life. Your ancestors ate the manna God gave them in the desert, but it didn't keep them from dying. Here is the bread that comes down from heaven. Whoever eats this bread will never die."

REFLECTION:

Manna came once a day. It couldn't be kept or stored over night. It was a blessing from God, but it wasn't enduring. Jesus, however, is the bread of God coming down out of heaven that gives lasting life. His words, his life, his body, his truth, are our sustenance. He gives life that never ends.

PRAYER:

Keep me hungry, dear LORD, for the only Bread that can fulfill, sustain, and give life. Keep my heart hungry for Jesus, my Bread of Life. In the name of the Lord Jesus Christ I pray. Amen.

CONTEXT: JOHN 6:41-59

RELATED REFERENCES: 1 JOHN 1:1-3; 1 CORINTHIANS 11:23-26; LUKE 22:19

Day: 132

THE FLESH OFFERED FOR LIFE

JOHN 6:51

"I am the living bread that came down from heaven. Whoever eats this bread will live forever. This bread is my body. I will give my body so that the people in the world can have life."

REFLECTION:

Jesus, unlike wheat that has to "die" to be made into flour, is alive. He died and rose again. He is living Bread. A person who eats this bread will live forever.

At first glance, this passage appears to be saying much the same thing that we celebrate in the Lord's Supper (Luke 22:19; 1 Cor. 11:23-24). However, Jesus pushes us deeper with his statements here. The word translated "body" in the passage above is a different word than is used in the passages about the Lord's Supper. Here, Jesus uses the actual words, "my flesh." It is a jarring phrase. It is a harsh phrase. We are to think of more than just eating the bread of the Supper. We must hear the deeper call of taking Jesus—his words, his life, his sacrifice, his bread—into our lives as our life sustaining food.

The gift of Jesus' flesh, taken to the Cross and sacrificed as a sin offering for us and then raised up on the third day, is offered so that the world can live—so that you and I can live forever! Jesus is the forever bread!

PRAYER:

Holy and righteous Father, thank you for making salvation so accessible in Jesus. Thank you for living in our world, facing our pain, enduring our ridicule, and facing a brutal death. Thank you for the hope that frees me from the fear of death because of your sacrifice for me. Thank you for the confidence this hope gives me in my times of trial. Thank you for giving me the living Bread of Jesus, in whose name I pray. Amen.

CONTEXT: JOHN 6:41-59

RELATED REFERENCES: JOHN 3:16-17; COLOSSIANS 1:19-23; JOHN 13:1-3

Day: 133
NO BACKING OFF!

JOHN 6:52-56

Then the Jews began to argue among themselves. They said, "How can this man give us his body to eat?" Jesus said, "Believe me when I say that you must eat the body of the Son of Man, and you must drink his blood. If you don't do this, you have no real life. Those who eat my body and drink my blood have eternal life. I will raise them up on the last day. My body is true food, and my blood is true drink. Those who eat my body and drink my blood live in me, and I live in them."

REFLECTION:

Sometimes Jesus made following him a real challenge. We sometimes forget this today when so much "bait" is used to attract people to Jesus. This chapter reminds us that Jesus challenged the pre-conceived and small-sized notions people had of him. He pushed them to make an all-or-nothing decision about him. He would not allow himself to become simply a miracle-working hero of the masses.

Jesus challenged the people of his day to either follow him as Lord with everything they had or to reject him and turn away. (If we are honest with ourselves, he is challenging us to do the same today.) Jesus is either everything God intends for us or he is a dangerous lunatic to be rejected. Which will it be for us?

Jesus refuses to be just a simple and kind religious leader; he challenges us to receive him as our life and sustenance. The question is not whether we believe this; it's whether we seek him, his lifestyle, and his character with all that we are.

PRAYER:

Father, I confess that I often times want following Jesus to be less demanding. I often want your truths to be more easily understood and more easily lived. I love Jesus with all my heart, but for some reason, I find myself not depending upon him as my life and my sustenance. Father, I ask not just for forgiveness but for a greater hunger for your Living Bread in my life. Feed me with his life as I seek to place him first in all I do. In his name, Jesus Christ the Lord, I pray. Amen.

CONTEXT: JOHN 6:41-59

RELATED REFERENCES: LUKE 18:18-27; LUKE 9:23-24; LUKE 14:33

Day: 134
LIVE FOREVER?

JOHN 6:57-59

"The Father sent me. He lives, and I live because of him. So everyone who eats me will live because of me. I am not like the bread that your ancestors ate. They ate that bread, but they still died. I am the bread that came down from heaven. Whoever eats this bread will live forever." Jesus said all this while he was teaching in the synagogue in the city of Capernaum.

REFLECTION:

Our power comes from a living Lord who was sent to us by the living Father! He allows us to receive his power. He blesses us with his life. Because of him, will live forever!

But how is this so? Won't we surely die? How is the promise Jesus makes here possible?

Our physical bodies will die. However, there is a part of us will never die. We belong to Christ. When our physical bodies die, we go to be with him. Then, when Christ comes again, we will be given new immortal bodies and go to be with him and all those who are his. We will share life with him, and all those who belong to him, forever! (Col. 3:1-4; 1 Thes. 4:13-18) No bread can give us this kind of life except the true Bread of Heaven, Jesus Christ God's Son!

But do we believe this? I believe that if you listen to that stirring in your spirit, the restlessness deep in your soul, you find that the deepest part of who you are longs for this to be true and recognizes that in Jesus, it is true!

PRAYER:

Father, please bless those on my heart who are struggling with broken, aging, and diseased physical bodies. We often find it hard to deal with our mortal physical bodies. However, dear God, please help those on my heart to not lose faith in Jesus' promise that the real and lasting part of them will never die—help them believe that they will live forever with Jesus. Give them courage and hope as they face the roughest part of their physical journey on their way to the best part of their spiritual journey. In Jesus' name I pray. Amen.

CONTEXT: JOHN 6:41-59

RELATED REFERENCES: JOHN 11:17-26; 2 CORINTHIANS 4:6-8; JOHN 8:51-52

Day: 135

HARD TO UNDERSTAND

JOHN 6:60-62

When Jesus' followers heard this, many of them said, "This teaching is hard. Who can accept it?" Jesus already knew that his followers were complaining about this. So he said, "Is this teaching a problem for you? Then what will you think when you see the Son of Man going up to where he came from?"

REFLECTION:

"Make it easy for them!" That seems to be the church growth slogan of today. "Don't put the bar too high!" In a sense, both of these slogans is correct. God came near us in Jesus because he wanted his grace to be accessible, understandable, and approachable. But he also wanted us to recognize that his grace calls us to leave our lives of sin and live under the Lordship of Jesus Christ and his teaching. This was not because he is a capricious or harsh God, but because obedience is for our good and our blessing and our protection—even when we don't understand why God makes some of the demands he makes.

Jesus didn't make following easy for folks who were only looking out for their own interests. Instead, he made his words even more challenging. He even made sure those seeking him knew the stakes involved, so for that reason, he refused to water down his challenging teaching for them.

While we want people to come to Jesus and receive his grace, we surely don't want to rob the Lord's message of its power or its demands. Jesus calls us to follow a tough road to a wonderful place of glory and grace. Don't let his challenging words put you off. He is the only way to real and lasting life.

PRAYER:

Give me a heart to follow only you and your messengers, O LORD. Please don't let me be deceived by those who are false or misled by those who don't know the way. Give me discernment so that I can know your will more completely and follow Jesus more passionately. In Jesus' name I pray. Amen.

CONTEXT: JOHN 6:60-71

RELATED REFERENCES: 2 PETER 3:15-16; MATTHEW 7:15-21; LUKE 13:22-24

Day: 136

LEAVING LIFE BEHIND?

JOHN 6:63-66

"It is the Spirit that gives life. The body is of no value for that. But the things I have told you are from the Spirit, so they give life. But some of you don't believe." (Jesus knew the people who did not believe. He knew this from the beginning. And he knew the one who would hand him over to his enemies.) Jesus said, "That is why I said, 'Anyone the Father does not help to come to me cannot come.'" After Jesus said these things, many of his followers left and stopped following him.

REFLECTION:

The Bible opens in Genesis with the creative and life-giving power of God's word revealed: he speaks and order is formed out of chaos and life out of inanimate dust. His Spirit hovers and fills his precious human creations, and they have life! Jesus claims to have this same creative and life-giving power in his words. His words bring life. His words set loose the Holy Wind of heaven and the Spirit brings life to those who are dead. (The word "spirit" means wind, breath and spirit!)

The people of Jesus' day couldn't handle such powerful claims, especially on the heels of such demanding and hard teaching. This part of the story in John 6 begins with the crowd wanting to make Jesus king, but he will not let them make him king on their terms. He calls them to follow him as heaven's King, to obey him as their Lord, and seek him as their source of life. Most cannot accept such a demanding call and they turn away from following him.

Is Jesus the King of your life or do you want him to just be your holy fix-it guy that you can summon on your own terms and for your own interests?

PRAYER:

Father, I confess that I sometimes try to make Jesus into the kind of king that I want him to be—one who fixes my problems and blesses my desires. Please forgive me! I don't want to be a fair-weather follower. I want to hear his words and obey no matter the cost. I really do want Jesus to be my Lord and my King. I ask for your power and grace to help me, in the name of Jesus, my Lord and King. Amen.

CONTEXT: JOHN 6:60-71

RELATED REFERENCES: GENESIS 1:26-27, 31; GENESIS 2:4-7; 1 CORINTHIANS 15:45

Day: 137

ARE YOU LEAVING, TOO?

JOHN 6:67-69

Jesus asked the twelve apostles, "Do you want to leave too?" Simon Peter answered him, "Lord, where would we go? You have the words that give eternal life. We believe in you. We know that you are the Holy One from God."

REFLECTION:

We come to many crucial decision points in our lives. None is more important than this one. What do we do with Jesus? He has been pressing us to decide about him all week as we have looked at John 6. Most of the world will turn away from him. Even though God's grace has prepared the way, the path is too narrow and the demands too difficult for most people. Most don't want to have to give up control of their lives to a real Lord. Most want a messiah whom they can tame, manipulate, and make into their own heavenly servant. Jesus won't settle for less than to be our King. He will not settle on being just our prince or prophet, rabbi or ruler, but our King and Lord. So will we turn away? Will we leave? No, for he is Lord and King, and he wants to be our Lord and King. Only he has the words of life.

PRAYER:

Father God, please sweep out of my heart any competing loyalty that would disrupt my whole-hearted devotion to Jesus. I want to follow him fully and obediently. Please help me find life in his words. In Jesus' name. Amen.

CONTEXT: JOHN 6:60-71

RELATED REFERENCES: LUKE 1:26-37; MARK 14:45-50; LUKE 4:31-35

Day: 138

TREACHERY LURKS IN THE SHADOWS

JOHN 6:70-71

Then Jesus answered, "I chose all twelve of you. But one of you is a devil." He was talking about Judas, the son of Simon Iscariot. Judas was one of the twelve apostles, but later he would hand Jesus over to his enemies.

REFLECTION:

We know the story before it happens. Lurking in the shadows is the traitor. Treachery is afoot. While we can speculate on why Judas would do such a terrible thing, Scripture doesn't completely tell us all we would like to know. The Holy Spirit only tells us that he did betray Jesus, that he kept the money bag for Jesus' followers and stole from it, and that the devil put it into his heart to do this this awful thing. From Jesus' vantage point, he knows that Judas will betray him.

Quite remarkably, Jesus will do the bulk of his ministry and offer his deepest and most genuine service to his followers, knowing all the while that one of them will hand him over to be tortured and killed. I don't know about you, but that is a bittersweet comfort to me. Bitter because I hate that the Lord Jesus had to face such a heartbreaking breach of trust. Sweet because I know he knows what it is like to be betrayed and sold out by someone close—and he knows, not just as God, but also as a brokenhearted friend who has been betrayed. Sounds like my world. Sounds even more like my Savior!

PRAYER:

Holy God, Creator and Sustainer of all that is, I thank you. I thank you for not being a god who is far off. I thank you for living in my world and bearing the brunt of its broken-ness and betrayal. Please bless me with confidence as I approach you, knowing that you know the deepest pains of my heart from experience and not just omniscience. Thank you for revealing yourself in Jesus, in whose name I pray. Amen.

CONTEXT: JOHN 6:60-71

RELATED REFERENCES: JOHN 13:1-5; MATTHEW 26:16; JOHN 13:21-30

Day: 139

NOT TO JUDEA

JOHN 7:1

After this, Jesus traveled around the country of Galilee. He did not want to travel in Judea, because the Jewish leaders there wanted to kill him.

REFLECTION:

Jesus stayed away ... at least for now ... until the time was God's time. (Verses 6-9)Jesus would not be hurried or rushed by the agenda of others. He followed God's timetable, not the crowds or his family's. He concentrated his work on places where there were many people who needed God's grace. He was wise and prudent when under pressure, but he didn't allow the threats of others to curtail his service—he simply found a more accepting place for his ministry or waited until God showed him to carry on his ministry in the face of opposition in the place he was hated.

What a powerful message for us today; especially for those of us who sometimes find ourselves in horrible and challenging circumstances with enemies fiercely opposing us.

PRAYER:

Give me strength, O God, and a pure heart for my journey to you. Don't let me be deterred by those who would seek to dilute my faith, derail my sense of mission, or harm me. At the same time, dear Father, please help me honor the people around me with respect. Give me wisdom to know how to honor those I should honor while still remaining true to you. In Jesus' name I pray. Amen.

CONTEXT: JOHN 7:1-9

RELATED REFERENCES: JOHN 10:39-42; JOHN 11:15-16; JOHN 11:45-53

Day: 140
THEY JUST DON'T GET IT!

JOHN 7:2-5

It was time for the Jewish Festival of Shelters. So his brothers said to him, "You should leave here and go to the festival in Judea. Then your followers there can see the miracles you do. If you want to be well-known, you must not hide what you do. So show yourself to the world. Let them see these things you do." Jesus' brothers said this because even they did not believe in him.

REFLECTION:

Imagine how hard it must have been for Jesus. His family just didn't get it. The Lord's physical half brothers and sisters didn't understand and didn't believe until after his resurrection. Jesus didn't do miracles to "show out" for his followers, but to give them a sign so they could look beyond what they were seeing and understand that he had come from God.

Jesus wasn't trying to be a public figure, but instead, resisted the crowd's desires to make him king. He trusted that the Cross would draw people to him and to God's love. His signs, the very miraculous things his brothers nudged him to perform, brought to some a stronger faith, but brought others only more questions and some an even more determined commitment to reject and silence Jesus. Jesus wouldn't be bullied, teased, or ridiculed into anything. He would follow God's timing and do things God's way.

PRAYER:

Holy and faithful Father, please give me more patience to wait for the right moment to do what you want me to do and the courage to do it with passion and faith. Give me strength to resist any negative peer influences upon me. Forgive me, loving Father, for the times I have gone with the crowd so I would be accepted rather than sticking to your plan no matter the cost. In Jesus' name I pray. Amen.

CONTEXT: JOHN 7:1-9

RELATED REFERENCES: MARK 3:31-35; ACTS 1:12-14; LUKE 12:8-9

Day: 141
POINTING OUT EVIL

JOHN 7:6-9

Jesus said to them, "The right time for me has not yet come, but any time is right for you to go. The world cannot hate you. But the world hates me, because I tell the people in the world that they do evil things. So you go to the festival. I will not go now, because the right time for me has not yet come." After Jesus said this, he stayed in Galilee.

REFLECTION:

So much is not said today because of the political correctness police. That's not said to give us an excuse for prejudicial or bigoted speech. Instead, refusing to call sin "Sin!" is my concern.

Jesus didn't just leave happy and healed people in the wake of his ministry. Some of the folks he met will reappear later in the story crying, "Kill him on a cross!" They didn't like it when he called their evil ways what it actually was. We must not either. Evil is still evil. Sin is still sin. Wrong is still wrong. Injustice is still injustice.

Truth often makes us uncomfortable with our sin and hopefully will lead us to change. Unfortunately, many don't want to be brought to the light of the truth. (John 3:16-21) Jesus was crucified for several key reasons, but we must realize that one of those reasons was simply this: many people, especially religious people, don't like being told they were sinners and did evil things. They had Jesus killed because they hated Jesus!

PRAYER:

Father, please give me greater wisdom so that I can demonstrate your love with compassion while at the same time stand up for your truth and righteousness. While I know others may not understand my faith, strengthen me through your Holy Spirit so that I will stand faithfully no matter how great the opposition and no matter how close to home that opposition might be. In the name of Jesus. Amen.

CONTEXT: JOHN 7:1-9

RELATED REFERENCES: JOHN 3:19-21; 1 PETER 4:2-5; 1 JOHN 3:1-3

Day: 142

CHALLENGE TO BELIEVING

JOHN 7:10-13

So his brothers left to go to the festival. After they left, Jesus went too, but he did not let people see him. At the festival the Jewish leaders were looking for him. They said, "Where is that man?" There was a large group of people there. Many of them were talking secretly to each other about Jesus. Some people said, "He is a good man." But others said, "No, he fools the people." But no one was brave enough to talk about him openly. They were afraid of the Jewish leaders.

REFLECTION:

People don't come to faith in a vacuum. The enemy of faith, the devil, is always trying to cast doubt and reinforce unbelief with fear. Throughout John's story of Jesus, we will see the struggle to believe take place in the context of fear and rejection.

How many people around you would be more willing to believe if you were more open about your faith? Is there someone, or something, keeping you silent because of fear or potential rejection? Faith is not just believing in our heads and hearts; it is believing with our lives—demonstrating our faith with our actions, words, and influence. Don't let fear silence your faith; someone around you has her or his salvation depending upon your willingness to share the message and life of Jesus!

PRAYER:

Father, please give me courage and wisdom to demonstrate my faith in appropriate and effective ways. I need your help to influence those around me to come to Jesus. I need your guidance as I try to be bold about my faith without turning off those around me. I need your wisdom to know when the hearts of those around are open to your grace. Please help me know the right time for these things. In Jesus' name I ask for your help to have a redemptive influence in my world. Amen.

CONTEXT: JOHN 7:10-24

RELATED REFERENCES: JOHN 12:37-44; JOHN 9:18-23; JOHN 19:38-40

Day: 143
RELIGIOUS ARROGANCE

JOHN 7:14-15

When the festival was about half finished, Jesus went to the Temple area and began to teach. The Jewish leaders were amazed and said, "How did this man learn so much? He never had the kind of teaching we had!"

REFLECTION:

Arrogance is such an unattractive and unnecessary trait. Not only is it sinful, it also shuts us off from truth. None of us has a corner on the market for truth. Education, experience, and training should not mean that we refuse to learn something from someone who does not have these advantages. Christian living is about faithfulness, not about the letters that come after a comma at the end of our name.

Jesus came from God. He spoke the truth of God. He called others to share God's message. He calls us to listen to others whose lives reflect the truth of that message and to learn from them without prejudice. Education, experience, and training can be fantastic tools when coupled with humility. Let's commit to be true followers of Jesus. Let's commit to be life-long learners!

PRAYER:

Father, forgive me for those times that I have not listened to others because I have thought that they had nothing to teach me. Humble me gently. Help me discern your truth no matter from whom I need to learn it. Give me a heart that is open to all that you want to teach me. In Jesus' name. Amen.

CONTEXT: JOHN 7:10-24

RELATED REFERENCES: ACTS 4:8-14; JOHN 3:1-2; JOHN 9:24-34

NOT MY OWN IDEAS

JOHN 7:16

Jesus answered, "What I teach is not my own.
My teaching comes from the one who sent me."

REFLECTION:

Jesus wants those who would reject him to know that his words do not find their origin in a man's opinion. His words come from God! He is more than a prophet. He is more than a teacher. They had better not discount him because they thought they knew where he was born and that he was not educated.

His message is divine. His ideas are heaven-sent. What we do with Jesus is what we decide about God.

PRAYER:

Almighty God, I thank you for revealing yourself to me in Jesus. Thank you for speaking
your words of truth through your Son. Help me as I seek to both understand and obey
Jesus' words and honor your will. Transform me to be more like your Son as I seek to honor
his words in my lifestyle. In Jesus' name I pray. Amen.

CONTEXT: JOHN 7:10-24

RELATED REFERENCES: JOHN 5:16-23; JOHN 8:23-30; JOHN 1:14-18

Day: 145
You Will Know!

John 7:17

"People who really want to do what God wants will know that my teaching comes from God. They will know that this teaching is not my own."

Reflection:

Who are you trying to honor? For whom do you want to live?

If you are seeking to honor God, then you will know what Jesus is about. If you are seeking the truth, you will find that Jesus opens the door for you to heaven. Come learn from him and you will know the way to God!

Prayer:

More than anything else, dear Father, I want to honor you. I confess that I sometimes lose focus and drift in my spiritual walk, but in my heart of hearts, I want to honor you. Forgive me for the times I have been lax in my spiritual fervor. Remind me how much I need to learn from Jesus everyday. Please gently turn me back to your way and to my holy passion when I become distracted. In Jesus' name I pray. Amen.

Context: John 7:10-24

Related References: Matthew 7:7-11; John 8:31-42; Matthew 11:28-30

Day: 146

THE HEART OF GOD'S MESSENGER

JOHN 7:18

*"If I taught my own ideas, I would just be trying to get honor for myself.
But if I am trying to bring honor to the one who sent me, I can be trusted.
Anyone doing that is not going to lie."*

REFLECTION:

What are you in it for? Why would you want to teach God's Word to someone else? Why would you want to share your faith with a friend? Why would you want to speak out for Christian values?

Jesus makes it very simple and clear: the motive of God's messenger is to honor the Father. So let's ask ourselves if what we say, teach, explain, expound, or suggest brings honor to God, or to ourselves!

PRAYER:

Father, may the words of my mouth and the meditations of my heart and the motives for my speech be pleasing to you and bring you glory. In Jesus' name I pray. Amen.

CONTEXT: JOHN 7:10-24

RELATED REFERENCES: HEBREWS 1:1-3; PROVERBS 25:13; 1 CORINTHIANS 6:19-20

Day: 147

BLINDED TO THE TRUTH BY OUR PRACTICE

JOHN 7:19-24

"Moses gave you the law, right? But you don't obey that law. If you do, then why are you trying to kill me?" The people answered, "A demon is making you crazy! We are not trying to kill you." Jesus said to them, "I did one miracle on a Sabbath day, and you were all surprised. But you obey the law Moses gave you about circumcision—and sometimes you do it on a Sabbath day. (Really, Moses is not the one who gave you circumcision. It came from our ancestors who lived before Moses.) Yes, you often circumcise baby boys on a Sabbath day. This shows that someone can be circumcised on a Sabbath day to obey the Law of Moses. So why are you angry with me for healing a person's whole body on the Sabbath day? Stop judging by the way things look. Be fair and judge by what is really right."

REFLECTION:

Jesus looks through the duplicity of his accusers and sees the bare, naked ugliness of their warped religion. He knew they were after him, not because they supported the truth, but because they twisted the truth to fit their own prejudicial conclusions. The heart of the Law God gave Moses was not their plumb line; instead, they interpreted the Law to fit their understanding. In the process, the heart of God got lost in all the religious practice. Isn't it interesting that we can clearly see this problem in them and miss it in ourselves! Our own traditions, and practices can literally blind us to God's truth. So before we get ready to pass judgment on others, let's humbly ask God for wisdom and clarity as we seek his will in our own lives.

PRAYER:

Father, I come to you acknowledging that my insight is shallow and my wisdom very limited. I don't want to see your will watered down by fuzzy, conviction-less religion that poses as Christianity. At the same time, Father, I don't want to find everyone else's faults while justifying my own. Please give me wisdom so that I can live my life with integrity, truthfulness, and honor. In Jesus' name I pray. Amen.

CONTEXT: JOHN 7:10-24

RELATED REFERENCES: JOHN 5:39-40; MATTHEW 7:1-5; 1 SAMUEL 16:1-6

Day: 148

SOMETIMES WE JUST SCRATCH THE SURFACE

JOHN 7:25-27

Then some of the people who lived in Jerusalem said, "This is the man they are trying to kill. But he is teaching where everyone can see and hear him. And no one is trying to stop him from teaching. Maybe the leaders have decided that he really is the Christ. But when the real Christ comes, no one will know where he comes from. And we know where this man's home is."

REFLECTION:

Jesus is from God. That is one of the primary declarations of the Gospel of John. However, many folks miss this truth about Jesus. There are a variety of reasons they miss this truth. Some thought that Jesus violated the Sabbath. Some thought he spent too much time with sinners. Some preferred the acceptance of their peers to the call of Jesus in their lives. Others thought that they knew where he came from, but hadn't dug deep enough to really know the truth.

John let's us, his readers, in on the truth. Jesus comes from God. He speaks the words of God. He does the work of God. He completes the mission God gave him to do. So have you come to terms with this true Jesus? Or is Jesus still just a religious figure you try to tame and manipulate for your own desires? Ask God to help you know Jesus more fully and honor him more completely with your life.

PRAYER:

Almighty God and heavenly Father, please help open the hearts of several of my friends who have rejected Jesus as Lord because they think they know more about him than they really do. Use me to help them open their hearts to the truth about Jesus. Empower me and bless my influence as I seek to serve them in Jesus' name. In Jesus' name I pray. Amen

CONTEXT: JOHN 7:25-36

RELATED REFERENCES: JOHN 8:42-47; JOHN 13:1-5; JOHN 14:1-11

Day: 149

MY FATHER SENT ME!

JOHN 7:28-29

Jesus was still teaching in the Temple area when he said loudly, "Do you really know me and where I am from? I am here, but not by my own decision. I was sent by one who is very real. But you don't know him. I know him because I am from him. He is the one who sent me."

REFLECTION:

Jesus came on a mission. It wasn't a mission of his own initiative. He wasn't looking for honor for himself. He was sent to do the Father's work, to accomplish the Father's mission, and to bring glory to the Father by completing his work. The cost was high; he gave his life to complete the Father's work.

The mission was clear: to reveal the Father to us. The amazing thing about it, however, is that when Jesus left this world, he gives us a very similar mission. "The Father sent me. In the same way, I now send you" (John 20:21). So let's live today following the example of our Savior: let's be fully committed to represent the one who sent us to reveal his glory and grace.

PRAYER:

Holy God and loving Father, I confess that sometimes I see life as monotonous and predictable. I lose sight of the opportunities to do your work with each new day. Sharpen my focus God, so that I will seize the opportunities each day to help others see you more clearly. Give me passion as I face the challenges, opportunities, and even the monotony of each day. Empower me to live as one sent on a mission. In Jesus' name I pray. Amen.

CONTEXT: JOHN 7:25-36

RELATED REFERENCES: JOHN 3:10-17; JOHN 10:22-25, 36-41; 1 JOHN 4:9-10

Day: 150

MANY PUT THEIR FAITH IN HIM

JOHN 7:30-31

When Jesus said this, the people tried to grab him. But no one was able even to touch him, because the right time for him had not yet come. But many of the people believed in Jesus. They said, "We are waiting for the Christ to come. When he comes, will he do more miraculous signs than this man has done?"

REFLECTION:

Even with pressure from the authorities not to believe, many still put their faith in Jesus. Why? They saw what he did and recognized that there had to be divine power behind it.

Today, when unbelievers look at our churches (that are supposed to be the bodily presence of Christ) what do they see? Do they see compelling deeds that cry out that God has to be behind what we do or we couldn't do it? Or, do they see predictable "church stuff"? Jesus promised that we would do even greater things than he did (John 14:25). So let's go out and be what he called us to be and do the life-changing work of the Kingdom, not just the housekeeping work of "churchiness."

PRAYER:

Dear LORD, God Almighty, please ignite my congregation of Christians, and me in particular, to a higher calling and a larger vision of what you want to do with us. Use us in our community, and beyond, to do the work of Jesus. Use us in ways that we don't even think is possible. Most of all, dear Father, help your work through us to lead others to believe in Jesus, in whose name I pray. Amen.

CONTEXT: JOHN 7:25-36

RELATED REFERENCES: JOHN 14:12-14; JOHN 4:39-53; JOHN 10:45-48

Day: 151
LIMITED TIME
JOHN 7:32-36

The Pharisees heard what the people were saying about Jesus. So the leading priests and the Pharisees sent some Temple police to arrest him. Then Jesus said, "I will be with you a little while longer. Then I will go back to the one who sent me. You will look for me, but you will not find me. And you cannot come where I am." These Jews said to each other, "Where will this man go that we cannot find him? Will he go to the Greek cities where our people live? Will he teach the Greek people there? He says, 'You will look for me, but you will not find me.' He also says, 'You cannot come where I am.' What does this mean?"

REFLECTION:

So often we find ways to put off doing the right thing by making excuses—or as in this case, posing religious sounding questions—for not responding to God in the proper way. I don't know how many times I've seen a husband or wife get serious about his or her marital commitment too late to make a difference. Opportunities to live for Jesus vibrantly and passionately can pass us by each day while our hearts grow more and more callused. One day, there will be no more opportunities. Our hearts may grow hard, our bodies grow too weak, our circumstances degrade, or our influence may be lost.

"I will be here a little longer," Jesus reminded his followers. Many missed the joy of Jesus' life because they found reasons to put off responding to him or found excuses to reject him. Let's not be guilty of wasting this limited-time offer. Instead, let's respond to Jesus with passion today before our hearts grow cold or our time runs out or our influence on those close to us is gone.

PRAYER:

LORD and Father, give me a sense of spiritual urgency about the decisions I make today. Give me a clear sense of what is at stake in what I choose, reject, and put off. Give me wisdom to see through all the distractions that can clutter my view and mislead my heart. Give me a holy passion to do what you want me to do. I don't want to waste a day of my life in your service. In Jesus name. Amen.

CONTEXT: JOHN 7:25-36

RELATED REFERENCES: 2 CORINTHIANS 6:1-2; HEBREWS 3:12-15; LUKE 19:5-10

Day: 152

LIVING WATER

JOHN 7:37-39

The last day of the festival came. It was the most important day. On that day Jesus stood up and said loudly, "Whoever is thirsty may come to me and drink. If anyone believes in me, rivers of living water will flow out from their heart. That is what the Scriptures say." Jesus was talking about the Spirit. The Spirit had not yet been given to people, because Jesus had not yet been raised to glory. But later, those who believed in Jesus would receive the Spirit.

REFLECTION:

A huge difference exists between a cistern and a well. A cistern has to be filled with water from the outside. It is not self-renewing and can easily run dry. An artesian well has flowing water that bubbles up with its cool and refreshing blessing.

This same difference exists between a person trying to be spiritual and a Spirit-filled person. When we become Christians, Jesus blesses us with his Spirit. That presence and power in our lives makes all the difference in the world. It is his Living Water inside of us, renewing us, refreshing us, empowering us, slaking our thirst, and giving us life. Living for Jesus is more than just a spiritual commitment on our part requiring our effort; it is also the gift and blessing of Jesus enabled by his Spirit.

PRAYER:

Holy God, my Righteous and Eternal Father, the gift of your Son is such a gracious and wonderful blessing. The gift of your Holy Spirit is such a daily treasure and sustaining grace. For these gifts, the two greatest of my life, I give you thanks and praise as I dedicate my life to your service in Jesus' name. Amen.

CONTEXT: JOHN 7:37-52

RELATED REFERENCES: JOHN 4:1-14; JEREMIAH 2:11-13; ROMANS 8:9-11

Day: 153
WHO DO YOU SAY JESUS IS?

JOHN 7:40-44

When the people heard the things that Jesus said, some of them said, "This man really is the Prophet." Other people said, "He is the Christ." And others said, "The Christ will not come from Galilee. The Scriptures say that he will come from the family of David. And they say that he will come from Bethlehem, the town where David lived." So the people did not agree with each other about Jesus. Some of the people wanted to arrest him. But no one tried to do it.

REFLECTION:

Who do you say Jesus is? Is he prophet, king, teacher, messiah, lord, master, imposter, pretender, fake, charlatan, or deceiver?

So often others try to make their decisions about Jesus on improper information. They think they know because they have heard about him in a Bible class or read about him in a magazine or have been told by someone else about him. The real issue, however, is whether or not each of us has personally gone on a quest to discover Jesus.

As you continue reading the Gospel of John this year, try to read the other three Gospels (Matthew, Mark, and Luke) as well. Ask God to help you meet Jesus and to know him as he really is. The most important question any of us will ever answer is this: "Who do you say Jesus is?"

PRAYER:

O God, Almighty and Everlasting Father, please reveal Jesus to me so that I can know him personally and follow him passionately. I don't just want to know him by reputation or report, but from personal knowledge and experience. Please reveal your Son to me and through me as I seek to know him better. It is in his name, Jesus the Christ, that I pray. Amen.

CONTEXT: JOHN 7:37-52

RELATED REFERENCES: MATTHEW 16:13-17; MATTHEW 2:1-12; JOHN 8:23-24

Day: 154

NEVER HEARD ANYONE TALK LIKE THIS

JOHN 7:45-46

The Temple police went back to the leading priests and the Pharisees. The priests and the Pharisees asked, "Why didn't you bring Jesus?" The Temple police answered, "We have never heard anyone say such amazing things!"

REFLECTION:

I love to listen to the accents of people from different parts of the world speak. In a world with so many words—spoken, written, hung on signs, blasted over radio waves, printed in newspapers and magazines, sent through cyberspace—I find that it is nice to hear something different. Then, every-once-in-a-great-while, someone comes along and speaks something in a fresh way; that person's words and accent are not just new, her or his message is refreshing and startling.

Jesus spoke with startling freshness. His message was not just new, but powerful. It had behind it the breath of heaven and the ring of truth that resonated in people's souls. It also had power to change hearts, alter circumstances, and force out darkness. While we live thousands of years later, if we will listen for his voice as we read his story, we too, can be touched and transformed. We too can say, "We have never heard anyone talk like this!"

PRAYER:

God of truth and grace, thank you for speaking to us in Jesus. I thank you for the message you spoke when you sent him to our world. I thank you for the very words he spoke while he was here. Make those words come alive in my heart as I read them. Transform me and refresh me through their power as I pledge my best to honor those words with my obedience. In Jesus' name I ask this. Amen.

CONTEXT: JOHN 7:37-52

RELATED REFERENCES: JOHN 6:63-69; JOHN 7:16-17; MARK 1:27-28

Day: 155

OPPOSITION TO THE WORD

JOHN 7:47-49

The Pharisees answered, "So he has fooled you too! You don't see any of the leaders or any of us Pharisees believing in him, do you? But those people out there know nothing about the law. They are under God's curse!"

REFLECTION:

Smug rejection is such an obnoxious trait. Yet we see it all the time. When others don't want to grapple with the truth of Jesus—the perplexing and demanding challenges of being a genuine follower—they smugly look down their noses and speak of believers as idiots and imbeciles. Some do it more subtly than others, but the smug arrogance is still there. "If only you were as educated or smart or street-wise as we are, you would know that Christianity is a bunch of fluff for the weak."

We also need to remember that many rejected Jesus because his demands were hard, not because his existence is questionable. The religious opposition in Jesus day was rooted in religionists' not wanting to have to change their lives, their perspectives, their places of power, or their positions.... So when they could not explain Jesus away, they had to put down his followers and any who had an interest in what he had to say. If you listen closely today, you will continue to hear their voices. Just don't heed them! Decide for yourself based on what you read and see of Jesus on your own.

PRAYER:

Father, I recognize that the Gospel of Jesus doesn't exist in a vacuum. I confess that I am frustrated by several of those around me that I love dearly, who will not accept the truth about Jesus. Please grant them a season of an open heart. Please bless them with an openness to truth. Please use me to point them to Jesus so they can decide about him honestly for themselves from an open heart. In Jesus' name I pray. Amen.

CONTEXT: JOHN 7:37-52

RELATED REFERENCES: JOHN 8:38-47; JOHN 9:30-34; 1 PETER 3:13-17

Day: 156

SLOW SEARCH FOR TRUTH

JOHN 7:50-51

But Nicodemus was there in that group. He was the one who had gone to see Jesus before. He said, "Our law will not let us judge anyone without first hearing them and finding out what they have done."

REFLECTION:

One of my favorite stories in the Gospel of John is the story of Nicodemus (John 3). This wonderful seeker of truth originally came to Jesus because he saw something of heaven in Jesus.

Nicodemus had a hard time giving his heart to Jesus all at once. God kept working on his seeking heart, leading him closer to Jesus through the events and circumstances of both Jesus' life and Nicodemus' role as a religious leader. Eventually, the events of the Cross captured Nicodemus' heart just as Jesus said they would (John 3:14-15; 19:38-40). Even in the hostile setting "in John 7," Nicodemus' search for truth and love of integrity called him to stand up for Jesus.

For me, Nicodemus is a great reminder not to give up hope on those around me who have not yet become Christians, but who keep having Jesus tug at their heart. Let's not give up on these precious people in our lives. Let's keep working with them and praying for them to come to see Jesus in light of the Cross and God's great love for all of us!

PRAYER:

Father, please be with the folks in my life who are good-hearted and genuine, but who haven't responded yet to the call of Jesus. Please help me as I try to make my life a consistent and helpful witness to Jesus and his transforming power. Guide my words and give me wisdom for the proper timing to know when to talk with them about Jesus. Most of all, please be at work in their lives just as you were in the life of Nicodemus, and bring them safely into your Kingdom through the drawing power of the Cross. In Jesus' name I pray. Amen.

CONTEXT: JOHN 7:37-52

RELATED REFERENCES: JOHN 3:1-3, 14-17; JOHN 19:38-42; 1 CORINTHIANS 1:18

Day: 157

IF YOU CAN'T BEAT 'EM, THEN CRITICIZE 'EM

JOHN 7:52

The Jewish leaders answered, "You must be from Galilee too! Study the Scriptures. You will find nothing about a prophet coming from Galilee."

REFLECTION:

One person against a group seldom wins the short-term battle. If the group is wrong with its information, it will be wrong in its conclusion no matter how many people stand up and speak in support of that conclusion. Rather than trying to deal with the truth of Nicodemus' statement, the rulers of Israel use a slur against Galileans and their wrong information about Jesus' city of origin to shame Nicodemus. However, Nicodemus was right and they were wrong. Nicodemus was a seeker and they were satisfied. Nicodemus stood for truth and they wanted to stay comfortable.

We must always put our conclusions up to the test of truth. Simply because a lot of other folks agree with us does not make it right and just because the majority of folks disagree with us doesn't mean that we are wrong.

When Jesus enters into a situation, he nearly always shakes up the status quo and tears down the sacred cows. Let's NOT be like the religious hypocrites of Jesus' day who loved their positions, their teachings, and their cronies more than they loved the truth and the One who embodied that truth.

PRAYER:

Father, forgive me for the times that I have shut my heart to the radical truth of your righteousness, justice, and mercy because I found myself comfortable with my own religious positions. Please keep the heart of a seeker—a truth-seeker, a people-seeker, and a Jesus-seeker—alive in me. Please continue to conform me to the character, compassion, and courage of Jesus. Protect me from the easy road of the religious hypocrites of Jesus' day who could not see above the ruts of their own traditions. In Jesus' name I pray. Amen.

CONTEXT: JOHN 7:37-52

RELATED REFERENCES: MATTHEW 7:7-14; MATTHEW 26:69-75; MATTHEW 4:12-16

Day: 158
THE GIFT OF TEACHING

JOHN 7:53-8:2

Then they all left and went home. Jesus went to the Mount of Olives. Early in the morning he went back to the Temple area. The people all came to him, and he sat and taught them.

REFLECTION:

Jesus gave people the gift of his teaching. His words were God's Word. He spoke and embodied God's Message. So when people gathered together, Jesus gave them his great gift of teaching. In this instance, he will teach them with his words and he will also teach them with his life and his actions. Let's never underestimate the importance of learning the truth from Jesus, both through his words and his deeds.

PRAYER:

Almighty God and tender Shepherd, guide me into your truth. Conform me to the character of your Son Jesus. I especially ask for the help of your Holy Spirit to conform my lifestyle to the things that I believe. Help me walk the talk and to put into practice the things I have learned. In Jesus' name. Amen.

CONTEXT: JOHN 7:53-8:11

RELATED REFERENCES: MATTHEW 7:21-29; JOHN 13:12-15; JAMES 1:19-24

Day: 159

Destroying People to Settle Arguments

John 8:3-6

The teachers of the law and the Pharisees brought a woman they had caught in bed with a man who was not her husband. They forced her to stand in front of the people. They said to Jesus, "Teacher, this woman was caught in the act of adultery. The Law of Moses commands us to stone to death any such woman. What do you say we should do?" They were saying this to trick Jesus. They wanted to catch him saying something wrong so that they could have a charge against him. But Jesus stooped down and started writing on the ground with his finger.

Reflection:

This was a trap set for Jesus—a question intended to use Jesus' compassion to crush him against the Law of Moses. The woman and her sin were props in this trap. Her well-being wasn't even considered by those who set the trap. She was just bait to them. It's sad how we can get so "amped up" about our religious discussions that we lose sight of God's heart and the needs of broken people.

God is a God of holiness and integrity as well as righteousness and steadfast love. The two pairs of attributes are inseparable. Those who call upon God must pursue these four aspects of his character with all their heart and strength. The religious leaders here remind us how easily we shift from being righteous students of the Law into vicious brutes pursuing self-justification.

Lost in the argument was the woman's humanity. She is no more than a bit of cheese in their religious mousetrap. Yet Jesus finds a way to deflect their venom from the woman and restore her dignity. People matter to God. They matter enough to him that he sent Jesus. Do they matter that much to us?

Prayer:

O LORD, God of Israel and Father of my Lord Jesus, I fear that I have not treated some people as you would have me treat them because they didn't fit into my religious comfort zone. Give me a more compassionate heart and greater skill to do the redemptive thing for people. In Jesus' name I pray. Amen.

Context: John 7:53-8:11

Related References: John 9:1-3; Joel 2:12-13; Romans 5:6-11

Day: 160

RESCUE AND RIGHTEOUSNESS

JOHN 8:7-9

The Jewish leaders continued to ask him their question. So he stood up and said, "Anyone here who has never sinned should throw the first stone at her." Then Jesus stooped down again and wrote on the ground. When they heard this, they began to leave one by one. The older men left first, and then the others. Jesus was left alone with the woman standing there in front of him.

REFLECTION:

The lynch mob doesn't want truth. It doesn't want redemption or righteousness either. By publicly shaming the unnamed woman, they had tasted blood. Now they wouldn't back down until their desire for more blood was satiated. No word could hold them back. They would press Jesus till they had what they wanted.

Then Jesus spoke a word they had not expected. It was a heaven-sent word. It was a word rooted in truth and a word that struck at their very soul. They knew they were not sinless. This word of truth penetrated to the hearts of those who were mature and knew both life and law.

As Jesus glanced away to write in the dust, he gave them permission to leave without being shown up. For a brief moment, righteousness triumphed over hatred and self-importance; bloodlust gave way to spiritual conviction. Those who were younger followed the example of the older and more mature, leaving the woman protected and safe with Jesus, alone. This is redemption in action. The Gospel is portrayed before our very eyes. Jesus takes the hate of hell and our own sinfulness and turns back the foe, leaving us safe and in his presence and out of the line of fire of shame and ridicule.

PRAYER:

How can I thank you, dear Father, for the salvation Jesus has purchased for me. Lord Jesus, thank you! These words seem so shallow and so small before your expansive grace. Use me to be a conduit of that grace to others. All glory to you, O Father who reigns above all, and to you, Lord Jesus, for you have triumphed over sin and death to rescue me. Amen.

CONTEXT: JOHN 7:53-8:11

RELATED REFERENCES: GALATIANS 3:33-28; COLOSSIANS 1:19-23; EPHESIANS 431:-5:2

Day: 161

FORGIVENESS AND DELIVERANCE

JOHN 8:10-11

He looked up again and said to her, "Where did they all go? Did no one judge you guilty?"
She answered, "No one, sir." Then Jesus said, "I don't judge you either.
You can go now, but don't sin again."

REFLECTION:

Can you imagine anything more wonderful? This woman was caught in the very act of adultery. She was publicly humiliated and used as bait to trap Jesus. She could have been killed as part of this dramatic trap. But Jesus steps in!

Suddenly, she was saved! Saved from the mob. Saved from the Law. Saved from her sin. She was given a fresh start and a new challenge.

This is what Jesus does for each of us! He forgives our sin and then delivers us to a new life with a new start (2 Cor. 5:17). So the challenge for each of us is this: what are we going to do with a new start?

PRAYER:

Help me please, dear Father, to live as your new creation. Help me fully take advantage of the forgiveness and deliverance that you have so graciously lavished on me by sending Jesus. In his name I pray. Amen.

CONTEXT: JOHN 7:53-8:11

RELATED REFERENCES: MATTHEW 7:1-5; JAMES 4:11-12; LEVITICUS 20:10

Day: 162

You Don't Have to Stumble

John 8:12

Later, Jesus talked to the people again. He said, "I am the light of the world. Whoever follows me will never live in darkness. They will have the light that gives life."

Reflection:

A night-light is so helpful when you wake up in a darkened room in the middle of the night. You don't have to stumble and fumble your way along in the darkness.

Jesus comes to us, trapped as we are in a world of darkness, and he tells us that if we will look to him, then we won't have to stumble and fumble our way along in life. In fact, his light not only will illuminate our paths now, but his light will lead us to life everlasting.

Prayer:

God Almighty, shine the light of Jesus into my life and help me make my way through this world of darkness without stumbling. Guide me away from any false light, and help me to find and follow Jesus' light. Use me to share that light with others so they can find their way home to you. In Jesus' name. Amen.

Context: John 8:12-20

Related References: Colossians 1:11-14; John 12:44-50; John 1:6-8

Day: 163

DISCERNING WHAT IS FALSE

JOHN 8:13-16

But the Pharisees said to Jesus, "When you talk about yourself, you are the only one to say that these things are true. So we cannot accept what you say." Jesus answered, "Yes, I am saying these things about myself. But people can believe what I say, because I know where I came from. And I know where I am going. But you don't know where I came from or where I am going. You judge me the way people judge other people. I don't judge anyone. But if I judge, my judging is true, because when I judge I am not alone. The Father who sent me is with me."

REFLECTION:

At first glance, we rush past these passages on false teaching. In a culture where the only real value is tolerance, we don't have much stomach for the possibility of dangerous false teaching. Jesus and his early followers knew there was a danger of false teaching. Just because Jesus was labeled a false teacher didn't mean he wasn't concerned about false teaching among his followers (1 John 4:1-4). In fact, the accusations against him give us some tools for denoting false teachers.

Do they do the work of God?

Do we know where they come from?

Have we seen the quality and character of God their lives?

Is their judgment and discernment reflective of God's truth?

Jesus, when examined, shows himself to be true. Do these teachers who claim to come in his name measure up?

PRAYER:

Father, I believe that Jesus is your standard of truth and righteousness. Please help me discern that truth in my life. Please help me guard my steps from those who claim to come in his name but who are false. Please guard my heart against those whose teaching does not come from you. In Jesus' name I pray. Amen.

CONTEXT: JOHN 8:12-20

RELATED REFERENCES: MATTHEW 7:15-20; 1 JOHN 4:1-6; ACTS 20:28-31

Day: 164
WHAT GREATER WITNESS?

JOHN 8:17-18

"Your own law says that when two witnesses say the same thing, you must accept what they say. I am one of the witnesses who speaks about myself. And the Father who sent me is my other witness."

REFLECTION:

What witnesses could Jesus call to prove he came from God? He needed at least two under Jewish law (Deut. 19:15). Jesus had more than two witnesses, but the first two are the most important. Jesus himself was a witness and so was his Father. Elsewhere in the Gospel of John, Jesus will list John the Baptist, his own mighty works, and even those who saw his miracles as his witnesses. However, only two really know that Jesus came from God—the Son and the Father.

Once again, Jesus is pushing people to make a hard and definitive choice: is he a blasphemer who is saying the unthinkable or is he really from God? Jesus leaves us no middle ground. He claims to be God's Son, sent from God, to speak the words of God, and to do the deeds of God.

PRAYER:

Father in heaven, I confess that I often find it hard to make difficult and potentially life-altering decisions. I don't like them. I fear making the wrong decision. But, dear Father, I really do want to honor you with all my heart and to live as a person of integrity. So I decide this day to once again fully believe that Jesus is your Son, that he came as your presence in our world, and that he showed us who you are in all your fullness. I commit to trust him as my Savior and to follow him as my Lord. I give you all thanks and praise in Jesus' name. Amen.

CONTEXT: JOHN 8:12-20

RELATED REFERENCES: JOHN 1:6-9; JOHN 5:31-38; JOHN 17:20-21

Day: 165

YOU DON'T KNOW MY FATHER

JOHN 8:19-20

The people asked, "Where is your father?" Jesus answered, "You don't know me or my Father. But if you knew me, you would know my Father too." Jesus said these things while he was teaching in the Temple area, near the room where the Temple offerings were kept. But no one arrested him, because the right time for him had not yet come.

REFLECTION:

People can be so incredibly gullible about charlatans and scam artists, yet push away those who genuinely want to help them. Many people who followed false messiahs and false teachers rejected Jesus. As Jesus does so often in the Gospel of John, he emphasizes that when they rejected him, they were also rejecting God who sent him. The very fact that they cannot and do not arrest him until it is God's timing is testimony that Jesus is who he claims to be.

As we read John for our own encounter with Jesus, the Lord continues his emphasis on the importance of our decision about who he is and about our relationship to him. We do not have God if we reject him. It may not be very politically correct in many places today, but Jesus' exclusive claims remind us that being politically correct is not nearly as important as being eternally correct. If we do not know Jesus, we do not know the Father. If we know Jesus, we know the Father as well.

PRAYER:

Holy and righteous God, it troubles my heart that so many people do not know Jesus. Even more painful, dear Father, many have rejected Jesus as your Son and their Savior. Please open the door of the hearts of the millions who need to know Jesus. Stir your people, your Church, to reach out to the lost of the world with more passion. Bless those who have already crossed cultural and language barriers to share you grace. Bring a time of deep longing in the hearts of the people of the world to know Jesus, in whose name I pray. Amen.

CONTEXT: JOHN 8:12-20

RELATED REFERENCES: JOHN 14:6-11; JOHN 5:43; JOHN 20:17

Day: 166
DIE IN YOUR SINS

JOHN 8:21-24

Again, Jesus said to the people, "I will leave you. You will look for me, but you will die in your sin. You cannot come where I am going." So the Jewish leaders asked themselves, "Will he kill himself? Is that why he said, 'You cannot come where I am going'?" But Jesus said to them, "You people are from here below, but I am from above. You belong to this world, but I don't belong to this world. I told you that you would die in your sins. Yes, if you don't believe that I AM, you will die in your sins."

REFLECTION:

Jesus came to deliver us from sin and its consequences. God sent Jesus as our Savior and Lord. Jesus makes the importance of his coming clear: those who die in their sins will not come to be with Jesus in heaven.

Unless people believe that he is God with us—"if you don't believe that I AM"—they will die in their sins. Jesus came from God, as God, to bring us back home to God. He is not from this world and is not bound by this world. He is from above and will return to take those who follow him back home with him to the Father.

PRAYER:

Father, thank you for my faith and all those who helped me come to faith. I know that my trust in Jesus as your Son and my Savior has changed my eternal destiny. Thank you for giving me a way to escape my sin and its guilt and to stand before you as your righteous child. I know that these gifts come from your love and grace. I thank you in Jesus' name. Amen.

CONTEXT: JOHN 8:21-29

RELATED REFERENCES: 2 CORINTHIANS 5:19-21; JOHN 3:31-36; JOHN 10:38

Day: 167

LIFTED UP TO SAVE US

JOHN 8:25-28

They asked, "Then who are you?" Jesus answered, "I am what I have told you from the beginning. I have much more I could say to judge you. But I tell people only what I have heard from the one who sent me, and he speaks the truth." They did not understand who he was talking about. He was telling them about the Father. So he said to them, "You will lift up the Son of Man. Then you will know that I AM. You will know that whatever I do is not by my own authority. You will know that I say only what the Father has taught me."

REFLECTION:

John uses such a simple vocabulary to tell the story of Jesus in such a magnificent way. The term "lifted up" can mean "to physically lift" something up or it can mean "to exalt." The latter use is more prominent in the New Testament.

For John, however, the two mean the same thing. Jesus is exalted when he is "lifted up" on the Cross. Far from being something of shame, the Cross was God's way of reaching the hearts of people. Jesus does what he does because it is the Father's way of touching people's hearts and showing them his love. Unfortunately, so many miss the wonders of this sacrificial love. Yet for those of us who have been touched by this display of grace, it is God's power to draw us to himself, to show his heart to us, and to transform us.

PRAYER:

For your wondrous love, O God, I praise and thank you. For your incredible sacrifice, Lord Jesus, I praise you for your obedience and thank you for your incredible love. Amen.

CONTEXT: JOHN 8:21-29

RELATED REFERENCES: JOHN 3:13-17; JOHN 12:23-33; MATTHEW 27:54

ALWAYS? ALWAYS!

JOHN 8:29
*"The one who sent me is with me. I always do what pleases him.
So he has not left me alone."*

REFLECTION:

The premarital counselor gave me this advice: "Never say to your wife 'you never,' 'you always,' or 'you're just like ....'"

None of us does "always" very well! We normally use the "always" phrase to exaggerate and emphasize something or we use it as a put down. But for Jesus, "always" fits. He does what is pleasing to God no matter what the public response might be or the price he has is to pay for doing it. He is always obedient, submissive, and sacrificial in doing God's will. Jesus is our model, our goal, and the perfect one toward whom the Spirit leads us. While we may not make "always" stick in our lives the way Jesus did, let's aim at always doing what pleases our heavenly Father!

PRAYER:

Righteous Father, please forgive my sins. I know they disappoint and disgust you. Thank you for providing your forgiveness for me through Jesus' atoning sacrifice for my sins. Be with me and empower me through your Holy Spirit as I seek to always please you—not out of a sense of guilt or fear, but out of a deep sense of joy, appreciation, and praise for your love and grace. In Jesus' name. Amen.

CONTEXT: JOHN 8:21-29

RELATED REFERENCES: 1 JOHN 2:1-2; HEBREWS 7:22-25; MATTHEW 28:19-20

Day: 169

THE PROOF IS IN THE DOING

JOHN 8:30-32

While he was saying these things, many people believed in him. So Jesus said to the Jews who believed in him, "If you continue to accept and obey my teaching, you are really my followers. You will know the truth, and the truth will make you free."

REFLECTION:

What is the secret to knowing the truth? Doing what Jesus says! It isn't in discovering a new idea, coming up with a new plan, or going in search of some lost mystery. Knowing the truth is found in living Jesus' teaching. The proof is in the doing!

PRAYER:

Father, give me a heart to obey Jesus' teaching. Give me a heart to obey even when I don't fully understand the "why" behind it. Give me a heart to obey even when I don't feel I fully have the capability of pulling it off. I know that so many of the valuable lessons I have learned from you have come when I trusted and obeyed. Bless me now as I seek to put this into practice more fully in my life. In Jesus' name ask for this grace. Amen.

CONTEXT: JOHN 8:30-47

RELATED REFERENCES: PHILIPPIANS 2:5-11; JOHN 13:12-17; PHILIPPIANS 4:9

Day: 170
THE SLAVE TRADE

JOHN 8:33-34
They answered, "We are Abraham's descendants. And we have never been slaves.
So why do you say that we will be free?"
Jesus said, "The truth is, everyone who sins is a slave—a slave to sin."

REFLECTION:

Sin captures us. Sin enslaves us. Sin abuses us. Sin brings us to death (James 1:13-15). When sin infects us and takes root, it becomes addictive and destructive. If we are going to enjoy the freedom the Lord longs to give us, then we must also make a commitment to live for him and turn away from sin. We can, by the Spirit's power, put to death the power of sin (Rom. 8:12-14). At the same time, we must also make it our commitment to leave it behind (Col. 3:5-10).

PRAYER:

Father, God of grace and power, please deliver me from the sin that entangles me and keeps me from being all that you have made me to be. In Jesus' name I pray. Amen.

CONTEXT: JOHN 8:30-47

RELATED REFERENCES: ROMANS 8:1-4, 12-14; ROMANS 6:12-14; JAMES 5:16

Day: 171
FREED COMPLETELY

JOHN 8:35-36

"A slave does not stay with a family forever. But a son belongs to the family forever. So if the Son makes you free, you are really free."

REFLECTION:

Salvation involves two great realities: 1) we are set free from our sins, and 2) we are made God's children and adopted into his heavenly family.

This means that Jesus is not only our Savior and Lord; he is also our older brother (Heb. 2:14-18). God is not just the Almighty; he is also Abba Father (Rom. 8:13-17). In Jesus, we are given our freedom to become all we are meant to be as God's children and Jesus' siblings!

PRAYER:

Abba Father, I thank you and praise you for my freedom from my sin and the privilege of being a child in your family. I thank you Jesus for paying the price of my ransom to set me free and to purchase my adoption into your family. Amen.

CONTEXT: JOHN 8:30-47

RELATED REFERENCES: GALATIANS 3:24-4:6; JOHN 3:3; 1 JOHN 3:1-2

Day: 172

PEDIGREE OR FAITH?

JOHN 8:37-40

"I know you are Abraham's descendants. But you want to kill me, because you don't want to accept my teaching. I am telling you what my Father has shown me. But you do what your father has told you." They said, "Our father is Abraham." Jesus said, "If you were really Abraham's descendants, you would do what Abraham did. I am someone who has told you the truth I heard from God. But you are trying to kill me. Abraham did nothing like that."

REFLECTION:

What is your claim for significance? Is it your wealth, education, health, appearance, or achievement? What about your family heritage, your neighborhood, or your reputation? What matters most is what you do with Jesus! Who or what are you going to trust to make a difference in the biggest part of life, the eternal part of your life? Are you going to trust in your pedigree or in your Savior?

Despite all that the apostle Paul had accomplished in his life as a devoted child of Israel, he realized that all of those achievements—all the trappings of his religious pedigree—were worth less than nothing (Phil. 3:3-9). Only what he did with Jesus mattered. Let's follow his example and put our trust in his Lord.

PRAYER:

Father, forgive me because I have sometimes been arrogant about my achievements and self-righteous because of my religious heritage. I recognize that I find my life, my hope, my joy, and my salvation in Jesus. In his name I offer you my life and my praise. Amen.

CONTEXT: JOHN 8:30-47

RELATED REFERENCES: PHILIPPIANS 3:3-9; COLOSSIANS 3:1-4; GALATIANS 6:14

Day: 173
KNOW YOUR ENEMY

JOHN 8:41-44

"So you are doing what your own father did."
But they said, "We are not like children who never knew who their father was. God is our
Father. He is the only Father we have." Jesus said to them, "If God were really your
Father, you would love me. I came from God, and now I am here. I did not come by my
own authority. God sent me. You don't understand the things I say, because you cannot
accept my teaching. Your father is the devil. You belong to him. You want to do what he
wants. He was a murderer from the beginning. He was always against the truth. There is
no truth in him. He is like the lies he tells. Yes, the devil is a liar. He is the father of lies."

REFLECTION:

Satan is behind the evil in all of its forms, including the religious evil that
sent Jesus to the Cross. Make no mistake, the devil distorts, deceives, and lies.
Satan opposes and destroys. His goal is our spiritual murder and destruction.
Let's not take him lightly. At the same time, let's not cower before his threats.
Jesus conquered him for us in the Cross and resurrection (Col. 3:15; Heb. 2:14-
15). Let's make sure that we stick with Christ, hold to his teaching, and live his
truth. Let's make it clear to the evil one that he will have no hold on us for our
allegiance is to the Lord Jesus.

PRAYER:

Almighty and powerful Father, deliver me from the evil one. I know that all power, all
honor, and all glory are yours. Help me make that true in my life and in my example.
In Jesus' name I pray. Amen.

CONTEXT: JOHN 8:30-47

RELATED REFERENCES: 1 PETER 5:8-9; 1 JOHN 3:10; JAMES 3:13-16 & 4:7

Day: 174

GOD'S CHILDREN

JOHN 8:45-47

"I am telling you the truth, and that's why you don't believe me. Can any of you prove that I am guilty of sin? If I tell the truth, why don't you believe me? Whoever belongs to God accepts what he says. But you don't accept what God says, because you don't belong to God."

REFLECTION:

God is the true Father of all people who look to his Son for their salvation. These people listen to Jesus and do what he says. It is not simply a list of notable people who have lived for Jesus in spectacular ways. No, the litmus test for all of us as children of God is this: Do we live what Jesus says?

PRAYER:

Father God, please help me as a follower of Jesus to make a difference in the way that I live my life as well as the way I use my language at prayer time. Please forgive me for sometimes letting my commitment to follow Jesus and my passion for the Lord not make it out my prayer and Bible study time and into my daily life. Empower me as I seek to show my love in the way that I live my life in obedience to Jesus' words.
In Jesus' name I pray. Amen.

CONTEXT: JOHN 8:30-47

RELATED REFERENCES: 1 PETER 1:14-15; 1 JOHN 3:10; 1 JOHN 5:1-2

Day: 175
WHO DETERMINES YOUR WORTH?

JOHN 8:48-50

The Jews there answered, "We say you are a Samaritan. We say a demon is making you crazy! Are we not right when we say this?" Jesus answered, "I have no demon in me. I give honor to my Father, but you give no honor to me. I am not trying to get honor for myself. There is one who wants this honor for me. He is the judge."

REFLECTION:

So often we succumb to peer pressure because we let the people around us determine our worth in our own eyes. To be labeled as a demon crazed person is about as bad a criticism as one could receive if he or she is seeking to live for God. Jesus, however, wasn't fazed. He knew who determined his worth. He would not be baited into useless arguments by people who could only criticize and call him names. He lived for his Father's glory, not his own—and certainly not for the acceptance of the masses.

Since Jesus was only trying to please his Father, he was very willing to leave the determination of his worth in his Father's hands. This allowed him to live with the freedom to be all that God had made him to be. What about you? Who determines your worth?

PRAYER:

Father, forgive me. I sometimes let the evaluation of others mean too much to me and compromise my mission and my integrity in your work. Bless me with strength, dear LORD, as I seek to leave the determination of my worth solely in your hands so that I am not swayed by the criticism of those who would seek to derail my life's mission. In Jesus' name I pray. Amen.

CONTEXT: JOHN 8:48-59

RELATED REFERENCES: JOHN 7:16-18; 1 CORINTHIANS 4:1-5; GALATIANS 1:10

NEVER DIE!

JOHN 8:51

"I promise you, whoever continues to obey my teaching will never die."

REFLECTION:

When we become Christians, when we are baptized into Christ, we die to our old selves and are raised to live a new life (Rom. 6:3-7). The old life is gone. The most important death that matters has already happened. Yes, eventually our bodies die. But as Christians, we are united with Christ and not even death can separate us from Christ (Rom. 8:32-39). The living part of us goes to be with Jesus and awaits his triumphant return to earth in glory when all that belong to him are changed and given immortal bodies and go to live with him forever. When we obey him, when we belong to him, death cannot claim the living part of us. We will never die, but live with the Lord forever. As Paul says, we should encourage one another with this message (1 Thes. 4:13-18).

PRAYER:

Almighty and eternal God, my Abba Father, thank you for making me yours and joining my life to Jesus so that death can claim only my body, but can never have the everlasting part of me. I look forward to the coming day of victory when I join with all of your children and celebrate and participate in your glory, forever! In Jesus' name and by his power I praise you. Amen.

CONTEXT: JOHN 8:48-59

RELATED REFERENCES: JOHN 11:17-25; ROMANS 6:3-9; 2 CORINTHIANS 5:6-9

Day: 177

ARE YOU GREATER? YES!

JOHN 8:52-55

The Jews said to Jesus, "Now we know that you have a demon in you! Even Abraham and the prophets died. But you say, 'Whoever obeys my teaching will never die.' Do you think you are greater than our father Abraham? He died, and so did the prophets. Who do you think you are?" Jesus answered, "If I give honor to myself, that honor is worth nothing. The one who gives me honor is my Father. And you say that he is your God. But you don't really know him. I know him. If I said I did not know him, I would be a liar like you. But I do know him, and I obey what he says."

REFLECTION:

Sometimes the doubts of the crowd become our reminder of the truth. "Are you greater than Abraham ... the prophets ... ?" they ask Jesus. That's the question we are to ask. The answer? Yes! He is and he is to be obeyed just as he obeyed. He knows the Father and reveals him to us. Yes! Jesus is greater because he is God's Son and our Lord and Savior, the Christ.

PRAYER:

All praise to you, God most high and all praise to Jesus, your Son and my Savior. You planned my deliverance, dear Father, and purchased my salvation through the gift of your Son who brought life and immortality to light in himself and in his message. I pledge to you, O God, my heart and my life. In Jesus' name. Amen.

CONTEXT: JOHN 8:48-59

RELATED REFERENCES: MATTHEW 12:38-42; MATTHEW 16:13-17; JOHN 20:24-29

Day: 178

BEFORE ABRAHAM

JOHN 8:56-59

"Your father Abraham was very happy that he would see the day when I came. He saw that day and was happy." The Jews said to Jesus, "What? How can you say you have seen Abraham? You are not even 50 years old!" Jesus answered, "The fact is, before Abraham was born, I AM." When he said this, they picked up stones to throw at him. But Jesus hid, and then he left the Temple area.

REFLECTION:

Like so many other things Jesus says in this chapter, this claim is audacious and bold. It is also true. Jesus didn't just happen on the scene when he came to earth; he existed before any created thing. When Jesus came to earth, he didn't come merely as a messenger of God, he also came as God himself among us, the great I AM (John 1:14-18). Three times in John 8, Jesus uses the name God used to identify himself to Moses (Ex. 3:14) as his own mark of identity (John 8:24, 28, 58).

Jesus is God, the great I Am, the covenant God of Israel, the great deliverer of the Old Testament. This is why it is so important that we pay attention to him. He not only sacrificed himself for us, but he left heaven's glory to come and live with us and show us God's love and great deliverance.

PRAYER:

Father, open my heart to the teaching and truth of Jesus and give me a greater sense of his authority, his majesty, and his lordship in my life. In Jesus' name I pray. Amen.

CONTEXT: JOHN 8:48-59

RELATED REFERENCES: JOHN 1:1-4; COLOSSIANS 1:15-17; PHILIPPIANS 2:5-11

Day: 179
HOW DO WE VIEW PEOPLE?

JOHN 9:1-3

While Jesus was walking, he saw a man who had been blind since the time he was born. Jesus' followers asked him, "Teacher, why was this man born blind? Whose sin made it happen? Was it his own sin or that of his parents?"
Jesus answered, "It was not any sin of this man or his parents that caused him to be blind. He was born blind so that he could be used to show what great things God can do."

REFLECTION:

If you look carefully in this chapter, you will find a number of different ways we sometimes look at people and dehumanize them for our own benefit—usually so we don't have to consider their real needs and address them, but simply set them aside. Jesus reminds that each person is someone made in God's image, an eternal person whom God intentionally created, and a real person in whom the work of God needs to be done! And what is that work of God? To believe that Jesus was sent from God to bring them God's love (John 6:29).

PRAYER:

Lord God, maker of all things and all people, give me greater sensitivity in the way that I treat others so that it more perfectly reflects your desire to work in each life to bless that person and bring that person to your grace and glory! In Jesus' name I pray. Amen.

CONTEXT: JOHN 9:1-12

RELATED REFERENCES: GENESIS 1:26-27; JAMES 3:7-12; PSALM 139:13-16

Day: 180

URGENCY!

JOHN 9:4

"While it is daytime, we must continue doing the work of the one who sent me. The night is coming, and no one can work at night."

REFLECTION:

Jesus recognizes that his time on earth is short. He feels a sense of urgency to get the work of God completed. He also feels urgency about getting his work done with his followers. Night is coming. There is a sense of real urgency about getting the work of God done before night falls!

With so many distractions crowding into our lives—some of them important and others very insignificant—how well do we place God's priorities first in our lives? Do we feel a sense of urgency to get done God's work in comparison to getting our other tasks done? Do we recognize the urgency to get God's work done before night falls in our own lives and in the lives of those we want to influence?

PRAYER:

Holy God, help me better know how to order my priorities. Please help me be more confident of the things you want most for me to do. Father, I gladly submit my will to be led by your Spirit and to live for your glory. Please guide my way. In Jesus' name I ask it. Amen.

CONTEXT: JOHN 9:1-12

RELATED REFERENCES: JOHN 13:21-30; JAMES 4:13-16; JOHN 11:9-10

LIGHT TO SEE

JOHN 9:5-7

"While I am in the world, I am the light of the world."
After Jesus said this, he spit on the dirt, made some mud and put it on the man's eyes.
Jesus told him, "Go and wash in Siloam pool." (Siloam means "Sent.") So the man went
to the pool, washed and came back. He was now able to see.

REFLECTION:

Jesus longs to bring us his blessings. Our most needed blessing is the sight to see things as they are and to be able to discern his will and follow it. So often we view obedience as a burden rather than a blessing. However, Jesus wants to bless us through our obedience just as he blessed the blind man. Obeying him, doing what he sends us to do, brings a much greater blessing than any burden it might entail. As with this man, our obedience to Jesus' commands helps us see his will and his purposes more clearly in our own lives.

PRAYER:

O gracious and generous Father, please make my heart pliable and open to your truth.
Help me move from merely understanding your will to obeying it with joy and expectation.
Forgive me for being reluctant to obey when I do not fully understand why you want me to
do something. Open my eyes to your will and your way in my world as I experience the joy
of obeying your Son. In Jesus' name. Amen.

CONTEXT: JOHN 9:1-12

RELATED REFERENCES: JOHN 13:12-17; MATTHEW 7:21-23; JAMES 1:21-25

Day: 182
BEYOND APPEARANCES

JOHN 9:8-12

His neighbors and some others who had seen him begging said, "Look! Is this the same man who always sits and begs?" Some people said, "Yes! He is the one." But others said, "No, he can't be the same man. He only looks like him." So the man himself said, "I am that same man." They asked, "What happened? How did you get your sight?" He answered, "The man they call Jesus made some mud and put it on my eyes. Then he told me to go to Siloam and wash. So I went there and washed. And then I could see." They asked him, "Where is this man?" He answered, "I don't know."

REFLECTION:

How often have you judged someone simply based upon his or her appearance? The folks who were supposed to be the neighbors of this man that Jesus healed knew him only as a label. That label was based upon his physical blindness and his need to beg—they saw him as the "man who always sits and begs." They never spent enough time to move beyond the label to the real person. They didn't know him; they only knew his label. They didn't bother to befriend him because he was a blind beggar.

Before we get too self-righteous, let's ask how different we are! We all need to ask ourselves, "Do I make unfair assumptions about people based on external appearances? Do I use labels to push people away so that I do not have to deal with them in everyday life?"

PRAYER:

Father, I confess that I often do not view people as you do. I too easily dismiss them based on appearances. Father, I don't want to waste my time worrying with folks who are chronically dependent and don't want to change. However, I don't want to neglect blessing anyone that you send my way who needs to experience your touch of mercy. Please give me the wisdom to know how to balance the two responses. In Jesus' name I pray. Amen.

CONTEXT: JOHN 9:1-12

RELATED REFERENCES: 1 JOHN 3:16-17; JAMES 2:12-13; LUKE 10:29-37

Day: 183

BENDING REALITY TO FIT OUR THEOLOGY

JOHN 9:13-17

Then the people brought the man to the Pharisees. The day Jesus had made mud and healed the man's eyes was a Sabbath day. So the Pharisees asked the man, "How did you get your sight?" He answered, "He put mud on my eyes. I washed, and now I can see." Some of the Pharisees said, "That man does not obey the law about the Sabbath day. So he is not from God." Others said, "But someone who is a sinner cannot do these miraculous signs." So they could not agree with each other. They asked the man again, "Since it was your eyes he healed, what do you say about him?" He answered, "He is a prophet."

REFLECTION:

Isn't it interesting how we can "bend" reality to make it fit our faulty theology? This man was healed. He was healed on the Sabbath. In the theological wrangling and maneuvering of the Pharisees, what Jesus did was a violation of the Sabbath so either Jesus was bad or the man hadn't really been healed. Unbelievable!

Some disagreements on obscure or much debated minor theological points are inconsequential. However, when we use these discussions to wall out and condemn people, or we use them to make God's good work appear to be something bad, then those theological positions become evil. That doesn't mean we water down the plain teaching of Scripture on personal morality or on the nature of Jesus; it does mean that we are a lot more humble and generous when it comes to the value of people. If Jesus' actions on the Sabbath show us anything, they show us that God values people supremely and wants to restore them to wholeness—that's what his day of rest and worship should be all about.

PRAYER:

Dear Heavenly Father, please forgive me for the times that I have wrongly used your Word to hurt other people. Empty me of my theological and doctrinal arrogance that could blind me to your work in the people around me. In Jesus' name I pray. Amen.

CONTEXT: JOHN 9:13-34

RELATED REFERENCES: JOHN 5:8-10; MATTHEW 23:13-15; MATTHEW 12:9-14

Day: 184
Parents Who Don't Parent
John 9:18-23

The Jewish leaders still did not believe that this really happened to the man—that he was blind and was now healed. But later they sent for his parents. They asked them, "Is this your son? You say he was born blind. So how can he see?" His parents answered, "We know that this man is our son. And we know that he was born blind. But we don't know why he can see now. We don't know who healed his eyes. Ask him. He is old enough to answer for himself." They said this because they were afraid of the Jewish leaders. The leaders had already decided that they would punish anyone who said Jesus was the Christ. They would stop them from coming to the synagogue. That is why his parents said, "He is old enough. Ask him."

Reflection:

While many parents are conscientious and dedicated to raising their children in the Lord, unfortunately many others view their children only as mere biological products. Their tie to their children is simply genetic; it is neither spiritual nor emotional. That's the kind of parents this newly healed man had. They were more concerned about their place in the synagogue than they were in their son's healing and spiritual development. They left their son on his own to defend himself and to fend for himself before the hostile Jewish religious leaders.

As God's people, we must remember his heart for the orphaned and abandoned and we must defend and care for them as God's people. We must care for our own as well as those who are abandoned and alone and love them as those in whom the work of God needs to be done!

Prayer:

Holy God, please help your people as we seek to care for the abandoned and helpless. We are incensed at some of the horrible things done to children in our world. We pray for courage to step forward and help protect them. We pray for the compassion and courage of Jesus to personally care for them no matter the cost. In Jesus name, and to Jesus' glory. Amen.

Context: John 9:13-34

Related References: Ephesians 6:4; Deuteronomy 6:4-9; Psalm 68:3-6

BOTTOM LINE FAITH

JOHN 9:24-25

So the Jewish leaders called the man who had been blind. They told him to come in again. They said, "You should honor God by telling the truth. We know that this man is a sinner." The man answered, "I don't know if he is a sinner. But I do know this: I was blind, and now I can see."

REFLECTION:

Sometimes we cannot answer all the intellectual or theological arguments about faith and the reasons we believe. Even though we might not be able to answer every question from the most seasoned skeptic, we do know God and have seen him work with power in our lives and in the lives of people we love. Our response is like the blind man's: "I don't have all the answers, but I have surely been changed by the one who does!"

PRAYER:

Father, make your presence known in my life so that others can see and know your love and grace through me. Give me courage to hang on to my faith in you no matter the people who criticize, attack, or belittle me for that faith. In Jesus' name I pray. Amen.

CONTEXT: JOHN 9:13-34

RELATED REFERENCES: JOHN 14:12-14; JOHN 8:31-32; MATTHEW 28:18-20

Day: 186

SEARCH AWAY FROM THE TRUTH

JOHN 9:26-27

They asked, "What did he do to you? How did he heal your eyes?"
He answered, "I have already told you that. But you would not listen to me. Why do you
want to hear it again? Do you want to be his followers too?"

REFLECTION:

Sometimes folks make themselves the enemies of the truth because they don't want to discover it. The interchange between the authorities and the man who was healed reaches the absurd and almost humorous point. The authorities interrogate the healed man because they want to find some discrepancy in his story to discredit Jesus. They don't want the truth, so the healed man chides them for their repeated questions.

This bitter irony helps us understand that the authorities rejected Jesus because they had already decided he is the enemy. Because of their wrong position on Jesus, they had to re-write the truth of his grace and power.

Unfortunately, there are people who do the same thing with Jesus today. Their evil deeds have alienated them from the truth and blinded them to the grace of God in Jesus. We, however, must love them, pray for their hearts to be changed, and live as people of character as we look for an opportunity to share the Savior's grace.

PRAYER:

Father, I have friends who are far from your Kingdom. I know that some of them have hardened their hearts because they are caught in sin. Others are stuck in religious ruts that have hidden the truth of Jesus from them and caused them to re-write the truth about Jesus to fit their own point of view. Please use me and my influence to bring them to Jesus. Please be actively at work in their lives to do all within your will to give them reasons to re-evaluate their lives and the way they are living. In Jesus' name I pray. Amen.

CONTEXT: JOHN 9:13-34

RELATED REFERENCES: COLOSSIANS 1:21-23; JOHN 12:37-39; EPHESIANS 2:1-5

Day: 187

ADMITTING THE TRUTH

JOHN 9:28-29

At this they shouted insults at him and said, "You are his follower, not us! We are followers of Moses. We know that God spoke to Moses. But we don't even know where this man comes from!"

REFLECTION:

"We don't even know where this man comes from!" Sadly, this is about the only truthful thing the authorities say about Jesus in this whole episode. But, if they really knew Moses, they would know Jesus. If they really knew God, they would know Jesus. So many people reject Jesus because they don't really know him—church experiences, church people, or chosen lifestyles get in their way of truly knowing Jesus. As we seek to reach the lost, we must remember that the core, the essence, the truth we share is centered in Christ Jesus. Rather than getting lost in a lot of church mumbo jumbo, let's share Jesus with them. Let's help them see the Savior.

PRAYER:

Dear heavenly Father, thank you for sending Jesus. I know that he is your greatest and most complete message. Forgive me for the times that I have gotten lost in religious arguments and forgotten to share Jesus with those who need him. Bless my efforts to share Jesus with those who do not recognize him as their Lord and Savior. It's in Jesus' precious and mighty name I pray. Amen.

CONTEXT: JOHN 9:13-34

RELATED REFERENCES: JOHN 1:16-18; JOHN 5:39-46; JOHN 17:25

Day: 188

I KNOW WHAT MY BIBLE SAYS!

JOHN 9:30-33

The man answered, "This is really strange! You don't know where he comes from, but he healed my eyes. We all know that God does not listen to sinners, but he will listen to anyone who worships and obeys him. This is the first time we have ever heard of anyone healing the eyes of someone born blind. This man must be from God. If he were not from God, he could not do anything like this."

REFLECTION:

The healed man reminds the authorities that his Bible and his experience line up: this person has to be from God because only someone from God could give him this gift.

One of the greatest tools we have to lead others to Christ is our own story about how God's promises in Scripture and our experience in life line up. Those who are open to the truth will be blessed. Unfortunately some folks are just like these religious authorities; they're not going to believe no matter what happens. So let's share our story with folks when we are given the opportunity and trust that God will use it to touch hearts that are open.

PRAYER:

Gracious God, my Abba Father, please help me to recognize the opportunities you give me to share the story of how Jesus has blessed my life. Give me eyes to see and ears to hear when that moment comes. Thank you for blessing me in so many ways and thank you for being so faithful to your promises. In Jesus' name I pray. Amen.

CONTEXT: JOHN 9:13-34

RELATED REFERENCES: 1 PETER 3:13-16; ACTS 26:9-18; JOHN 6:66-68

Day: 189

A HEAVIER JUDGMENT ON TEACHERS!

JOHN 9:34

The Jewish leaders answered, "You were born full of sin! Are you trying to teach us?" And they told the man to get out of the synagogue and to stay out.

REFLECTION:

God despises the abuse of power. He warns those who teach and lead in his Kingdom that they had better do so honorably or they will stand under harsher judgment (James 3:1-2; Luke 12:41-48). When these religious authorities cannot discount the truth of the healed man's statements and they cannot discredit Jesus, they resort to shaming the man and to expelling him from their society. In other words, they want to get rid of the witness and the evidence. Such behavior is damnable. Let's be warned—especially if we are leaders—of how awful such behavior is and how God abhors it.

PRAYER:

Almighty and holy Father, please give me the courage to always look for truth. Help me never be so self-deceived that I resort to such deplorable actions as these religious leaders. Give me a teachable heart that yearns for your truth and a heart of compassion for those seeking you. In Jesus' name. Amen.

CONTEXT: JOHN 9:13-34

RELATED REFERENCES: JAMES 3:1; MATTHEW 23:27-36; JOHN 7:16-17

Day: 190

THE PROOF IS IN THE PERSON

JOHN 9:35-38

When Jesus heard that they had forced the man to leave, he found him and asked him, "Do you believe in the Son of Man?" The man said, "Tell me who he is, sir, so I can believe in him." Jesus said to him, "You have already seen him. The Son of Man is the one talking with you now." The man answered, "Yes, I believe, Lord!" Then he bowed and worshiped Jesus.

REFLECTION:

Jesus shows he is who he claims to be by his actions. When everyone else abandons and casts out the healed man, Jesus goes and finds him. The man shows he is a true God-seeker because when Jesus shares with him his identity, the man worships him. Let's show who we are by our actions and trust that Jesus will never forsake us or abandon us!

PRAYER:

Dear God, thank you that Jesus does not abandon me when everyone else does. Thank you for your steadfast faithfulness toward me even when no one else believes in me. Please form my character so that I can be steadfast and faithful as well. In Jesus' name I pray. Amen.

CONTEXT: JOHN 9:35-41

RELATED REFERENCES: JAMES 2:14-20; 2 TIMOTHY 2:11-13; MATTHEW 11:27-30

Day: 191

FOR THOSE WHO SEEK

JOHN 9:39-41

*Jesus said, "I came into this world so that the world could be judged. I came so that people
who are blind could see. And I came so that people who think they see would become
blind." Some of the Pharisees were near Jesus. They heard him say this. They asked,
"What? Are you saying that we are blind too?" Jesus said,
"If you were really blind, you would not be guilty of sin.
But you say that you see, so you are still guilty."*

REFLECTION:

Jesus is the Savior for those who are seeking God's truth. As long as we
recognize that we don't have all the answers and that we need his grace and
healing, then God is ready to bless us super-abundantly. However, if we let
arrogance capture our hearts and think that we are important, then we had
better beware. Pride and arrogance often get in the way of truth. This is never
more true than in matters of spiritual truth. Let's openly recognize that we
need God's help to discern the truth.

PRAYER:

*Father, without your help, I would not be able to know the truth. I confess that my wisdom
is but a grain of sand on the seashore of your wisdom. Thank you for placing Jesus in such
an accessible place for me to find him and receive his gracious light. Please give me
wisdom to live for you. In Jesus' name. Amen.*

CONTEXT: JOHN 9:35-41

RELATED REFERENCES: PROVERBS 16:18; 1 CORINTHIANS 2:1-5; JAMES 1:5-7

Day: 192
THE SHEPHERD USES THE GATE

JOHN 10:1-2

Jesus said, "It is certainly true that when a man enters the sheep pen, he should use the gate. If he climbs in some other way, he is a robber. He is trying to steal the sheep. But the man who takes care of the sheep enters through the gate. He is the shepherd."

REFLECTION:

If you want to know the attributes of God's shepherd—or of God as Shepherd—then this is the chapter for you. Of course the ultimate Shepherd is God and Jesus comes to us as God in human flesh. Jesus didn't sneak into a leadership position or hide himself and run some subversive movement. Instead, he publicly ministered to God's people in open sight. There were no secret meetings to determine policy and no clandestine rendezvous to plan the overthrow of the current leadership. Instead, Jesus did what he did openly before the people and in the presence of God. Any other way, and any other shepherd, is not to be trusted.

PRAYER:

Father, bless me as I follow Jesus as my Shepherd. Thank you for his public ministry before the people. Thank you for sharing that ministry through the Gospels in the Bible. In Jesus' name I thank you. Amen.

CONTEXT: JOHN 10:1-21

RELATED REFERENCES: JOHN 18:19-21; ACTS 20:28-31; MARK 6:34

Day: 193

THE VOICE OF THE SHEPHERD

JOHN 10:3-4

"The man who guards the gate opens the gate for the shepherd. And the sheep listen to the voice of the shepherd. He calls his own sheep, using their names, and he leads them out. He brings all of his sheep out. Then he goes ahead of them and leads them. The sheep follow him, because they know his voice."

REFLECTION:

Even today, sheep in Israel are separated from other flocks by the sound of their shepherd's voice. They follow their shepherd while sheep from other flocks follow their own shepherd. This is true even if the flocks are intermingled for a time.

Jesus wants us to know that as our Shepherd, he knows us intimately and will call us by name.

We, in turn, need to learn to recognize his voice when he calls us. But how do we learn to do that? By reading his words in the Gospels (Matthew, Mark, Luke, & John in the Bible) and learning to recognize his ways and his will. He will lead us where he wants us to go and bless us as we need to be blessed, but we need to be able to distinguish his voice from the many false religious voices that crowd into our world today. The only way to do that is to listen and follow the words God has given us from Jesus in the Scriptures. Let's renew our passion to know the Jesus of the Gospels and follow those words!

PRAYER:

Gracious God, please help me follow your Son as my Shepherd as I commit to spend more time with him in the Gospels. Bless me as I learn to recognize his work and his leading in my life. In the name of Jesus, my Lord and Shepherd, I pray. Amen.

CONTEXT: JOHN 10:1-21

RELATED REFERENCES: ACTS 20:11-16; PSALM 23; HEBREWS 13:20-21

HIS MASTER'S VOICE

JOHN 10:5-6

"But sheep will never follow someone they don't know. They will run away from him, because they don't know his voice." Jesus told the people this story, but they did not understand what it meant.

REFLECTION:

The old RCA logo had a dog listening to an old gramophone and underneath it was written, "Listening to His Master's Voice." That's what the sheep do with their true Shepherd. They have so trained themselves to recognize him and so trust him because of his love for them, that that they will not follow anyone who does have the voice of their Shepherd. Jesus is our Shepherd. He speaks and we hear the Master's voice. We follow him as Lord, and him alone.

PRAYER:

O God, give me a heart to follow only Jesus and an ear to recognize any imposter that might seek to steal away my heart from my Lord. In Jesus' name I pray. Amen.

CONTEXT: JOHN 10:1-21

RELATED REFERENCES: JOHN 20:24-28; 1 PETER 2:25; 2 CORINTHIANS 11:2

Day: 195

THOSE THAT CAME BEFORE ME

JOHN 10:7-8

So Jesus said again, "I assure you, I am the gate for the sheep. All those who came before me were thieves and robbers. The sheep did not listen to them."

REFLECTION:

False christs had come and gone. People were constantly looking for a messiah. Many religious leaders were ready to claim that role. But only one was sent by God. Only one did the will of God. Only one was willing to fully lay down his life for the sheep of God. This kind of shepherd not only entered through the gate, but he was also willing to lay down his own body to be the gate in the make-shift pens in the open fields to protect the sheep and to calm their restlessness and fears. Jesus was not seeking his own good or glory, but came to serve God's sheep—including us. Why? Because that is what God wanted him to do and that is because that is what a real shepherd does!

PRAYER:

Lord God, I refuse to listen to the false voices of self-appointed religious leaders who are unwilling to sacrifice for your sheep and instead want to fleece them for their own benefit. Thank you, Jesus, for being the one real Shepherd that I can follow. By the authority of your name I offer my prayer and praise. Amen.

CONTEXT: JOHN 10:1-21

RELATED REFERENCES: EZEKIEL 34:7-10; MARK 10:42-45; MATTHEW 24:24

Day: 196
LAYING DOWN HIS BODY

JOHN 10:9-10

"I am the gate. Whoever enters through me will be saved. They will be able to come in and go out. They will find everything they need. A thief comes to steal, kill, and destroy. But I came to give life—life that is full and good."

REFLECTION:

When a shepherd would take his sheep to open pastureland he would sometimes place them in a small pen at night. This pen didn't have a gate. The shepherd would actually sleep in the opening to the pen. He was their protector during the night. When daylight came, he would get up and lead them to good pasture grass.

The shepherd left the comforts of home to bring the sheep to good pasture. The shepherd slept out in the open land to offer protection and company for the sheep. Why? His desire was that the sheep be healthy, fed, and protected.

The parallels to Jesus leaving heaven, laying down his life for us, and doing all he can to give us health and life are clear. O what a Savior! O what love! That's how Jesus cares for you and me.

PRAYER:

What words, dear Father, can truly describe my appreciation for your love for me. What "thank you" is suitable for your sacrifice, Lord Jesus? I confess that some days I lose sight of your amazing love for me and your desire to give me life. I know that it is on those days that I am most vulnerable to Satan's temptations. Please forgive me. I know you have come to give me life that is rich here and knows no boundaries when I arrive at home with you and the Father. Thank you, Lord Jesus and I pray to the Father in your name. Amen.

CONTEXT: JOHN 10:1-21

RELATED REFERENCES: JOHN 1:14-18; JOHN 3:16-17; JOHN 20:30-31

HIS SHEEP

JOHN 10:11-13

"I am the good shepherd, and the good shepherd gives his life for the sheep. The worker who is paid to keep the sheep is different from the shepherd. The paid worker does not own the sheep. So when he sees a wolf coming, he runs away and leaves the sheep alone. Then the wolf attacks the sheep and scatters them. The man runs away because he is only a paid worker. He does not really care for the sheep."

REFLECTION:

Will God run? Yes, he will run to meet us when we return to him from rebellion (Luke 15:11-32). Will Jesus run? No, he will not run away from us when we are in danger or face hardships and attacks. They both love us intensely and want us safe and home with them and will do anything and everything we will let them do to make sure that happens.

Don't let the evil one make you doubt God's love. Human shepherds are fallible and will sometimes stumble, fall, and let us down. Our heavenly Shepherd, however, will not fail us, will seek and find us, and has already paid the horrible price required to ransom us from sin, death, and destruction.

PRAYER:

O Father, may I never ever outlive my love for you. May I never doubt your love and steadfast care for me. In Jesus' name I ask this. Amen.

CONTEXT: JOHN 10:1-21

RELATED REFERENCES: JOHN 15:9-17; EZEKIEL 34:7-10; PSALM 23:4

Day: 198

KNOWING AND KNOWN

JOHN 10:14-15

"I am the shepherd who cares for the sheep. I know my sheep just as the Father knows me. And my sheep know me just as I know the Father. I give my life for these sheep."

REFLECTION:

Jesus knows us. He knows our hearts. He knows our fears. He knows our temptations. He knows us inside and out. We do not have to try to vainly pretend he knows us and loves us. We do not have to be afraid in his presence. We know he wants what is best for us. He demonstrated it by allowing himself to be born into our world and placed in a corn crib in a stable at Bethlehem. He made it clear by allowing himself to be arrested, mistreated, falsely tried, and then crucified on the cross at Golgotha. We can know him and trust him because of his demonstrated love!

PRAYER:

Father, because of your love and because of Jesus, who is interceding for me now, I pour out to you my deepest concerns that are on my heart today .... I know that you will hear my cries and minister to my needs. I do not mean to be selfish today, O God, but I do want to be honest in your presence knowing that I can come to you openly and receive your grace. Thank you for such love, understanding, and assurance which were given to me at such a high price. In Jesus' name I pray. Amen.

CONTEXT: JOHN 10:1-21

RELATED REFERENCES: JOHN 2:23-25; HEBREWS 2:14-18; 1 JOHN 2:1-2

Day: 199

One Flock from Many Pastures

John 10:16

"I have other sheep too. They are not in this flock here. I must lead them also. They will listen to my voice. In the future there will be one flock and one shepherd."

Reflection:

Jesus didn't come to save a few. Jesus didn't die just for one race or one people. Jesus came for the entire world. His desire is for us to lay aside our differences and find our peace in him. When we listen to his voice, when we all are drawn closer to our one true Shepherd, we will find each other closer to one another and can then lie down and trust one another in peace.

Prayer:

Father, I long for the day when all the barriers that divide the people of earth are gone and we find joy and peace in your presence. I long for the time when all peoples can join with one voice to praise you for your grace, holiness, mercy, faithfulness, justice, righteousness, and might. Maranatha—come O Lord! Amen.

Context: John 10:1-21

Related References: John 12:31-33; John 3:13-17; Matthew 28:18-20

Day: 200

THE POWER TO LAY IT DOWN

JOHN 10:17-18

"The Father loves me because I give my life. I give my life so that I can get it back again. No one takes my life away from me. I give my own life freely. I have the right to give my life, and I have the right to get it back again. This is what the Father told me."

REFLECTION:

Jesus didn't just die; he died with power and authority. His life wasn't taken from him; he laid it down willing to die for our sins. His crucifixion was an apparent defeat for him, but he turned it into a lasting defeat for the evil one who sought to use his death to win a victory over God.

No one could take Jesus' life. He gave it willingly to save us and purchase us from death. The Cross is God's power demonstrated in humanity's worst forum. The Cross is Jesus' most humiliating and exalted moment as he was both ridiculed by hell and evil people and praised for his obedience by the eternal Father. Most of all, Jesus' voluntary gift of his life for us on the Cross is our glory!

PRAYER:

Father, as the old hymn says, "My glory all the Cross." I thank you for purchasing me from sin and death through the gift of Jesus. I trust in Jesus' sacrifice to atone for my sins. I entrust my life to Jesus as Lord. He alone had the power both to lay down his life for me and then to take that life back up again for my eternal salvation. Praise and glory be to you, dear Father, and to the Son who is to be forever praised. Amen.

CONTEXT: JOHN 10:1-21

RELATED REFERENCES: 1 JOHN 3:16; 1 JOHN 4:7-12; JOHN 15:9-17

Day: 201

TIME TO DECIDE AGAIN

JOHN 10:19-21

Again the Jews were divided over what Jesus was saying. Many of them said, "A demon has come into him and made him crazy. Why listen to him?" But others said, "These aren't the words of someone controlled by a demon. A demon cannot heal the eyes of a blind man."

REFLECTION:

Sometimes we fail to hear the bite in Jesus' words because we have heard them so many times before. For Jesus to claim to have the power to lay down his life and take it back up again is to claim the impossible and preposterous. The crowd reacts, as it often did, to his strong claims with clamoring. They recognize that they either have to believe him and put their trust in him, or else recognize him as self-deluded and crazy.

As John tells us the story of Jesus, he makes sure we are confronted again and again by the voices of those who have to decide about Jesus. He does this for two reasons. First, he knows that life is only found in Jesus. Second, he knows that his readers—that's you and me—have to continually make this choice in our lives or else we drift apart from our passionate faith in Jesus as Lord. So, what's your choice? You cannot be neutral about Jesus. He is either Lord or liar, Christ or crazy man. Let's make sure that we trust him and give our lives to God's Son as both our Lord and Christ!

PRAYER:

Father, I choose to believe that Jesus is your Son and want him to be my Lord. Fill me with your Spirit and with passion to live this truth and to share it with others. In Jesus' name I pray. Amen.

CONTEXT: JOHN 10:1-21

RELATED REFERENCES: ACTS 2:36-41; ROMANS 10:9-13; 1 CORINTHIANS 12:3

Day: 202

LOOK AT WHAT I DO, THEN DECIDE

JOHN 10:22-25

It was winter, and the time came for the Festival of Dedication at Jerusalem. Jesus was in the Temple area at Solomon's Porch. The Jewish leaders gathered around him. They said, "How long will you make us wonder about you? If you are the Christ, then tell us clearly." Jesus answered, "I told you already, but you did not believe. I do miracles in my Father's name. These miracles show who I am."

REFLECTION:

Many people can claim to be something they are not. Jesus repeatedly reminded his followers (including us), that the proof of a follower's identity is not in what he or she claims, but in what he or she does.

Jesus' proof of identity was in what he did, too! His miracles were signs that pointed to his true identity. So do you really want to have a good idea who Jesus is? Then notice what he did and how he lived while doing it.

PRAYER:

Father, please empower me as I seek to live up to what I profess and to practice what I preach. I want my life to genuinely reflect the values I hold in my heart. I want to walk the talk and put my life where my mouth is. In Jesus' name I pray. Amen.

CONTEXT: JOHN 10:22-42

RELATED REFERENCES: JOHN 14:10-11; MATTHEW 7:21-23; JAMES 2:14, 18-20

Day: 203
Can't Take them Away

John 10:26-29

"But you do not believe, because you are not my sheep. My sheep listen to my voice. I know them, and they follow me. I give my sheep eternal life. They will never die, and no one can take them out of my hand. My Father is the one who gave them to me, and he is greater than all. No one can steal my sheep out of his hand."

Reflection:

How strong a grip do you have? Well know this: Jesus' grip is stronger! As your Shepherd he will never let you go.

Prayer:

Father, I trust my life, my hope, and my future to you. I trust that as I seek you, you will never let me go. Give me strength so that I can respond to such assurance and grace with passion for you, for your kingdom, and for your holiness. In Jesus' name. Amen.

Context: John 10:22-42

Related References: Romans 8:31-39; John 18:1-9; Psalm 23:4

Day: 204

EQUAL WITH GOD?

JOHN 10:30-33
"The Father and I are one."
Again the Jews there picked up stones to kill Jesus. But he said to them, "The many wonderful things you have seen me do are from the Father. Which of these good things are you killing me for?" They answered, "We are not killing you for any good thing you did. But you say things that insult God. You are only a man, but you say you are the same as God! That is why we are trying to kill you!"

REFLECTION:

They're getting the message! The "I AM" statements, the great deeds of Jesus, and his self-identification as God's Son were being understood by Jesus' opponents. He is claiming to be God in human flesh, God among humans, and God with us. Either they had to receive him or reject him. They had to obey him or oppose him. They had to believe him or berate him.

As so often happens, Jesus' words and actions in John make clear that there can be no middle ground. The same is true for us. Jesus must be our Lord or he is nothing to us at all. He comes and challenges us to a radical faith in him. Don't you want to be radical for Jesus?

PRAYER:

Give me courage, great God and Father, to live with Jesus as my Lord. Keep me from lukewarm faith and a shallow commitment to follow Jesus. Do what it takes to fan into flame the faith I have in Jesus and make it burn brightly for your glory and for the sake of the Gospel. In Jesus' name I pray. Amen.

CONTEXT: JOHN 10:22-42

RELATED REFERENCES: JOHN 1:1-5; COLOSSIANS 1:15-17; TITUS 2:13

Day: 205

WINNING AT THEIR GAMES

JOHN 10:34-36

Jesus answered, "It is written in your law that God said, 'I said you are gods.' This Scripture called those people gods—the people who received God's message. And Scripture is always true. So why do you accuse me of insulting God for saying, 'I am God's Son'? I am the one God chose and sent into the world."

REFLECTION:

The religious leaders of Jesus' day used all sorts of rabbinic arguments—"ancient rabbi logic"—to win their religious debates. Several times in Jesus' ministry, especially toward the end of his ministry when he was in Jerusalem and they were trying to trick him with religious questions, Jesus defeats the religious teachers and leaders at their own game using their own methods of debate and logic.

In this instance, they want to charge Jesus with blasphemy because they won't believe. Even without forcing them to believe in him, Jesus uses their own logic to show why they can't convict him of blasphemy. They can't win at their own games because Jesus is greater than they are and he knows what is in their heart. Let's use this as our reminder that if we play religious games, Jesus can see through them. He challenges us to come to him and find life. Let's not settle for shallow religiosity or feelings of self-righteous superiority.

PRAYER:

Forgive me, Father, for sometimes playing religious games. I truly want to have genuine faith and I know that you long to give me life through that faith. Mold me and make me more into a person of character and faith. I ask this in Jesus' name. Amen.

CONTEXT: JOHN 10:22-42

RELATED REFERENCES: MATTHEW 22:41-46; JOHN 2:18-25; JOHN 8:24

Day: 206
LOOK AT WHAT I DO!

JOHN 10:37-38

"If I don't do what my Father does, then don't believe what I say. But if I do what my Father does, you should believe in what I do. You might not believe in me, but you should believe in the things I do. Then you will know and understand that the Father is in me and I am in the Father."

REFLECTION:

As Jesus said several times in John, "Look at my work and you will know whether I am telling the truth or not." The issue isn't Jesus' identity, but our honesty and desire to honor God. The truth about Jesus resonates in the hearts of those seeking to find God and know him. His actions and his words call us to believe him. If we don't believe him, we must reject or belittle him. There is no middle ground. We must look at the way he treated people, the things he taught, the way he lived his life, and the great works he did. Then, we must decide: Is this the work of a mad man or is he God's Messiah? Is he the Son of God come in human flesh or son of Joseph and a self-deluded wretch?

PRAYER:

Father, I thank you for making yourself accessible to me through Jesus. I know you are ever near, but Jesus' life on earth somehow makes that even more real and personal to me. Thank you for loving me so much in Jesus, in whose name I praise and thank you. Amen.

CONTEXT: JOHN 10:22-42

RELATED REFERENCES: JOHN 7:16-18; JOHN 20:24-29; JOHN 3:12

Day: 207

THE LEGACY OF JOHN

JOHN 10:39-42

They tried to get Jesus again, but he escaped from them. Then he went back across the Jordan River to the place where John began his work of baptizing people. Jesus stayed there, and many people came to him. They said, "John never did any miraculous signs, but everything John said about this man is true." And many people there believed in Jesus.

REFLECTION:

Isn't it amazing the power a godly legacy has on the hearts of those who loved the one who left them the legacy?

John the Baptist is dead, but his teaching is very much alive. He told great things about Jesus. He helped prepare the way for the Messiah, his cousin from Nazareth. Even though Herod had John executed, John's voice and influence weren't stilled.

While none of us will probably ever be a John the Baptist to such a large host of people, we all can be like John to a few folks. We can be people of character who help them find Jesus. That's a legacy that can live for generations and make an eternal difference in the lives that follow us! Let's commit to leave that kind of lasting legacy.

PRAYER:

Father, glorious God of the ages, please use me to lead others to Jesus. Help me make a difference in the lives of those around me. Use me to be a John the Baptist to those in my influence. In Jesus' name. Amen.

CONTEXT: JOHN 10:22-42

RELATED REFERENCES: JOHN 1:6-9, 15; JOHN 1:19-28; 2 TIMOTHY 3:10-17

Day: 208
BAD THINGS, GOD'S PEOPLE

JOHN 11:1-2

There was a man named Lazarus who was sick. He lived in the town of Bethany, where Mary and her sister Martha lived. (Mary is the same woman who later put perfume on the Lord and wiped his feet with her hair.) Mary's brother was Lazarus, the man who was now sick.

REFLECTION:

This story of Lazarus' death is part of a much bigger story. Martha, Mary, and Lazarus are Jesus' followers. Jesus knows them and loves them deeply. Their loyalty and love are without fault. Along the way, Lazarus gets sick and dies. Grief rips at their hearts. Jesus isn't there and Lazarus is buried and his body begins to decay. Separation tears at the hearts of this loving family.

This is also our story. We can find our answers to life's most painful reality and several of its most confusing questions in this story. Bad stuff does happen to God's people, but Jesus will not allow the bad stuff to win. Jesus triumphs! Jesus is glorified. Those who love Jesus enjoy reunion. These are the ultimate truths of this story for Martha, Mary, and Lazarus. These are the ultimate truths for us as well.

Let your heart settle here for the next couple of weeks. Let the questions as well as the faith of Martha and Mary become your own. As a mere mortal, you know that dark days will come. However, if you will walk with Martha, Mary, Jesus, and Lazarus, you will find an even surer truth: Jesus has the final word over death's separating power and you will have the final joy of his power over death!

PRAYER:

Father, please deepen my faith and stitch these words of faith and comfort on my heart these next two weeks walking with Martha, Mary, Lazarus, and Jesus. Give me hope beyond my fear of death and trust beyond my limited sight. In Jesus' name I pray. Amen.

CONTEXT: JOHN 11:1-16

RELATED REFERENCES: LUKE 10:38-42; JOHN 12:1-8; HEBREWS 2:14-15

Day: 209
CRYING OUT TO JESUS

JOHN 11:3-4

So Mary and Martha sent someone to tell Jesus, "Lord, your dear friend Lazarus is sick." When Jesus heard this he said, "The end of this sickness will not be death. No, this sickness is for the glory of God. This has happened to bring glory to the Son of God."

REFLECTION:

Sometimes we have no answers and all we can do is cry out to Jesus and ask for his help! We don't know what he knows. We can't see all the way to the end of the matter. Everything looks lost from our end. So in our desperation, we cry out for help.

But why does it take desperation to cry out to him and ask for his help? Why don't we start each day by crying out to him for help? Why not begin each day asking him to enter into our world, our homes, our lives, and our hearts? The reminder that Jesus stands at the door of our hearts and knocks (Rev. 3:20) wasn't written to the lost, but to the saved who had begun to take their walk with Jesus for granted. So let's not wait till desperation sets in to cry out and to invite him in.

PRAYER:

Father, thank you for being ever near. Thank you for coming all the way here. Thank you for making Jesus available. And now, dear Savior, I cry out and ask you into my heart. I know you are always here and always near, but I want you to know you are welcome in my heart. I willingly open myself to you. Your wisdom, strength, care, healing, guidance, love, inspiration, tenderness, strength,and power are always welcome in my life. Please come alive in me and live in me as Lord. Amen.

CONTEXT: JOHN 11:1-16

RELATED REFERENCES: REVELATION 3:19-22; MARK 1:40-41; ROMANS 7:23-24

Day: 210

NOT FOR A LACK OF LOVE

JOHN 11:5-6

Jesus loved Martha and her sister and Lazarus. So when he heard that Lazarus was sick, he stayed where he was two more days and then said to his followers, "We should go back to Judea."

REFLECTION:

Most of us will face the long dark night of the soul when it seems as if God is absent and our prayers are nothing more than wasted breath. God doesn't respond when we want him to respond. His delay in acting seems uncaring. We can feel abandoned and unloved by the God on whom we depend and for whom we seek to live. While we are not alone in these feelings, we can often be discouraged and disheartened by them (Psalm 13:1-4).

I claim no great wisdom in understanding the how or even the why of those times. They are as varied as we are. The mystery of God's actions during those times are known only to him. However, I do know three things:

First, I know we can honestly cry out and share our deepest disappointments with our Father—after all, he gave us many Psalms that do just that.

Second, I know from this story that the Lord's apparent absence is not based on a lack of love for us.

Third, I know that in the end, Jesus will triumph in us and through us.

Jesus' journey with Martha, Mary, and Lazarus reminds us that the Lord will lead us to life and victory if we will hang on to our faith in him.

PRAYER:

Father of glory and might, please give me strength to face those times when you seem absent. I pray that you will please make your presence known to those I know and love who are facing agonizing times right now. Please use me to help be a blessing to them in their time of loneliness and loss. Fill them with your Holy Spirit so that their strength will not fail. In Jesus' name I pray. Amen.

CONTEXT: JOHN 11:1-16

RELATED REFERENCES: PSALM 5:1-3; ROMANS 8:37; COLOSSIANS 3:1-4

Day: 211
WAKE UP CALL

JOHN 11:7-15

... and then said to his followers, "We should go back to Judea." They answered, "But Teacher, those Jews there tried to stone you to death. That was only a short time ago. Now you want to go back there?" Jesus answered, "There are twelve hours of light in the day. Whoever walks in the day will not stumble and fall because they can see with the light from the sun. But whoever walks at night will stumble because there is no light." Then Jesus said, "Our friend Lazarus is now sleeping, but I am going there to wake him." The followers answered, "But, Lord, if he can sleep, he will get well." They thought Jesus meant that Lazarus was literally sleeping, but he really meant that Lazarus was dead. So then Jesus said plainly, "Lazarus is dead. And I am glad I was not there. I am happy for you because now you will believe in me. We will go to him now."

REFLECTION:

Jesus will awaken each of us that belong to him. Death cannot sever our relationship with the Lord. When we die, we are still tied to him (Phil. 1:19-24). In addition, he will return one day and summon each of us from our graves. His victory over death at the empty tomb and his triumph over death for Lazarus in this story both remind us that at its worst, death is just a restful sleep. Jesus will snatch us from death's clutches with a simple call of our names. He will bring us unto himself in glory and victory. We will hear his wake up call and rise to be with him for death does not claim us. We died with Christ in baptism so that sin and death no longer have a claim over us. We await the full realization of his resurrection in our lives, but know that time will come. We have a wake up call in our future!

PRAYER:

Father, thank you for a hope that cannot be destroyed by death. Stir the urgency and passion in my heart to live victoriously because of that hope.
In Jesus' name I pray. Amen.

CONTEXT: JOHN 11:1-16

RELATED REFERENCES: JOHN 5:25-29; HEBREWS 9:27-28; 1 THESSALONIANS 4:13-14

Day: 212
Faith to Follow

John 11:16

*Then Thomas, the one called "Twin," said to the other followers, "We will go too.
We will die there with Jesus."*

Reflection:

Martha and Mary will soon be challenged to believe in what they cannot understand. Before they face their challenge, however, the followers of Jesus must follow even though they don't understand and know that they are risking their lives to follow Jesus.

They are our examples. Do we have faith to follow in the face of danger and confusion? Do we have faith to follow in the face of grief, delay, and loss? These people become God's great reminder that we can follow in times of confusion and danger. In fact, in the middle of confusion, danger, grief, delay, and loss, there is no one else we should follow. Only in Jesus can we find life and reunion beyond our greatest earthly troubles. So let's have faith to follow!

Prayer:

Almighty God, I love you and want to live your purpose for my life. Please give me the courage and faith to follow when I don't understand, when I am afraid, when I mourn, and when I feel alone. I want my life to be lived for you and guided by your hand. However, I know there are times when I do not and cannot understand what you are doing. So please, dear Father, give me courage to follow and may I never outlive my love for you. In the name of Jesus I pray. Amen.

Context: John 11:1-16

Related References: Romans 8:28-30; Luke 9:21-27; Luke 9:62

Day: 213
LORD OF HOPELESS CAUSES

JOHN 11:17-19

Jesus arrived in Bethany and found that Lazarus had already been dead and in the tomb for four days. Bethany was about two miles from Jerusalem. Many Jews had come to see Martha and Mary. They came to comfort them about their brother Lazarus.

REFLECTION:

Did you ever notice that Jesus is the Lord of hopeless causes? Can you think of a funeral he attended that he didn't "ruin" by raising the dead person to life? Remember the time he provided a picnic for 5,000 from one boy's picnic basket of "sardine sandwiches"? Do you recall how he about sank the futile fisherman's boat with an amazing catch of fish? Wasn't it amazing when he saved the terrified sailors by calming the seas they feared would sink them?

So in what area of your life do you find yourself or your situation hopeless? Have you ever just admitted that you are powerless to face it and invited Jesus into that situation? It might be a bumpy ride, but he is still the Lord of hopeless causes! Cry out and ask for his help. Admit your need for his help right now. Then go share that admission and ask for prayer and accountability from another brother or sister in Christ. I believe you will discover that the Lord can put the hope back in your cause!

PRAYER:

Give me hope, O Lord, for I rely on you and trust in your gracious power to carry me through. I cannot win the battle I now face without your power, presence, and mercy. Please be near with power. In Jesus' mighty name I pray. Amen.

CONTEXT: JOHN 11:17-37

RELATED REFERENCES: JOHN 6:1-8; JOHN 9:19-24; HEBREWS 11:39-40

Day: 214
FAITH BEYOND MY FEELINGS

JOHN 11:20-22

When Martha heard that Jesus was coming, she went out to greet him. But Mary stayed home. Martha said to Jesus, "Lord, if you had been here, my brother would not have died. But I know that even now God will give you anything you ask."

REFLECTION:

Wow! Martha spoke words that actually were greater than her understanding and her faith. Jesus would and could give her whatever he asked from the Father.

Sometimes we let the evil one deceive us into thinking that if somehow Jesus were here with us, it would be easier to believe and we could get many more fantastic things done. Jesus reminds us that just the opposite is true. Because he has gone to the Father, we can pray in his name and he will ask the Father and we will receive (John 14:12-14). Let's ask for faith that is greater than our feelings and beyond our understanding, knowing that when we ask in Jesus' name, God hears our prayer and blesses us with heaven's best answer!

PRAYER:

Father, I do believe that you long to bless me as I pray to you in the name of Jesus, your Son and my Lord. I believe that you can do mighty things in response to my cries. So I pray that you act powerfully in the following situations that are upon my heart .... In Jesus' mighty and authoritative name I pray. Amen.

CONTEXT: JOHN 11:17-37

RELATED REFERENCES: JOHN 14:12-14; JOHN 15:14-17; JOHN 16:23-27

Day: 215

RESURRECTION DAY!

JOHN 11:23-24

Jesus said, "Your brother will rise and be alive again." Martha answered, "I know that he will rise to live again at the time of the resurrection on the last day."

REFLECTION:

There is a resurrection day for all of us. For Christians, this is a day of joy, reunion, victory, celebration, glory, and revelation. It is a day to cherish and anticipate, not a day to fear. This is our day, when our faith in the Lord will be shown to be true. This is Jesus' day, when all peoples of the earth will bow their knees and proclaim that he is Lord. This is the Father's day, because he will bring all of his earthly children home to himself. This is the Spirit's day, as he raises us back to life and brings us into the full glory that is ours as children of God. However, Jesus decides to give Martha, Mary, and us a glimpse of that day when he raises Lazarus! Now we can catch a glimpse of that day and say with certainty, "Ah! Won't that resurrection day be sweet!"

PRAYER:

Father, thank you for giving me something that I can look forward to no matter what is going on in my life. I pray for the repentance and salvation of several people who are close to me and confess to you that this is my only reluctance in asking for Jesus' swift return. I do look forward to his coming and the dawn of that glorious reunion on resurrection day! In Jesus' name I anticipate that day and pray. Amen.

CONTEXT: JOHN 11:17-37

RELATED REFERENCES: 1 PETER 1:3-9; 1 THESSALONIANS 4:16-18; 2 TIMOTHY 4:7-8

Day: 216

UNTOUCHABLE LIFE!

JOHN 11:25-26

Jesus said to her, "I am the resurrection. I am life. Everyone who believes in me will have life, even if they die. And everyone who lives and believes in me will never really die. Martha, do you believe this?"

REFLECTION:

"You will never really die!" Did you catch that promise embedded in Jesus' words? Jesus says: 1) Lazarus will be raised (right now); 2) those whose bodies die will be raised to live again; and 3) those who believe in me will never die!

We readily accept the first two, but most of us have never really grasped the third one. However, Paul tells us that when we are baptized, we share in Jesus' death and die to sin (Romans 6:3-7). That means we've died the only death that truly matters, because now we are alive to God in Christ Jesus. My life—your life—and his life are fused. His future is our future. His glory will be our glory. His resurrection is our resurrection (Col. 3:1-4). Do you really believe this? If you do, then nothing can ever be the same again!

PRAYER:

Glorious God, my Abba Father, I ask for help to believe more strongly the words of Jesus. I want to live vibrantly, always alive to the promise that the true life that is me is tied to Jesus and Satan cannot defeat, destroy, or take that life from my Lord. Stir me to live more passionately, always alive to the moment knowing that my future with you is secure. In Jesus' name I pray. Amen.

CONTEXT: JOHN 11:17-37

RELATED REFERENCES: ROMANS 8:35-39; COLOSSIANS 1:25-27; COLOSSIANS 3:1-4

Day: 217

YES, I BELIEVE

JOHN 11:27

Martha answered, "Yes, Lord. I believe that you are the Christ, the Son of God. You are the one who was coming to the world."

REFLECTION:

Do you believe this? True faith hinges on believing that what Martha said is true and then living based upon that belief. Do you believe that Jesus is God's Son, the Lord, the Christ (Messiah), who came to the world from God? That faith is crucial. So say it out loud! "Yes, Lord. I believe that you are the Christ, the Son of God. You are the One that was coming to the world." Share it with someone else.

Someday, every knee will bow and every tongue will confess that these titles of Jesus are true. So let's say it now to the praise of his glory! And let's remember that not even disappointment, death, misunderstanding, and loss could strip this faith from Martha ... or us!

PRAYER:

To the praise of your glorious grace, dear Father, I confess that I believe with all my heart that Jesus is your Son and my Savior, the Christ, the Messiah promised your people, who lived as one of us and was Immanuel, God with us! I want him to rule my life as Lord. In Jesus' name I praise you and confess his glorious identity. Amen.

CONTEXT: JOHN 11:17-37

RELATED REFERENCES: PHILIPPIANS 2:9-11; LUKE 12:8; JOHN 20:24-29

Day: 218

FAITH IN THE MIDDLE OF LOSS

JOHN 11:28-30

After Martha said these things, she went back to her sister Mary. She talked to Mary alone and said, "The Teacher is here. He is asking for you." When Mary heard this, she stood up and went quickly to Jesus. He had not yet come into the village. He was still at the place where Martha met him.

REFLECTION:

I love the faith of the three key women named Mary in Jesus' life. Mary, Jesus' mother, is such a powerful example of faith and piety as she accepts the angel's proclamation of God's miraculous conception of her child (Luke 1:26-38). Mary Magdalene had been rescued from demon possession (Luke 8:2) and devotedly considered Jesus her Lord even after he is placed in the tomb and all appears to be lost; even in the face of his death she still views him as her Lord (John 20:1-2). In this situation, Jesus is still Mary's hope, even though her brother Lazarus has already died. She believes Jesus could have prevented it (John 11:32).

The important thing about all three of these women is this: they may not have had all the answers to all of their important questions, but they knew the One who is The Answer. While life will deal us some misfortunes and Satan will do what he can to wound and destroy us, we must not let the confusion of the moment steal our faith in Jesus as Lord. We must hold on to the truth that Jesus is the ultimate answer to our biggest challenges. We will not have answers to all of our questions, but we do have The Answer to the biggest one! Who assures my relationship with God, both now and forevermore? Jesus!

PRAYER:

Gracious and loving Father, please give me a faith like these three women. I want to be useful to him as a loving and faithful servant. I want to keep believing in Jesus as my Lord no matter what happens in my life or what confusing issues cloud my mind. Jesus, in those moments I ask that you make your presence very real in my life, not just for my benefit, but so that those around me can know your glory. Amen.

CONTEXT: JOHN 11:17-37

RELATED REFERENCES: JOHN 20:1-2; JOHN 6:66-69; JOHN 20:30-31

Day: 219

WORSHIP IN THE SHADOWS
OF CONFUSION AND GRIEF

JOHN 11:31-32

The Jews who were in the house comforting Mary saw her get up and leave quickly. They thought she was going to the tomb to cry there. So they followed her. Mary went to the place where Jesus was. When she saw him, she bowed at his feet and said, "Lord, if you had been here, my brother would not have died."

REFLECTION:

"Where could I go but to the Lord?" These words to an old hymn speak the truth of Mary's heart. Through her confusion and loss she comes and falls at the feet of Jesus. So often the evil one convinces us that our doubts, fears, confusion, and grief make us unacceptable to the Lord. But where else can we or should we go with these soul-wrenching concerns. If there is anything that the ministry of Jesus should teach us it should be this: we can come honestly to Jesus for truth, mercy, grace, help, forgiveness, cleansing, power, and love. Even if we don't know the "What?" or the "Why?" about the things going on in our lives, we can know that there is one waiting for us who will share the burden of our hearts. All we have to do is fall at his feet and call out for his help. His name is Jesus.

PRAYER:

Dear heavenly Father, I have some folks that are truly on my heart that need your presence and your blessing. I'm not sure if they can hold on to their faith much longer. Please minister in clear ways to them. I will continue to encourage them to come to you, but please, dear Father, they need your help today and they desperately need to know the presence of your Son is with them. In Jesus' name I ask for this blessing. Amen.

CONTEXT: JOHN 11:17-37

RELATED REFERENCES: HEBREWS 2:17-18; HEBREWS 4:14-16; MATTHEW 11:25-30

Day: 220
JESUS' ENEMY AND JESUS' FRIEND
JOHN 11:33-35

When Jesus saw Mary crying and the people with her crying too, he was very upset and deeply troubled. He asked, "Where did you put him?" They said, "Lord, come and see." Jesus cried.

REFLECTION:

I don't know about you, but I am truly blessed by the Lord's displays of human need and human emotion in the Gospels. To know he was tired, hungry, and thirsty is reassuring—he knows these very basic human needs. To know that he grew angry, was frustrated, felt sorrow, and even was indignant ("very upset ... deeply troubled") gives me great comfort—he knows the roller coaster of human emotion.

I know I don't always use those emotions righteously, so it is nice to know that he had to wrestle with them, too, even though he used these emotions righteously.

I especially love the power of this moment and the honesty with John's description: Jesus is "very upset" and "deeply troubled" with the power of death. He is also sorrowful at the grief involved in Lazarus' death. These emotions capture where I am a lot at funerals. I am mad at the devil and his awful tool (death) of hurting and separating families and friends. I am broken-hearted for those who have lost their loved one.

Jesus loves us. Jesus hates death. Thank God he defeated death and will one day set it aside forever! Yet in the face of death, it's nice to know that he still sees death as his enemy (1 Cor. 15:25-26) and is upset, troubled, and grieved when it wounds us.

PRAYER:

Thank you, God, for a Savior who has been here and felt our pain, suffered our grief, and experienced our anger in the face of death. Thank you for the promise that lies behind a Savior who "ruined" every funeral he attended by raising the dead person back to life. I trust that in my sorrow, his promise will sustain me and those who have lost the ones they love. In Jesus' conquering name I pray. Amen.

CONTEXT: JOHN 11:17-37

RELATED REFERENCES: 1 CORINTHIANS 15:25-26; HEBREWS 2:14-15; 1 CORINTHIANS 15:51-58

Day: 221
DISCOUNTED LOVE

JOHN 11:36-37

And the Jews said, "Look! He loved Lazarus very much!" But some of them said, "Jesus healed the eyes of the blind man. Why didn't he help Lazarus and stop him from dying?"

REFLECTION:

Satan has a way of trying to distort any good thing and corrupt it. We shouldn't be surprised that he would try to distort Jesus' genuine love for Lazarus by casting doubt on why he was so late in coming to help Lazarus: "Jesus healed the eyes of the blind man. Why didn't Jesus help Lazarus and stop him from dying?"

The evil one also helps us ask those questions about the Lord's intentions for us as well. He stirs our minds with doubts, trying to make us question the Lord's love for us. But we won't let the evil one steal God's love for us in our moments of shock, sorrow, and loss. We know the Lord is there and cares for us. He demonstrated that when he suffered and died for us. So while we may not have the answer to our "Why?" questions, we don't let that keep us from the right answer to the "Who?" question.

Jesus is our answer! Jesus is our hope! Why? Because he demonstrated his love for us and nothing can rob the nails of Calvary from God's triumphant message to us: "I have a never-ending love for you!"

PRAYER:

Holy Father, please give me wisdom to discern the false and deceptive voice of Satan as he seeks to work discouragement and doubt in me through the confusing and hurtful times of my life. Hold my heart with the love your Son showed me at Calvary. In Jesus' name I pray. Amen.

CONTEXT: JOHN 11:17-37

RELATED REFERENCES: JOHN 3:16-17; ROMANS 5:6-11; 1 JOHN 4:9-10

Day: 222
REMOVING THE STENCH OF DEATH

JOHN 11:38-40

Again feeling very upset, Jesus came to the tomb. It was a cave with a large stone covering the entrance. He said, "Move the stone away." Martha said, "But, Lord, it has been four days since Lazarus died. There will be a bad smell." Martha was the sister of the dead man. Then Jesus said to her, "Remember what I told you? I said that if you believed, you would see God's divine greatness."

REFLECTION:

Gritty. The reality of Lazarus' death—the sorrow, disappointment, friendship, finality, cemetery, and stench—is told in plain, straightforward, and gritty truth. Lazarus is long gone. His tomb is shut. His body stinks. His sisters are disappointed by Jesus' absence in his illness and tardiness in his death. All those close to Lazarus grieve his passing.

All these realities, however, have to give away to one greater reality: Jesus and his glory! Jesus contradicts our mortal realities—illness, death, grief, and confusion. At least that is what our faith reminds us. Each of us will face the bitter realities of death when it hits close to our home. Do we have faith that Jesus and his glory offer us a greater reality?

PRAYER:

Holy God, please bless those that I know and love who now grieve because death has hit close to their home. Bless them with faith so they can believe in the greater reality of Jesus' return in glory. Father, I also ask for confident faith in that same greater reality. Give me courage, grace, and faith as I face my own mortality and the mortality of all those I love. In Jesus' glorious name I pray. Amen.

CONTEXT: JOHN 11:38-44

RELATED REFERENCES: 1 THESSALONIANS 4:13-14; 1 CORINTHIANS 15:50-57; MATTHEW 25:31

Day: 223

THE FATHER HEARS THE SON

JOHN 11:41-42

So they moved the stone away from the entrance. Then Jesus looked up and said, "Father, I thank you that you heard me. I know that you always hear me. But I said these things because of the people here around me. I want them to believe that you sent me."

REFLECTION:

While he hasn't taught his followers the key principle yet, he is proving it beforehand. The Father hears the Son and responds to his requests. There can be no more clear example of this than his thanks to the Father for hearing his request to raise Lazarus—who is clearly (four days) dead. This demonstration of Jesus' conversation with the Father is for our benefit, so that we can believe that God had sent him.

Jesus had earlier promised that the dead would hear his voice and be raised to life (John 5:28-29). We see it happen with Lazarus! Jesus will later promise that we will be able to pray through him and the Father will do what the Son asks (John 14:12-14). We get a glimpse of that truth here as Jesus asks the Father and Lazarus comes out of the grave! So let's seek the Father's will and glory, asking Jesus for his power to be released through our prayers.

PRAYER:

Father, thank you for the assurance that when I pray in Jesus' name, you hear me. Please give me wisdom and boldness as I pray in Jesus' name. Amen.

CONTEXT: JOHN 11:38-44

RELATED REFERENCES: JOHN 16:23-27; 1 TIMOTHY 2:5-6; 1 JOHN 2:1-2

LET HIM GO!

JOHN 11:43-44

After Jesus said this he called in a loud voice, "Lazarus, come out!" The dead man came out. His hands and feet were wrapped with pieces of cloth. He had a handkerchief covering his face. Jesus said to the people, "Take off the cloth and let him go."

REFLECTION:

I love Jesus' words, "Take the cloth off of him and let him go." Because of Jesus' powerful words, death cannot bind Lazarus anymore, so his grave clothes shouldn't bind him either!

Think of the power of this statement! One day, Jesus will speak our name, call us to himself, and forbid death to bind us. Lazarus is the great example of what we anticipate—receiving back those who have died and gone to the Lord before us. One day, we will receive our call to be set free from the demands of our mortal bodies and the bondage of death. Jesus will call us to himself and share his glory with us.

PRAYER:

Lord God Almighty, the Father of all that lives, thank you for giving us back what we throw away with sin—the opportunity to live with you forever. Thank you for the assurance that I will be united with those that I love who have died in faith because of Jesus' sacrificial life, powerful resurrection, and authoritative word. Thank you for the assurance that death cannot hold me captive when Jesus knows my name. In his mighty name I pray. Amen.

CONTEXT: JOHN 11:38-44

RELATED REFERENCES: HEBREWS 2:14-15; 1 CORINTHIANS 15:53-58; JOHN 5:25-28

Day: 225

DETERMINED NOT TO BELIEVE

JOHN 11:45-46

There were many Jews who came to visit Mary. When they saw what Jesus did, many of them believed in him. But some of them went to the Pharisees and told them what Jesus did.

REFLECTION:

Some folks just won't believe. It doesn't matter what they see or what others say; they are determined not to believe in Jesus. How do we explain this kind of thing?

Jesus told us that people have to want to do God's will if they are going to believe (John 7:17). If they play with sin, then they open their hearts for Satan to block their believing. Religion can sometimes be a tool Satan uses to foster unbelief—more often than we would like to imagine I fear. Something like that happens here. Rather than rejoice that Lazarus has been raised, the protectors of the religious status quo will try to get rid of both Jesus and Lazarus.

However, we don't give up because God can use the circumstances in people's lives to open their hearts. We are not sure how many of the skeptics and unbelievers at this stage of Jesus' ministry later became believers as the Gospel spread and the early church grew. Undoubtedly, more than a few (Acts 2:33-41; Acts 6:7).

PRAYER:

Holy and almighty God, please use me and the circumstances of the lives of the following people, to open their hearts to Jesus ... I pray this in Jesus' name. Amen.

CONTEXT: JOHN 11:45-57

RELATED REFERENCES: JOHN 7:16-18; COLOSSIANS 1:21-22; ROMANS 1:18

Day: 226
WHAT CAN BE DESTROYED?

JOHN 11:47-48

Then the leading priests and Pharisees called a meeting of the high council. They said, "What should we do? This man is doing many miraculous signs. If we let him continue doing these things, everyone will believe in him. Then the Romans will come and take away our Temple and our nation."

REFLECTION:

What do you value most in your life? What do you have the greatest trouble relinquishing to the Lordship of Christ? These two questions are crucial, because they help define the battleground on which you will have to fight your adversary—Satan. He will do everything he can to distort those values and have them displace the will of God in your heart and the Lordship of Jesus Christ in your life.

The Temple was one of the most important symbols of Jewish life and faith. Yet it was not more important than the will of God. The Scriptures were essential to God's people, but not more important than God's Son, his living message. The religious leaders were important to Jewish heritage, but never more important than Israel's true King, God! The Pharisees and high council were so intent in keeping what they had, they rejected what God wanted and planned for their blessing. They couldn't even see the good things Jesus did because their true treasure was in what they had and not in the God they served and his promises for their future. What about us? What would keep us from welcoming the exclusive call of Christ upon our hearts and lives?

PRAYER:

Purify my heart, O God, and renew a right attitude in me. Cleanse me from my sin and guard me from competing distractions that could become an idol for me. I want no claim upon my heart other than your will for me. Keep my heart, soul, and mind in devotion to you and to the work of your Kingdom. In Jesus' name I pray. Amen.

CONTEXT: JOHN 11:45-57

RELATED REFERENCES: MATTHEW 6:19-24; JOHN 5:39-44; MATTHEW 22:34-40

Day: 227
ONE TO DIE FOR THE PEOPLE

JOHN 11:49-50

One of the men there was Caiaphas. He was the high priest that year. He said, "You people know nothing! It is better for one man to die for the people than for the whole nation to be destroyed. But you don't realize this."

REFLECTION:

Jesus came to live as God among us and to die for our sins to bring us to God. However, we are saved from destruction because of grace, not because of some corrupt religious leader's decision. This was God's plan, so that a perfect sacrifice could be offered that would completely take away our sin. Jesus is our atoning sacrifice. He died so that we could live. What incredible love! What overwhelming grace!

PRAYER:

LORD God Almighty, thank you for your incredible mercy and grace demonstrated through the sacrifice of your Son! Thank you, Jesus, for bearing my sin and shame so that I could receive your salvation. May my life be a worthy response of praise to all that you have done, and all that you will do, to bless me and make me yours. Amen.

CONTEXT: JOHN 11:45-57

RELATED REFERENCES: JOHN 3:16-17; ROMANS 3:21-26; 1 PETER 3:18

Day: 228
A Promise for the Nations

John 11:51-53

Caiaphas did not think of this himself. As that year's high priest, he was really prophesying that Jesus would die for the Jewish people. Yes, he would die for the Jewish people. But he would also die for God's other children scattered all over the world. He would die to bring them all together and make them one people. That day the Jewish leaders began planning to kill Jesus.

Reflection:

God can even use those who oppose him to declare his grace. His plan was to save his people, Israel, and also reach the non-Jewish nations of the world through Jesus. We should remember that grace triumphs over even the most evil plots! God will not be deterred. His will is going to triumph. His glory will be declared even by those who have opposed Him. That is the power of the Gospel and the God who authored it and the Lord Jesus who made that power available to us.

Prayer:

Thank you, dear Father, that your grace is for all peoples of the earth. Please bless my brothers and sisters in Christ all over the world, especially those who live out their faith in hostile situations. Please spread the power of the Gospel throughout the world in this generation so that every nation, culture, language, and people have a chance to know the name and experience the grace of Jesus. In the name of the Lord Jesus I pray. Amen.

Context: John 11:45-57

Related References: John 10:14-16; John 12:31-32; 1 John 2:1-2

Day: 229

FOLLOWER TIME

JOHN 11:54

So Jesus stopped traveling around openly among the Jews. He went away to a town called Ephraim in an area near the desert. He stayed there with his followers.

REFLECTION:

In all four Gospels (Matthew, Mark, Luke, John), we learn that the last part of Jesus' ministry is specifically focused on teaching and preparing his followers. Many in the crowd turn away and the determination of his opponents to kill him is growing. Jesus recognizes that he has a short time to prepare his followers for his "departure" and the responsibilities they will carry in his absence.

Despite Jesus' clear and powerful example, many of us fail to share our vision and our ministries with others who can carry them on after we are gone as well as help us take advantage of the opportunities that God is giving us now. Let's learn from Jesus' example the vital importance of sharing our visions, dreams, and ministries with others while we still have time.

PRAYER:

Father of grace and mercy, thank you for giving me the abilities that I have and the opportunities to use them for your glory and for the work of your Kingdom. Open my eyes, dear Father, to those around me with whom I can share the passion, understanding, experience, and ministry opportunities that you have given me. In Jesus' name I ask it. Amen.

CONTEXT: JOHN 11:45-57

RELATED REFERENCES: MARK 3:13-15; JOHN 15:9-17; PHILIPPIANS 3:17

Day: 230

REFUSING DELIVERANCE

JOHN 11:55-57

It was almost time for the Jewish Passover festival. Many people from the country went to Jerusalem before the Passover. They went to do the special things to make themselves pure for the festival. The people looked for Jesus. They stood in the Temple area and asked each other, "Is he coming to the festival? What do you think?" But the leading priests and the Pharisees had given a special order about Jesus. They said that anyone who knew where he was must tell them so that they could arrest him.

REFLECTION:

Why is it so hard for those caught up in wrong things—wrong ideas, destructive addictions, harmful relationships—to accept the opportunity for deliverance? There are many partial answers, but one clear answer: Satan has blinded them to the truth because he doesn't want them to be freed from his clutches. Despite the inexplicable healing of Lazarus, some would not believe. Despite the freedom that Jesus comes to offer them, some will not receive it. In fact, some are determined to be rid of Jesus because they are happily settled in the fog Satan has brought over them. As much as we may try to convince them otherwise, some will not believe until they reach the point where they cannot believe (John 12:39). There is not much we can do except to pray for their hearts to change; to ask God to give them an opportunity to reconsider their relationship with Jesus; to live before them with a consistent example of character and faith; and to be ready to help when they face difficulty or find themselves open to the truth.

PRAYER:

Father, please minister to my discouragement. I have some friends whom I love deeply who are caught in Satan's traps. Make my life a consistent example of genuine compassion and godly character before them. Please help me see the opportunities when these friends are more open to your grace and please use me to share that grace at the appropriate time. In Jesus' name I pray. Amen.

CONTEXT: JOHN 11:45-57

RELATED REFERENCES: ACTS 26:15-18; EPHESIANS 2:1-2; 1 PETER 1:18-21

Day: 231

MEMORIES OF EXTRAVAGANCE

JOHN 12:1-3

Six days before the Passover festival, Jesus went to Bethany. That is where Lazarus lived, the man Jesus raised from death. There they had a dinner for Jesus. Martha served the food, and Lazarus was one of the people eating with Jesus. Mary brought in a pint of expensive perfume made of pure nard. She poured the perfume on Jesus' feet. Then she wiped his feet with her hair. And the sweet smell from the perfume filled the whole house.

REFLECTION:

Our sense of smell is powerful. Smell can attract or repulse us. It can excite or inhibit us. Most of all, it can deeply embed a memory and call it back powerfully to the surface of our emotions when the fragrance reappears.

Mary's anointing of Jesus filled the whole house with the sweet smell of perfume. This smell would be anchored in the memory of all who participated and would be re-told by those present every time they caught even the faintest whiff of that aroma. Mary's extravagant love prepared Jesus for his death and primed our hearts for the extravagant love he showed for us on the Cross.

The people present at that dinner would also remember the beautiful aroma of Mary's extravagant love. When we truly know that Jesus loves us and has ransomed us from death, how can we not be extravagant in our display of love for him? Let's be like Mary, who was more concerned to extravagantly display her love for Jesus and less concerned about the criticism of those around her!

PRAYER:

Father, I confess that way too often my display of love for Jesus is passionless and predictable. For some reason, I find myself holding back—not wanting to call attention to myself and not sure what is an appropriate display of my affection. I truly love and appreciate you, Jesus, for your unbelievable sacrifice and the victory over death that you purchased for me. O Father, help me to be less concerned about the criticism of others and more free to show my love for my Savior. In Jesus' precious name I pray. Amen.

CONTEXT: JOHN 12:1-19

RELATED REFERENCES: JOHN 11:29-32, 39-44; MARK 14:1-9; 2 CORINTHIANS 9:15

Day: 232
PIOUS SOUNDING CRITICS
JOHN 12:4-7

Judas Iscariot, one of Jesus' followers, was there—the one who would later hand Jesus over to his enemies. Judas said, "That perfume was worth a full year's pay. It should have been sold, and the money should have been given to the poor people." But Judas did not really care about the poor. He said this because he was a thief. He was the one who kept the money bag for the group of followers. And he often stole money from the bag.

REFLECTION:

Ever notice how some people at church criticize much more freely than they praise, encourage, or serve? Satan has a way of finding small and selfish hearts to criticize those who sacrifice and lavishly express their love for God.

Does that mean we give up on the church? Well, did Jesus give up on his followers because one of them was a greedy traitor, the rest were often confused, and none of them proved reliable at their first big test? Of course not! Where else would we want a person wrestling with heart problems than among God's people?

The real issue for our churches today is whether those who lead give in to pious sounding critics or if they will respectfully and firmly confront them with the truth. Jesus did not let Judas' words become the final word spoken in this moment. He immediately confronted Judas ("Don't stop her") and praised Mary ("It was right for her to save this perfume for today.") Too many who sacrifice and serve are not affirmed simply because someone else criticizes their extravagant expressions of love with pious sounding words. Jesus shows us this must not be the case with his people!

PRAYER:

Holy and loving God, please open my eyes to people who are serving you extravagantly, then use me to affirm them and encourage them in their service and sacrifice to your Kingdom. In Jesus' name I pray. Amen.

CONTEXT: JOHN 12:1-19

RELATED REFERENCES: LUKE 3:21-22; 1 THESSALONIANS 1:2-3; 2 CORINTHIANS 8:1-5

Day: 233

PUTTING POVERTY IN PERSPECTIVE

JOHN 12:7-8

Jesus answered, "Don't stop her. It was right for her to save this perfume for today—the day for me to be prepared for burial. You will always have those who are poor with you. But you will not always have me."

REFLECTION:

Scripture is clear: we are to help the poor, feed the hungry, and care for widows, orphans, and aliens among us (Deut. 10:18-19; James 1:27). There will always be a tug of war about our priorities in how to give—what do we give specifically and extravagantly to help the poor among us and what do we give to generously support other facets of the Lord's work. Each is important. Each can honor God.

Let's not be critical of those who give extravagantly to any of God's works. God knows the heart of each giver and we need to rejoice in each act of kindness and generosity offered to honor him and bless his cause. Even more, we need to be generous both with the Lord and with those in need! After all, Jesus himself reminds us that when we care for those less fortunate, we are actually doing it for him (Matthew 25).

PRAYER:

Loving and gracious Father, mold my heart to be more like yours. Bless me with gracious-ness, generosity, thankfulness, and a forgiving spirit. Open my eyes to all that Jesus has done, is doing, and will do for me so that I will more freely share with others my love, possessions, money, and time. In Jesus' name, and because of Jesus' love, I pray. Amen.

CONTEXT: JOHN 12:1-19

RELATED REFERENCES: 2 CORINTHIANS 8:7; 2 CORINTHIANS 9:6-8; MATTHEW 25:31-40

Day: 234
I Could Never Do That!

John 12:9-11

Many of the Jews heard that Jesus was in Bethany, so they went there to see him. They also went there to see Lazarus, the one Jesus raised from death. So the leading priests made plans to kill Lazarus too. Because of him, many Jews were leaving them and believing in Jesus. That is why they wanted to kill Lazarus too.

Reflection:

How could a religious movement intent on doing good become murderous and treacherous? Over the centuries, many atrocities have been committed in the name of religion. (There have also been many atrocities committed against religious people.) The hatred of the religious elite that was aimed at Jesus boils over against Lazarus. Killing Jesus is no longer enough. They must now kill Lazarus to get rid of the proof of Jesus' power!

This hatred is a sad reminder of what happens when people no longer pursue the will of God and settle for the preservation of their religion. This is a sobering warning. When we have to find creative ways to justify how we could do something ungodly to one of God's children, we need to scrutinize our actions very carefully. God's two great commands to us still apply: Love the Lord your God and love your neighbor as yourself. Being religious does not give us the right to hate or brutalize someone in the name of God!

Prayer:

Holy and righteous God, fill me with your Spirit and your wisdom. I do not want to ever push away someone who is searching for your will or harm anyone who is seeking you no matter how much I might not understand them or agree with them. In addition, dear Father, I don't want my religious biases and my entrenched traditions to cause me to blindly reject someone in your family. Give me wisdom, character, patience, and grace when I deal with all people. In Jesus' name I ask for this help. Amen.

Context: John 12:1-19

Related References: Luke 12:28-31; Matthew 5:43-48; 1 John 4:20-21

Day: 235

Clearly Praised for a Few Days

John 12:12-13

The next day the people in Jerusalem heard that Jesus was coming there. These were the crowds of people who had come to the Passover festival. They took branches of palm trees and went out to meet Jesus. They shouted, "'Praise Him! Welcome! God bless the one who comes in the name of the Lord! God bless the King of Israel'!"

Reflection:

The people hope Jesus is their conquering savior sent to deliver them from the Romans. They hail him as the great King David's heir. Jesus, however, identifies with the servant and peaceful Savior of Zechariah's prophecy (Zech. 9:8-10). He comes as a peacemaker, not as a warrior on a conquest.

When Jesus refuses to be the conqueror and submits to arrest and torture, the crowds who hailed him one week earlier are gone and are replaced by a crowd that cries, "Crucify him!" If Jesus is to be our Savior, he must also be our Lord. We come to him on his terms or we miss him and we miss the peace he came to bring to us. Jesus is both the Lion of the Tribe of Judah and the Lamb that was slain. He is both conquering warrior and gentle Savior. We must follow wherever and however he leads us, for he is Lord.

Prayer:

Holy God, my Abba Father, thank you for sending Jesus to be our mighty Savior and humble Servant King. Help me understand all that this means and empower me to follow him no matter the cost. In Jesus' mighty name I pray. Amen.

Context: John 12:1-19

Related References: Zechariah 9:9-12; Luke 13:34; Matthew 2720:-23

Day: 236
A SEED UNTIL THE RESURRECTION!

JOHN 12:14-16

Jesus found a donkey and rode on it, as the Scriptures say, "Do not be afraid, people of Zion! Look! Your king is coming. He is riding on a young donkey."
The followers of Jesus did not understand at that time what was happening. But after he was raised to glory, they understood that this was written about him. Then they remembered that they had done these things for him.

REFLECTION:

Jesus must be regarded differently because of his resurrection. If Jesus hadn't been raised from the dead, then our Christian walk has been a sad investment of faith, time, and hope. Since Jesus was raised, our lives are full of hope and promise, no matter how we might be threatened physically. We have the blessing of knowing how Jesus' story on earth ends—not with a cross and a tomb, but with a resurrected Savior! Once we truly grasp the crucial reality of the resurrection, everything is different and we are more than conquerors through our peaceful Savior.

PRAYER:

Father, thank you for redeeming me from death and the fear of death through Jesus' victory at the cross and the empty tomb! Never let me forget that you are the God who raises the dead and restores life to the lifeless. I pray this in the name of Jesus my Lord. Amen.

CONTEXT: JOHN 12:1-19

RELATED REFERENCES: JOHN 2:19-21; COLOSSIANS 3:1-4; 1 CORINTHIANS 15:4

Day: 237
WHEN LOST IS WON!

JOHN 12:17-19

There were many people with Jesus when he raised Lazarus from death and told him to come out of the tomb. Now they were telling others about what Jesus did. That's why so many people went out to meet him—because they had heard about this miraculous sign he did. So the Pharisees said to each other, "Look! Our plan is not working. The people are all following him!"

REFLECTION:

Those opposed to Jesus lost! The will of God won! While clearly hyperbole, the religious enemies of Jesus proclaim the will and the word of God: "All the people are following him!" While the religious leaders who hated Jesus didn't give up on their murderous plots, they pronounce their own ultimate defeat with these words.

Little did they know that their plan to stop Jesus by crucifying him would end up handing Jesus the ultimate victory. When Jesus is crucified, when he is lifted up on the Cross and fulfills God's will, he then conquers those opposed to God's will and calls all people seeking God to himself through the message and the triumph of God's grace. Thanks be to God for our victory in Christ Jesus, our Lord and Savior.

PRAYER:

Holy and gracious God, thank you for your victory over death, Satan, and false religion through the death, burial, and resurrection of Jesus. Please use me to help the people around me come to know Jesus better as Lord and Savior. Solidify my confidence, O LORD, in your ultimate plan of victory for me. As I see your mighty hand at work overcoming the awful events that follow these words, strengthen me so that I will resolutely hold to my faith in the times of trial that will surely come. I pray in the name of your Son, Jesus. Amen.

CONTEXT: JOHN 12:1-19

RELATED REFERENCES: JOHN 3:16-17; MATTHEW 28:18-20; JOHN 12:31-33

Day: 238

THE WORLD COMES KNOCKING

JOHN 12:20-23

There were some Greeks there too. These were some of the people who went to Jerusalem to worship at the Passover festival. They went to Philip, who was from Bethsaida in Galilee. They said, "Sir, we want to meet Jesus." Philip went and told Andrew. Then Andrew and Philip went and told Jesus. Jesus said to them, "The time has come for the Son of Man to receive his glory."

REFLECTION:

The enemies of Jesus proclaimed it. The non-Jewish Greek seekers demonstrate it. Jesus has won. The world is looking for Jesus as Savior. All people are following him. The only thing Jesus' enemies can think of doing now is to crucify him. That will make him a martyr and open the door to the world's greatest miracle and eternity's greatest turning point—Jesus' resurrection.

Jesus has been saying all throughout the Gospel of John, "The right time for me has not yet come." With the Greek seekers approaching him and his enemies recognizing his victory, Jesus knows that his time has now come. He will enter his glory by doing what the Father asks—he will faithfully offer his life as a sacrifice for sins by dying on the Cross. It will be a brutal and painful glory for Jesus, but it will guarantee glory for all who truly follow him.

PRAYER:

Lord God Almighty, I confess that I am stunned when I realize the cost of your plan to save me. Thank you for this incredible gift placed so firmly in the world in which I live. I praise you and give you all glory for your plan, your sacrifice, and your grace shared with me in your gift of Jesus, in whose name I pray. Amen.

CONTEXT: JOHN 12:20-36

RELATED REFERENCES: 1 CORINTHIANS 1:22-25; ROMANS 1:16; COLOSSIANS 1:25-27

Day: 239

PLANTED FOR THE HARVEST

JOHN 12:24-26

"It is a fact that a grain of wheat must fall to the ground and die before it can grow and produce much more wheat. If it never dies, it will never be more than a single seed. Whoever loves the life they have now will lose it. But whoever is willing to give up their life in this world will keep it. They will have eternal life. Whoever serves me must follow me. My servants must be with me everywhere I am. My Father will give honor to anyone who serves me."

REFLECTION:

So much of what we want to do for God we try to do by ourselves. Our motives are right. Our heart is right. Our plans are made with prayer. The problem is that we end up doing everything except the crucial thing: we are not willing to die.

Our identity gets involved in pulling off our plans. Our hopes and our feelings about Christian service get tangled up in our own sense of success in the plan. Jesus reminds us that there is no harvest without death—the seed has to be planted and die before it can germinate and grow. Jesus submitted everything, including his fears and his friends, to the will of God. It cost him his life. It won him the harvest.

What have you not surrendered to God? Why?

PRAYER:

Forgive me, Father. I confess that I have wanted my following Jesus and my ministry to be done my way, or at least for them to result in the outward trappings of success. After thinking about Jesus' words today, I want to die to my will and have yours come to life in me. Please show me how to do that because I want to be an agent of your great harvest. In the name of your submissive and triumphant Son, Jesus, I pray. Amen.

CONTEXT: JOHN 12:20-36

RELATED REFERENCES: LUKE 9:23-26; LUKE 10:2; JOHN 4:34-38

Day: 240
THE REAL BENEFIT

JOHN 12:27-30

"Now I am very troubled. What should I say? Should I say, 'Father save me from this time of suffering'? No, I came to this time so that I could suffer. Father, do what will bring you glory!" Then a voice came from heaven, "I have already brought glory to myself. I will do it again." The people standing there heard the voice. They said it was thunder. But others said, "An angel spoke to him!" Jesus said, "That voice was for you and not for me."

REFLECTION:

Wouldn't it be nice to be so sure you are living in God's will that you wouldn't need reassurance that you are doing the right thing? I don't know about you, but I have a hard time not envying Jesus' assurance expressed in this passage.

While we may never have the confidence of walking in God's will quite like Jesus did at this moment, we do have several incredible blessings that should give us great confidence about living in God's will.

First, we can pray for wisdom and be assured we will receive it.

Second, we can take confidence that God is going to work in our lives for our good.

Third, we can trust the Holy Spirit will help lead us and guide in God's will.

While we may not receive as visible a form of assurance as Jesus did in this passage, we need to rest in the confidence that God will get us where we need to be to honor him if we are genuinely seeking his will and are willing to do what he asks of us.

PRAYER:

O God Almighty, God of Abraham and Isaac and Jacob, please give me wisdom to know your will, the courage to follow it, and the grace to do all this in a way that blesses others. In Jesus' name I pray. Amen.

CONTEXT: JOHN 12:20-36

RELATED REFERENCES: JAMES 1:5-8; ROMANS 8:26-30; GALATIANS 5:22-26

Day: 241

HOW DARKNESS IS DEFEATED

JOHN 12:31-33

"Now is the time for the world to be judged. Now the ruler of this world will be thrown out. I will be lifted up from the earth. When that happens, I will draw all people to myself." Jesus said this to show how he would die.

REFLECTION:

The Cross was the place where the prince of this world, Satan, lost at his own game. Satan had intended to use Jesus' horrible death to destroy God's work. Instead, God used Jesus' death on the Cross to be a sacrifice for our sins. Through the resurrection of Jesus, God then defeated the power of sin and death. The powers of darkness that had controlled the world lost their victory at Calvary because of Jesus' obedience to the will of God and his love for us! Then, they lost their power when Jesus triumphed over death and emerged victorious as God's powerful Son.

PRAYER:

Father, please give me the courage to live with the confidence that darkness, and the prince of darkness, are defeated because of Jesus' death, burial, and resurrection. In Jesus' name. Amen.

CONTEXT: JOHN 12:20-36

RELATED REFERENCES: 1 CORINTHIANS 15:1-6, 54-58; HEBREWS 2:14-15; ROMANS 4:25

Day: 242
LIMITED OPPORTUNITIES

JOHN 12:34-36

The people said, "But our law says that the Christ will live forever. So why do you say, 'The Son of Man must be lifted up'? Who is this 'Son of Man'?"
Then Jesus said, "The light will be with you for only a short time more. So walk while you have the light. Then the darkness will not catch you. People who walk in the darkness don't know where they are going. So put your trust in the light while you still have it. Then you will be children of light." When Jesus finished saying these things, he went away to a place where the people could not find him.

REFLECTION:

So often, people think they will have plenty of opportunities to decide about Jesus. Satan ensures that this is not true, while still trying to make people think that it is. This was brought home tragically to me when a good friend of mine in high school was killed in a motorcycle accident a few months after I had tried to share Christ with him. He said, "I will do that when I am older. Christianity is for old people."

He didn't take advantage of the light when he had the opportunity. His words will forever haunt me and remind me that God wants his grace to reach its mark. Jesus' words of urgency are still true today, "So put your trust in the light while you still have it." Let's share Christ with a greater sense of urgency for we don't know when the opportunity for someone to come to the Light will end.

PRAYER:

Father, forgive me for not living with a greater sense of urgency, especially in my relation-ship with my non-Christian friends. Please be with me as I try to share my faith in Jesus with the following people....In Jesus' name I pray. Amen.

CONTEXT: JOHN 12:20-36

RELATED REFERENCES: 2 CORINTHIANS 6:2; JOHN 5:19-24; ACTS 26:19-26

Day: 243
COULDN'T BELIEVE

JOHN 12:37-41

The people saw all these miraculous signs Jesus did, but they still did not believe in him.
This was to give full meaning to what Isaiah the prophet said, "Lord, who believed what
we told them? Who has seen the Lord's power?" This is why the people could not believe.
Because Isaiah also said, "God made the people blind. He closed their minds. He did this
so that they would not see with their eyes and understand with their minds. He did it so that
they would not turn and be healed." Isaiah said this because he saw Jesus' divine greatness.
So he spoke about him.

REFLECTION:

This is a tough Scripture. These people didn't believe because they couldn't believe. Of course, this statement needs to be put together with other passages in John where we learn that they wouldn't believe and that if people would genuinely seek God they could come to believe.

What is the point? Some people can't and won't believe the truth about Jesus even when God's truth is clearly spoken, authentically lived, and truthfully shown. One reason is that their hearts are hardened to the truth. When we are sharing Christ with others, some just won't believe—they refuse to believe. We are never quite sure why they don't, but God knows. Let's always ask the Father to open the door to their hearts through circumstances in their life that will make them more readily available to receive God's message in Jesus. And, let's be ready when the doors to their hearts come open.

PRAYER:

O gracious and sovereign God, I do not understand all the ways you work in the lives and
upon the hearts of your human children. So I pray for those I know that are not near to
you. I pray for those who have rejected you. Please work in their lives to give your people a
chance to share your grace with them. Work in their lives in ways that challenge them to
think and open themselves up to your grace. In Jesus' name. Amen.

CONTEXT: JOHN 12:37-50
RELATED REFERENCES: JOHN 5:39-47; JOHN 10:24-32; JOHN 7:17

Day: 244

THE IDOL OF POPULARITY

JOHN 12:42-43

But many people believed in Jesus. Even many of the Jewish leaders believed in him, but they were afraid of the Pharisees, so they did not say openly that they believed. They were afraid they would be ordered to stay out of the synagogue. They loved praise from people more than praise from God.

REFLECTION:

What would make you afraid to show your faith? Be honest, now, because there are things we would all have a hard time losing.

To lose ones place in the synagogue was a huge loss for someone in Jesus' day. While we rightfully are disgusted with the lack of courage and integrity by those mentioned in this verse, we need to ask ourselves how often have we failed to stand up for Jesus when the stakes were much less high.

The real issue with fear and faith is our confidence in what we believe. If we truly believe in Jesus, how could we give him up? If we truly want to honor God, then how could the approval of mere mortal people become more important? God calls us to love him without rival. Anything that would interfere with our honoring God becomes our idol, even if it is the fear of rejection or the desire for popularity.

PRAYER:

Father, give me courage to stand up and confess my faith in Jesus with graciousness. I truly believe that you sent Jesus to die for my sins and give me power over sin and death. Please help me live that faith before the people with whom I interact regardless of their acceptance or rejection of me because of that faith, In Jesus' name. Amen.

CONTEXT: JOHN 12:37-50

RELATED REFERENCES: LUKE 12:8-9; JOHN 9:41-44; LUKE 9:23-26

Day: 245

IF YOU TRUST ME, YOU'RE TRUSTING GOD

JOHN 12:44-45

Then Jesus said loudly, "Everyone who believes in me is really believing in the one who sent me. Everyone who sees me is really seeing the one who sent me."

REFLECTION:

Want to know what God says? Listen to Jesus! Want to know how God treats people? Watch what Jesus does! Want to know what God looks like? Look at Jesus! Jesus claims to speak, act, and reveal God throughout the Gospel of John. As we reach this crucial point in John's Gospel, do you believe that Jesus was God living among people to show them who God is, how he feels about them, and what he wants them to do?

PRAYER:

Holy and almighty God, please forgive my little faith. Please bless me as I continue to seek to know you better by reading and meeting your Son, Jesus, in the Gospel of John. I ask that you make yourself known to me as I seek to live for you each day and seek to know you more fully by studying the life of your Son. In the name of the Lord Jesus I pray. Amen.

CONTEXT: JOHN 12:37-50

RELATED REFERENCES: JOHN 14:1-11; JOHN 1:17-18; HEBREWS 1:1-2

Day: 246

ESCAPE FROM DARKNESS

JOHN 12:46

"I came into this world as a light. I came so that everyone who believes in me would not stay in darkness."

REFLECTION:

At one time or another, most of us have been trapped in a darkened room and could not see anything until our eyes adjusted. Then, no matter how faint or far away, we began to move toward the light. Light casts out darkness. Light leads us away from darkness. Light triumphs over darkness. Jesus is our light! Let's move toward him and leave the darkness behind us.

PRAYER:

Holy and righteous Father, on the darkest nights of my soul, when all seems so discouraging, please help me see your light in Jesus. I confess that I often try to solve my own problems with my own limited wisdom. Instead of escaping my darkness, I find myself more deeply entangled in that darkness. Please lead me to Jesus so I can find the light of life! In Jesus' name I pray! Amen.

CONTEXT: JOHN 12:37-50

RELATED REFERENCES: JOHN 1:3-9; JOHN 3:16-21; JOHN 9:4-5

Day: 247

THE IMPORTANCE OF JESUS' WORDS

JOHN 12:47-50

"I did not come into the world to judge people. I came to save the people in the world. So I am not the one who judges those who hear my teaching and do not obey. But there is a judge for all those who refuse to believe in me and do not accept what I say. The message I have spoken will judge them on the last day. That is because what I taught was not from myself. The Father who sent me told me what to say and what to teach. And I know that whatever he says to do will bring eternal life. So the things I say are exactly what the Father told me to say."

REFLECTION:

Would you listen to a message if your life depended upon it? Would you follow the instructions carefully? Jesus makes clear that he speaks God's truth. What we do with that truth has eternal consequences and benefits. While obedience may not be a popular concept in modern culture, Jesus reminds us that it is essential that we obey his teaching.

God longs to save us through Jesus. He is not looking to trip us up on some fine point of Jesus' teaching that we have missed. But, our hearts need to be willing to do all that Jesus says because obedience is a blessing—it protects us from some things that we should never have to face and leads us to blessings that are found only when we do things God's way. Jesus' words are important. We should listen to them as if eternity depends on what we do with them—because it does.

PRAYER:

Holy and loving Father, thank you for revealing your will in human words taught us by Jesus. Open my mind to understand Jesus' teaching more completely and open my heart to accept those words more willingly as I commit to live by Jesus' words more completely. In Jesus' name. Amen.

CONTEXT: JOHN 12:37-50

RELATED REFERENCES: JOHN 6:61-69; MATTHEW 28:18-20; MATTHEW 7:24-28

Day: 248

LOVE'S DEFINING MOMENT

JOHN 13:1

*It was almost time for the Jewish Passover festival. Jesus knew that the time had come for
him to leave this world and go back to the Father. Jesus had always loved the people in the
world who were his. Now was the time he showed them his love the most.*

REFLECTION:

Many poems, songs, books, and movies have been written about true love.
Jesus defines it. On the eve of his own torture and death, knowing what lies
ahead, Jesus does the lovingly unthinkable!

Of the twelve men in the room with him, ten men will desert him, one will
deny him, and the final one will betray him. Yet Jesus stoops and does the work
of a slave by washing their feet. He loves them to the end. He shows them the
full extent of love. We had better pay attention if we want to know what love is!

As John tells his Spirit-inspired story of Jesus, he doesn't leave it to our sense
of discernment to pick up on the message. If we want to know about true love,
we should watch and listen to Jesus in verses that follow in John 13. This is a
love story without compare.

PRAYER:

*Holy God, I recognize that love is your very nature. I believe that your relationship with me
is built upon your great love for me and your desire to demonstrate that love to me. I
confess, dear Father, that I am still learning to love as I should. So teach me to love like
Jesus loves. Teach me to redeem others through that love. Free me from my inhibitions and
selfishness that block me from loving others like Jesus did. In Jesus' name I pray. Amen.*

CONTEXT: JOHN 13:1-17

RELATED REFERENCES: JOHN 3:16-17; JOHN 15:9-13; 1 JOHN 4:7-12

Day: 249

THE DEVIL HAS A PLAN

JOHN 13:2

Jesus and his followers were at the evening meal. The devil had already persuaded Judas Iscariot to hand Jesus over to his enemies. (Judas was the son of Simon.)

REFLECTION:

We must never forget that the events of the Cross—from Judas' plan to betray Jesus to Jesus' opponents all the way to the death of Jesus on the Cross being mocked by the crowds—were all a part of the devil's plan.

More than entering the upper room with Jesus and his followers, we have joined them on the battlefield. The evil one will not leave these events alone. He will orchestrate the hatred, jealousy, mockery, injustice, brutality, cruelty, betrayal, treachery, and death that follow. This is his desire for all who seek God and goodness. Choosing Jesus is not only crucial, it is also a battle. Let's never forget that Jesus faced the devil to win the victory for us. Let's also be aware that the devil will use all his deceptive powers to turn us against the Lord just like Judas. Yes, this is a war for our souls!

PRAYER:

Lord God Almighty, my Abba Father, please give me wisdom to see the crafty ways of the devil as he seeks to deceive and to destroy my faith in you and my love for you. Strengthen me by your Spirit in my inner being so that I can be strong enough to face down my enemy when he attacks. Most of all, deliver me from the evil one and bring me into your glorious presence with the great joy of eternal victory. In the name of Jesus, my conquering Savior, I pray. Amen.

CONTEXT: JOHN 13:1-17

RELATED REFERENCES: EPHESIANS 6:10-12; 2 THESSALONIANS 3:3; ROMANS 16:20

Day: 250

SERVICE IS ROOTED IN CONFIDENCE

JOHN 13:3-4

The Father had given Jesus power over everything. Jesus knew this. He also knew that he had come from God. And he knew that he was going back to God. So while they were eating, Jesus stood up and took off his robe. He got a towel and wrapped it around his waist.

REFLECTION:

Confidence in his walk with God enabled Jesus to serve others and to submit his will to God sacrificially—Jesus demonstrates this by washing his followers' feet which is detailed in the following verses. From the beginning of his ministry, God had affirmed Jesus' identity and importance: "You are my Son, whom I love; with you I am well pleased" (Mark 1:11 NIV).

In this crucial time before his death and knowing his identity, Jesus serves his followers showing them that the power of authority is found in loving service to others—not in demanding or expecting service from them.

PRAYER:

Father, please give me the courage and confidence to serve others sacrificially. I know you have made me your child, so please use me as your child to be a blessing to others and to serve them as Jesus did. In the name of your Son I pray. Amen.

CONTEXT: JOHN 13:1-17

RELATED REFERENCES: 1 JOHN 3:1-2, 16-18; 1 JOHN 5:13-15; 1 JOHN 4:17

GETTING REAL

JOHN 13:5

Then he poured water into a bowl and began to wash the followers' feet. He dried their feet with the towel that was wrapped around his waist.

REFLECTION:

"Get real, man!" It's a slang expression intended to force someone into reality—no exaggeration, no pretending, no imaginary tale, it's time to tell the unadulterated truth. Well, this is where God's becoming human flesh gets real!

Jesus, God in human flesh, takes water and washes the dirt and grime off his followers' feet. God becomes soiled with the dirt and stench of the world to show his love to the ignorant and ungrateful. The same dirt from which he made humanity is now the dirt he must wash away to recreate humanity.

Jesus gets real! This, my friend, is the crux of the Jesus story—that God would come to our world to bring us to his home at such great cost. Will you believe that this incredible story is true? If you do, everything is different! And part of that everything is how you see greatness—not on a pedestal receiving glory, but on the floor with a wash basin, taking care of folks most think are unworthy of your attention.

PRAYER:

Almighty and loving Father, I praise you for your work in creating me in your image. I thrill at the thought that you fashioned me in my mother's womb. I am overjoyed that you have re-created me new in Jesus. I thank you for being willing to get your hands dirty with the dirt of my world and my life to bring me home to you. In Jesus' name I praise you. Amen.

CONTEXT: JOHN 13:1-17

RELATED REFERENCES: GENESIS 2:7; PSALM 139:13-16; COLOSSIANS 3:8-11

WORDS OR DEEDS?

JOHN 13:6-9

He came to Simon Peter. But Peter said to him, "Lord, you should not wash my feet." Jesus answered, "You don't know what I am doing now. But later you will understand." Peter said, "No! You will never wash my feet." Jesus answered, "If I don't wash your feet, you are not one of my people." Simon Peter said, "Lord, after you wash my feet, wash my hands and my head too!"

REFLECTION:

Peter hasn't learned the lesson. Jesus wants his followers to demonstrate their faith and love. Talk is cheap. Peter is a big talker. Even in this moment of Jesus' example and sacrifice, Peter wants to talk big.

Jesus, however, stoops low and washes Peter's feet, too. Peter may not understand at that moment, but he will for the rest of his life just a few days later. He will then live to demonstrate his faith and loyalty and not just talk about it!

PRAYER:

Lord God, please forgive me when my deeds don't match up to my worship words. I know that kind of hypocrisy turns your stomach so I ask that you forgive me. In addition, dear Father, please help me become the person I say that I want to be. Humble me gently until I am like Jesus, in whose name I pray. Amen.

CONTEXT: JOHN 13:1-17

RELATED REFERENCES: MATTHEW 7:21; JAMES 1:22-25; JAMES 2:17

Day: 253

NOT EVERYONE IS CLEAN

JOHN 13:10-11

Jesus said, "After a person has a bath, his whole body is clean. He needs only to wash his feet. And you are clean, but not all of you." Jesus knew who would hand him over to his enemies. That is why he said, "Not all of you are clean."

REFLECTION:

Jesus can clean their dirty feet, but they have to offer their hearts for him to clean them. Judas' heart was dirtier than his feet, but Jesus still gave Judas this moment to receive his Master's loving service.

At that moment, Judas had to choose to stick to his scheme or be touched by the Savior. He chose not to be touched by Jesus' love, example, and service.

What about you, have you been touched? Have you offered your heart to Jesus? Jesus' example here reminds us that offering him our heart means more than just accepting him and being baptized into him. It means choosing to live a life of sacrifice and service like he did. It means loving those who don't love us in return and who may even do us harm. It means caring for the uncaring and loving the unlovable. So, have you really offered your heart to Jesus?

PRAYER:

Father, be with me this week as I seek to serve the following people....Please bless my service and use it to draw them closer to your Son. May every effort of grace I make be motivated out of love. In Jesus' name I pray. Amen.

CONTEXT: JOHN 13:1-17

RELATED REFERENCES: ROMANS 5:6-11; 1 JOHN 4:10; 1 JOHN 1:14

Day: 254
DO AS I HAVE DONE TO YOU!

JOHN 13:12-15

When Jesus finished washing their feet, he put on his clothes and went back to the table. He asked, "Do you understand what I did for you? You call me 'Teacher.' And you call me 'Lord.' And this is right, because that is what I am. I am your Lord and Teacher. But I washed your feet. So you also should wash each other's feet. I did this as an example for you. So you should serve each other just as I served you."

REFLECTION:

Jesus didn't just teach with words. His life was a conscious example lived before his followers and recorded in the Gospels for us. Jesus' life teaches us two crucial truths: 1) how God would live as a human, and 2) how we should live as humans. Our challenge is not just to know the words and deeds of Jesus' life. We need to understand those words and deeds as something God wants us to incorporate into our own lives. Jesus' life calls us to follow in his steps! He has set the example and he has called us to follow!

PRAYER:

Father, I thank you for the many truths that Jesus taught and the many deeds that he performed. Help me move, dear Father, from knowledge and admiration to obedience and emulation. Please have your Son's character and compassion come alive in me. In Jesus' name I pray. Amen.

CONTEXT: JOHN 13:1-17

RELATED REFERENCES: 1 PETER 1:21-25; COLOSSIANS 1:26-29;
2 CORINTHIANS 3:17-18

JUST DO IT!

JOHN 13:16-17

"Believe me, servants are not greater than their master. Those who are sent to do something are not greater than the one who sent them. If you know these things, you will be happy if you do them."

REFLECTION:

A good friend once remarked: "I've yet to meet a Christian whose knowledge didn't exceed his obedience." His point was simple: most Christians know far more of God's truth than they live.

That doesn't mean we don't quit searching and seeking God's truth, of course, but it does mean that we need to practice what we know to be the truth! Jesus said it before Nike® every thought of it, "Just do it!" The blessings in the words of Jesus can be found by putting them into practice daily!

PRAYER:

Forgive me, Father, for the times I've piddled at learning more about the words of Jesus so I didn't have to get around to obeying them. Father, I do want to keep learning and growing in knowledge of you and your truth. I also ask, dear God, that you give me the courage to live with obedience to your Son's words in my life now as well as having a passion to learn his teaching. In Jesus' name. Amen.

CONTEXT: JOHN 13:1-17

RELATED REFERENCES: LUKE 6:40; MARK 3:33-35; JAMES 1:21-25

Day: 256

PREPARING THEM IN HIS MOMENT OF SORROW

JOHN 13:18-19

"I am not talking about all of you. I know the people I have chosen. But what the Scriptures say must happen: 'The man who shared my food has turned against me.' I am telling you this now before it happens. Then when it happens, you will believe that I AM."

REFLECTION:

Nothing hurts quite like someone you love betraying you. Jesus knows what is going on with Judas. He also knows that the rest of the twelve will turn away from him for at least a little while. Yet in the middle of all this betrayal, Jesus prepares his followers for his death, resurrection, and return to heaven. Jesus serves his followers to the end!

Jesus carefully plants seeds of faith in his closest followers. These seeds are promises and teachings that will germinate after the horrors of the next few days pass and they can view his ministry through the lens of the resurrection. After all is said and done, Jesus helps them to realize that God, the great "I AM" of the Old Testament, had been with them (John 20:28).

Jesus' actions are powerful examples for us as we face our last days. His concern for those he will leave behind overrides his concern for his own well being. Will we muster the faith to do the same for our loved ones? How can we prepare those we love for our absence? How can we soften the blow of our death and departure from the family? How can we help them have faith after we are gone? These shouldn't just be our thoughts before our impending death; they should be the questions that guide our daily lives before those we love!

PRAYER:

God of grace and mercy, give me courage to live my life in ways that inspire those I love to believe now as well as after I am gone. Use my life to sow the seeds of lasting faith in the hearts of those I love. Especially, dear Father, please help me reach the following people _____ with your grace. In Jesus' name I pray. Amen.

CONTEXT: JOHN 13:18-38

RELATED REFERENCES: 1 CORINTHIANS 10:31-11:1; PHILIPPIANS 4:9; 2 TIMOTHY 2:1-2

ANGUISH

JOHN 13:20-22

"I assure you, whoever accepts the person I send also accepts me. And whoever accepts me also accepts the one who sent me." After Jesus said these things, he felt very troubled. He said openly, "Believe me when I say that one of you will hand me over to my enemies." His followers all looked at each other. They did not understand who Jesus was talking about.

REFLECTION:

Jesus felt "very troubled"! What his followers did mattered to him emotionally. He didn't distance his heart from the reality of pain simply because he was God. So his caring acts for his followers were carried out as he battled his own anguish and faced his own personal countdown to death. He even taught and served his followers right to the end of his life, even though they would cause a significant part his anguish.

Think of the incredible message this sends us about the love of God. The Son of God felt anguish at the betrayals and failures of those closest to him. Incredibly, the infinite and eternal God made himself vulnerable to emotional pain. Remarkably, God allowed this pain to be inflicted upon him by the finite and powerless mortals that he had made. Yet, God loved them—God loved us—so much that he allowed this all to happen.

The eternal, immortal, Sovereign God loved us so much that he chose to suffer in our world at our hands so that we could come to be with him in his world. There can be no greater love.

PRAYER:

I am moved, Abba Father, to speechless wonder that you should love me so. In the incredible expanse of your creation, why should you care for our tiny little planet and for the rebellious people who live here? Yet you know me, dear LORD, and it matters to you how I respond to your offer of love. Father, I choose to love, honor, cherish, and live for your glory. In Jesus' name I offer my thanks. Amen.

CONTEXT: JOHN 13:18-38

RELATED REFERENCES: GENESIS 6:5-6; MATTHEW 26:36-46; LUKE 13:32-35

Day: 258

LOVE AND BETRAYAL

JOHN 13:23-27

One of the followers was next to Jesus and was leaning close to him. This was the one Jesus loved very much. Simon Peter made signs to this follower to ask Jesus who he was talking about. That follower leaned closer to Jesus and asked, "Lord, who is it?" Jesus answered him, "I will dip this bread into the dish. The man I give it to is the one." So Jesus took a piece of bread, dipped it, and gave it to Judas Iscariot, the son of Simon. When Judas took the bread, Satan entered him. Jesus said to Judas, "What you will do—do it quickly!"

REFLECTION:

Part of me wants to shout at Jesus, "No! No! Stop him. You can stop Judas!" But, you see, he won't stop him. Jesus will not abuse his power to make Judas remain loyal. He has warned him. He has declared the truth. Judas could have responded. But Jesus won't trap him or overwhelm him or force him to remain faithful. Love must be offered voluntarily or it is not love. Following must be offered willingly or it is not really following. Jesus will not make us follow him. He will not make us reject Satan's knock at the door of our hearts. We must choose Jesus because we have caught a glimpse of his love for us. He will not force us!

PRAYER:

Almighty God, I cannot fathom the intricacies of grace, free will, pre-destination, and faith. I do understand, however, that you want my love for you to be the genuine response from a heart full of faith and gratitude. Dear Father, I offer you my heart willingly, without fear or question because of all you have done to save me. In Jesus' name I pray. Amen.

CONTEXT: JOHN 13:18-38

RELATED REFERENCES: GENESIS 4:2-7; ROMANS 5:6-11; 1 CORINTHIANS 10:13

Day: 259
NIGHT DESCENDS

JOHN 13:28-30

No one at the table understood why Jesus said this to Judas. Since Judas was the one in charge of the money, some of them thought that Jesus meant for him to go and buy some things they needed for the feast. Or they thought that Jesus wanted him to go give something to the poor. Judas ate the bread Jesus gave him. Then he immediately went out. It was night.

REFLECTION:

Jesus had warned that night was coming. He knew he was to battle the forces of darkness on their home turf in the world of darkness. From this point forward, the powers of darkness will try to assert themselves and destroy Jesus. As night descends, war begins. In the subsequent events of Jesus' ministry, we will see the battle of all that is good against all that is bad.

What are we to learn from this? There are many lessons. We'll focus on just two of them today. First, Jesus loves us enough to go face to face with darkness, evil, Satan, and the demons for us. Second, all it takes for Satan to bring great hardship on the people of God is for just one of Jesus' followers to sell out their Lord. The first of these lessons offers great comfort and grace. The last one, however, should make us all pause and examine our hearts!

PRAYER:

I praise you, O God my heavenly Father, for your love and mercy demonstrated to me in Jesus. Please, dear Father, may I never be a stumbling block to your children or a rebellious child that opens the door for Satan to attack. Not only forgive me, dear God, but purify my heart and empower me by your Spirit. In Jesus' name I pray. Amen.

CONTEXT: JOHN 13:18-38

RELATED REFERENCES: MATTHEW 18:4-6; EPHESIANS 2:1-2; EPHESIANS 6:10-12

Day: 260

A New Definition for Glory

JOHN 13:31-32

When Judas was gone, Jesus said, "Now is the time for the Son of Man to receive his glory. And God will receive glory through him. If God receives glory through him, he will give glory to the Son through himself. And that will happen very soon."

REFLECTION:

John has hinted throughout his gospel that Jesus would redefine the concept of glory. The word for exalt or glorify actually means to lift up on high. For Jesus, his glory involved being "lifted up" on the Cross out of love for us and in obedience to God. He brought the Father glory by fulfilling the Father's plan to bring God's people deliverance from their bondage to sin and death. He accomplished this through his death, burial and resurrection. By submitting to God's plan, he also glorified the Father through his obedience and sacrificial love.

What is God calling you to do to bring him glory? How will you glorify Jesus as your Lord? What price are you willing to pay? What word are you willing to obey?

PRAYER:

Give me courage, O God my Rock and my Redeemer, to accept the same kind of road to glory that Jesus walked ahead of me. I pray this in his powerful and holy name. Amen.

CONTEXT: JOHN 13:18-38

RELATED REFERENCES: HEBREWS 12:1-3; ROMANS 5:2; ROMANS 6:10-14

Day: 261
LOVE AS YOU HAVE BEEN LOVED

JOHN 13:33-34

Jesus said, "My children, I will be with you only a short time more. You will look for me, but I tell you now what I told the Jewish leaders: 'Where I am going you cannot come.' I give you a new command: Love each other. You must love each other just as I loved you."

REFLECTION:

The standard of love has been set for us. We are to love each other as Jesus has loved us—he came to us, he served us, and he sacrificed for us. Jesus shows us that love is personal, practical, and extravagant. He now wants us to demonstrate these same qualities with our love for each other—whether it is through the towel or the Cross!

PRAYER:

Father, I confess that my love is often shallow and selfish. I know that your Spirit has worked on me to help broaden and deepen my understanding of true love. Now bless me, O LORD, as I seek to share Jesus' love with my family, my friends, and my coworkers. In Jesus' name I pray. Amen.

CONTEXT: JOHN 13:18-38

RELATED REFERENCES: 1 JOHN 3:16-18; 1 JOHN 4:9-12; JOHN 3:16-17

THE PROOF

JOHN 13:35
"All people will know that you are my followers if you love each other."

REFLECTION:
Want to know which churches are really Jesus' true followers? Simple! Administer the love test. Do they truly love each other?

PRAYER:
Father, please help me and my church family to pass the love test!
In Jesus' name I pray. Amen.

CONTEXT: JOHN 13:18-38

RELATED REFERENCES: 1 JOHN 3:9-17; JOHN 15:9-13; COLOSSIANS 3:12-15

Day: 263

OVERSTATED COMMITMENT

JOHN 13:36-38

Simon Peter asked Jesus, "Lord, where are you going?" Jesus answered, "Where I am going you cannot follow now. But you will follow later." Peter asked, "Lord, why can't I follow you now? I am ready to die for you!" Jesus answered, "Will you really give your life for me? The truth is, before the rooster crows, you will say three times that you don't know me."

REFLECTION:

Most of us have done it. We've overstated, or at least over-estimated, the level of our commitment, abilities, or strength. Our intentions, at the time, were probably good. We just didn't realize Satan's power to combine circumstance, fear, doubt, disillusionment ... into a concoction brewed just perfectly to bring us to our knees.

Peter had a tendency to overstate everything in his early years as a follower. However, once Peter suffered through his personal embarrassments and failures, Jesus had a leader fully prepared to lead powerfully while also walking humbly. Let's not let our failures keep us from following Christ and being used for his glory. In addition, let's not overstate our ability to handle temptations, trials, difficulties, challenges, or problems. God's strength is made perfect when we realize our weakness and vulnerability; then rely on his strength to sustain us!

PRAYER:

Father, please forgive me for the times I've failed after I overestimated my ability to handle a problem. I know that I cannot face the challenges of life and faith without your power and presence. Strengthen me for the days ahead so that I can be a blessing to others and honor you with faithfulness in my life. In Jesus' name. Amen.

CONTEXT: JOHN 13:18-38

RELATED REFERENCES: 2 CORINTHIANS 12:6-10; 2 CORINTHIANS 4:5-7; 1 CORINTHIANS 1:22-29

Day: 264
SEE ME AS GOD UP CLOSE

JOHN 14:1
Jesus said, "Don't be troubled. Trust in God, and trust in me."

REFLECTION:

All their lives, Jesus' followers were taught to trust God. Their childhoods had been filled with great stories of God's faithfulness. Jesus' words—which later follow in John 14—will stretch their understandings past the breaking point. He will equate himself with God. They will struggle to understand. Much of what happens will remain an impenetrable mystery to them until Jesus' resurrection and the coming of his Spirit.

For Jesus' original hearers, and for us, these words take on deep significance. "You trust in Almighty God, so trust in me, too!" His point? It's like he's saying, "Trust me! I'm God up close for you!" Jesus is the great reminder of God's concern and understanding of our dilemmas. He is God up close.

PRAYER:

Righteous and holy God, my Abba Father, I praise you for your love and grace. Thank you for entering our world and drawing close to us in Jesus. Thank you for giving us Jesus so we can know your love and compassion more clearly. I put my trust in him as I pray in his mighty name. Amen.

CONTEXT: JOHN 14:1-14

RELATED REFERENCES: JOHN 1:14-18; JOHN 5:24; JOHN 12:44-50

Day: 265

A LOOK INTO OUR HEAVENLY HOME

JOHN 14:2-3

"There are many rooms in my Father's house. I would not tell you this if it were not true. I am going there to prepare a place for you. After I go and prepare a place for you, I will come back. Then I will take you with me, so that you can be where I am."

REFLECTION:

At this moment in his earthly ministry, Jesus is about to leave the earth and return to to heaven. He is going back to heaven to prepare a place for his followers—and for us. When the time is right and everything is ready, Jesus promises that he will return to take his followers to their heavenly home.

However, the greatest blessing Jesus promises is not just going to heaven; it's getting to go to heaven and be with the Lord forever! Jesus is more than just the direction and goal of our hope, he is also the basis for it! Because of Jesus, we're going home to be with God!

PRAYER:

Loving Father and holy God, thank you for knowing my needs, my weaknesses, my dreams, and my future. I trust you completely with my future. I look forward to the day Jesus returns to bring me home to you. Thank you for the assurance that I will get to be with you, as well as all those I love who have belonged to you. In Jesus' name I pray! Amen.

CONTEXT: JOHN 14:1-14

RELATED REFERENCES: 1 THESSALONIANS 4:15-18; JOHN 5:19-21; 2 CORINTHIANS 5:6-9

THE WAY HOME

JOHN 14:4-7

"You know the way to the place where I am going."
Thomas said, "Lord, we don't know where you are going, so how can we know the way?"
Jesus answered, "I am the way, the truth, and the life. The only way to the Father is
through me. If you really knew me, you would know my Father too. But now you know the
Father. You have seen him."

REFLECTION:

I sometimes give way too many instructions when giving directions. So
today, I want to keep it clear and simple. Want to know the way home to God?
It's Jesus! Turn to him. Focus on him. Follow him. He is the way home!

PRAYER:

Father, please be with your people so that we will passionately share our hope in Jesus so
others can be assured of finding their Way home to you! In Jesus' name. Amen.

CONTEXT: JOHN 14:1-14

RELATED REFERENCES: ACTS 4:10-12; ACTS 2:32-42; 1 JOHN 2:1-2

Day: 267
SHOW US THE FATHER

JOHN 14:8-11

Philip said to him, "Lord, show us the Father. That is all we need."
Jesus answered, "Philip, I have been with you for a long time. So you should know me.
Anyone who has seen me has seen the Father too. So why do you say, 'Show us the Father'?
Don't you believe that I am in the Father and the Father is in me? The things I have told
you don't come from me. The Father lives in me, and he is doing his own work. Believe me
when I say that I am in the Father and the Father is in me. Or believe because of the
miracles I have done."

REFLECTION:

Philip felt that all of his problems would be solved if only he could see God.
Moses had requested something similar of God when he was asked to lead
God's people (Exodus 33:18-20). Jesus' reply was something he had said again
and again, "If you've seen me or heard me then you have seen or heard the
Father!" Jesus lived to do the Father's will. He came to earth to demonstrate the
Father's love. Jesus is God's presence on earth. When you have seen Jesus, you
have seen God!

PRAYER:

Jesus, my Lord and Savior, thank you for coming to this world and showing me God. The
more I get to know you through the Gospel of John, the more I am moved by the love the
Father has for me. Thank you for not only being the way to the Father, but also the clear
expression of who the Father is and how the Father feels about me. Amen!

CONTEXT: JOHN 14:1-14

RELATED REFERENCES: 1 JOHN 1:1-3; JOHN 17:20-24; JOHN 1:18

Day: 268

GREATER WORKS

JOHN 14:12-14

"I can assure you that whoever believes in me will do the same things I have done. And they will do even greater things than I have done, because I am going to the Father. And if you ask for anything in my name, I will do it for you. Then the Father's glory will be shown through the Son. If you ask me for anything in my name, I will do it."

REFLECTION:

Incredible! Jesus promises that his followers will do "even greater things" than he did. And if you read the book of Acts and take all the things they accomplished through their many ministries, it's true. How is that possible? It almost sounds blasphemous even to suggest such a thing. But then, it is the Lord who made the promise. So how do we do "even greater things" than Jesus did?

Jesus is still at work through his followers. The church is his Body, his presence in the world. What he does through his church and its people is absolutely amazing. So in one sense, the church does "even greater things" than Jesus did if we consider its world-wide impact and influence. Jesus also tells us specifically how his followers can do these "greater things." He told his followers to use prayer to release his power and bring his blessing. After all, he sits at the Father's side and will present our requests to God when we pray in his name.

When we serve and pray in Jesus' name, incredible things happen! Jesus does "even greater things" through us than we can imagine—greater than he did in his earthly ministry (Eph. 3:20-21).

PRAYER:

Father, I come to you praying by the authority of your Son, Jesus. I ask that you use us in mighty ways to bless others to your glory. I pray that you stir your people worldwide, so that we will live more passionately for your glory. Give us all a bigger sense of the ways we can do your great work in the world. In the mighty name of Jesus I pray. Amen.

CONTEXT: JOHN 14:1-14

RELATED REFERENCES: EPHESIANS 3:20-21; ACTS 1:1; 1 JOHN 5:13-15

Day: 269

ANOTHER COUNSELOR, A LASTING COMFORTER

JOHN 14:15-17

"If you love me, you will do what I command. I will ask the Father, and he will give you another Helper to be with you forever. The Helper is the Spirit of truth. The people of the world cannot accept him, because they don't see him or know him. But you know him. He lives with you, and he will be in you."

REFLECTION:

It is so hard to adequately translate the term Jesus uses for the Holy Spirit in John 14. Translators make several different choices—Helper, Advocate, Counselor, and Comforter. Some coin a new word out of the original Greek word—Paraklete.

How we translate the word is not nearly as important as our understanding of Jesus' promise to send the Holy Spirit as the Helper to his followers. In addition, Jesus makes several promises that define who the Helper is by what he does for us. The abiding presence of our Helper—the Holy Spirit—is one of the most crucial and distinguishing characteristics of a Christian (Rom. 8:9). The world cannot recognize the Helper's presence, much less receive Him personally (1 Cor. 2:14). Christians, however, are given the Holy Spirit as a gift when they are saved (Acts 2:38-39; 1 Cor. 12:13). The Spirit makes them pure and holy and then lives inside them, making them God's holy Temple (1 Cor. 6:9-11, 18-20). What's more, the Spirit's presence is lasting. Our Helper won't leave us! As Jesus says, he will be with us "forever."

PRAYER:

Father and LORD, you are the holy and righteous God. Your majesty and might are incomparable. But, dear Father, I am a sinner. I have fallen short of your holy standards. I am not worthy to enter your presence. So I thank you today, knowing that your Spirit, my Helper, has purified my and now lives inside me. By the power of your abiding presence, the Holy Spirit who is my Helper, transform me to be like Jesus, in whose name I pray. Amen.

CONTEXT: JOHN 14:15-31

RELATED REFERENCES: ACTS 2:38-39; 5:32; 1 CORINTHIANS 6:19-20; 2 THESSALONIANS 2:13-14

Day: 270

I Will Not Abandon You

JOHN 14:18-20

"I will not leave you all alone like orphans. I will come back to you. In a very short time the people in the world will not see me anymore. But you will see me. You will live because I live. On that day you will know that I am in the Father. You will know that you are in me and I am in you."

REFLECTION:

Jesus' return to the Father is essential. He is going to prepare a place for us. He is at the Father's side to intercede for us as our counselor and comforter. However, just because he has gone to the Father's side does not mean that he has abandoned us. Jesus sends the Holy Spirit to be his living presence inside us. We are not alone. Far from it! We have the abiding reminder of Jesus' victory over death and his ascension to heaven living inside us through the Holy Spirit, the Helper sent from heaven to be with us and live in us!

PRAYER:

Your grace, dear heavenly Father, is really beyond my comprehension to fully grasp. I know even now, as I pray, your grace makes my prayer significant because the Holy Spirit intercedes for me according to your will. Father, when I find myself in difficult times, I confess that I sometimes try to rely too much on what I can do because I get to feeling like no one is there helping me. Please, dear Father, don't just forgive me, but remind me of your abiding presence in me through the Helper you sent to me, the blessed Holy Spirit. In Jesus' name I thank you for your many rich and gracious gifts to me. Amen.

CONTEXT: JOHN 14:15-31

RELATED REFERENCES: ACTS 1:6-8; 1 JOHN 2:24-29; 1 JOHN 3:24

Day: 271

THE SON AND THE FATHER FIND A HOME

JOHN 14:21-23

"Those who really love me are the ones who not only know my commands but also obey them. My Father will love such people, and I will love them. I will make myself known to them." Then Judas (not Judas Iscariot) said, "Lord, how will you make yourself known to us, but not to the world?" Jesus answered, "All who love me will obey my teaching. My Father will love them. My Father and I will come to them and live with them."

REFLECTION:

Do you know how God chooses a place to live? Jesus said that he looks for someone who is obedient to him, then the Father and the Son come to live in that person through the Helper, the Holy Spirit. Not only do they live there, Jesus promised that he would show himself to them. In other words, Jesus has gone to heaven to prepare a place for us there (John 14:1-4). However, until we can come live with him, he comes to live in us (John 14:19-23). Our invitation for him to come and live in us is shown by our obedience to Jesus as Lord.

PRAYER:

Holy and righteous Father, I love you and want you to inhabit my life, to mold my character, and to be pleased by my obedience to your will. Thank you for sending your Helper to encourage and empower me in these holy tasks.
In Jesus' name I pray. Amen.

CONTEXT: JOHN 14:15-31

RELATED REFERENCES: MATTHEW 7:21-27; ACTS 5:32; MARK 3:31-35

Day: 272

TWO GREAT BLESSINGS TO KNOW JESUS' WILL

JOHN 14:24-26

"But anyone who does not love me does not obey my teaching. This teaching that you hear is not really mine. It is from my Father who sent me. I have told you all these things while I am with you. But the Helper will teach you everything and cause you to remember all that I told you. This Helper is the Holy Spirit that the Father will send in my name."

REFLECTION:

Jesus' words are God's words. When we obey him, we obey the Father. When we disobey Jesus, we disobey the Father.

So how do we know what Jesus wants us to do? Two great blessings help us to know. One blessing is Scripture—especially the Gospels (Matthew, Mark, Luke, and John) that tell us about Jesus' life and words. The other blessing is the Holy Spirit, the Helper Jesus promised that God would send to us. The Helper enables us to understand Jesus' words, reminds us of Jesus' words when we are trying to live for him, and leads us to become more like Jesus as we seek after him.

PRAYER:

Father, please bless me as I seek to obey Jesus and live according to his words and your will for my life. Thank you for the Holy Spirit, the Helper you sent me, who is at work to bring those words to life in me. Forgive me, dear Father, when I have not sought to know more about Jesus in Scripture or when I have resisted the work of your Helper to transform me to be more like my Lord. In Jesus' name I pray. Amen.

CONTEXT: JOHN 14:15-31

RELATED REFERENCES: 1 JOHN 2:26-27; 2 CORINTHIANS 3:17-18; GALATIANS 5:22-26

Day: 273

JESUS' GIFT OF PEACE

JOHN 14:27-28

"I leave you peace. It is my own peace I give you. I give you peace in a different way than the world does. So don't be troubled. Don't be afraid. You heard me say to you, 'I am leaving, but I will come back to you.' If you loved me, you would be happy that I am going back to the Father, because the Father is greater than I am."

REFLECTION:

The Holy Spirit, our comforter and counselor, will bring us peace. This peace is not an absence of difficulties, an end to all strife, or the cessation of all disagreements. We know that those things will not happen in our fallen world as we know it now.

However, the grace of God's presence, the gift of Jesus' guidance, and the blessing of the Holy Spirit as our Helper mean that we can have peace in our storms, struggles, and fallen world. God is present within us through the Helper to guide, strengthen, comfort, lead, inspire, motivate, bless, and so much more.

We are not alone as we face any challenge in our lives. God is not only with us, he is within us! Jesus' return to heaven is not a loss of peace or his abandonment of us. It is his going away so that he can send us the gift of the Holy Spirit, our Helper, who brings us God's peace.

PRAYER:

Holy God, give me a deeper appreciation of your abiding presence within me. Lead me by your Spirit to know you more completely. Inspire me by your Spirit to do your work more joyously. Enlighten me by your Spirit to make better decisions each day. Thank you, God, for sending your Helper for me, the Holy Spirit, and your gift of grace, presence, and peace. I pray in the name of the Lord Jesus Christ. Amen.

CONTEXT: JOHN 14:15-31

RELATED REFERENCES: JOHN 16:33; ROMANS 5:1-5; TITUS 3:3-7

Day: 274
GIVING IN WHEN YOU DON'T HAVE TO
JOHN 14:29-31

"I have told you this now, before it happens. Then when it happens, you will believe. I will not talk with you much longer. The ruler of this world is coming. He has no power over me. But the world must know that I love the Father. So I do exactly what the Father told me to do. Come now, let's go."

REFLECTION:

The principle here is tough. Jesus gives in to an enemy and faces personal anguish, agony, and humiliation even though he has power over his enemy. Why does he do it? Why would he let the devil, who has no real power over him, do such horrifying things to him? He is honoring the will of God and showing his love for God to the world. God told him this must be done, so he does it.

Jesus' example here is a tough one to follow—giving in to redeem bad situations, even if it means suffering greatly even though we have the power to stop it from happening. Why would we do such a thing? Because God told us to do it! Go back and read the Sermon on the Mount (Matt. chapters 5-7), or the teaching on restoration and forgiveness (Matt. 18), or the call to families to honor Jesus as Lord by submitting to one another (Eph. 5:21-6:4) and you find God's call to do this in our daily lives!

PRAYER:

Father, I admit that Jesus' example is often hard for me to follow. When I am wronged or falsely accused, I don't want to give in. Sometimes, I don't even want to forgive. I want to vindicate myself. Please give me spiritual discernment to know the difference between being a doormat that lets others needlessly run over me and being redemptive. Please help me to know when to give in on matters so that others are spared the heartache of unnecessary conflict as I try to honor you by being a person of character. Thank you my Lord and Christ, for being willing to suffer abuse and injustice so that my sins could be forgiven. Please help me grow to have a heart that is more in tune with yours. Amen.

CONTEXT: JOHN 14:15-31

RELATED REFERENCES: MATTHEW 5:43-48; 1 PETER 2:19-24; 1 CORINTHIANS 6:1-8

Day: 275

FINDING WHERE WE BELONG

JOHN 15:1

Jesus said, "I am the true vine, and my Father is the gardener."

REFLECTION:

Jesus' statement is radical. The vine was a symbol of Israel in the Old Testament (Hos. 10:1). Jesus is saying that he is the place God's people will find their life and their identity. When people are in Christ, they will find themselves tended and cared for by God himself.

This concept is both radical and comforting. Jesus reminds us that God cares for the sparrows, so he surely cares for us. The Father knows the number of hairs on our heads. He knows what we need before we ask for it. God is not a God far off, but a God up close and personal. He knows us and will be involved in every aspect of our lives.

PRAYER:

Holy God, LORD Almighty, I am humbled and awed that in your incredible majesty you have also chosen to know me personally. Thank you for working in my life. Conform me to your will. In Jesus' name. Amen.

CONTEXT: JOHN 15:1-17

RELATED REFERENCES: PSALM 139:13-16; ROMANS 8:28; PHILIPPIANS 2:13

Day: 276
GOD AT WORK HERE!

JOHN 15:2-3

"He cuts off every branch of mine that does not produce fruit. He also trims every branch that produces fruit to prepare it to produce even more. You have already been prepared to produce more fruit by the teaching I have given you."

REFLECTION:

God is at work in the vine and in each individual branch of the vine. He does exactly what is needed so that the vine, and each individual branch of the vine, can be productive. He longs to enjoy the abundant harvest from his healthy vine. He works with each branch so that it achieves its maximum production.

How is God working in your life right now to make you a more productive person? What is he doing to help you find truly abundant living? What does God need to be trimming and cleaning out of your life right now?

PRAYER:

Dear God, my Father in heaven, I ask you to correct me and mold me so that I can be the person you want me to be. Make my life count. Discipline and nurture me as is needed to make my life joyous and productive for your Kingdom and glory. In Jesus' name I pray. Amen.

CONTEXT: JOHN 15:1-17

RELATED REFERENCES: GALATIANS 5:22-23; JOHN 10:10; 2 PETER 1:3-9

Day: 277

THE SECRET OF FRUITFULNESS

JOHN 15:4-5

"Stay joined to me and I will stay joined to you. No branch can produce fruit alone. It must stay connected to the vine. It is the same with you. You cannot produce fruit alone. You must stay joined to me. "I am the vine, and you are the branches. If you stay joined to me, and I to you, you will produce plenty of fruit. But separated from me you won't be able to do anything."

REFLECTION:

The key to fruitfulness is not effort; though effort will be necessary. The key to fruitfulness is not circumstance; though how we handle our circumstances is important. The key to fruitfulness is not our personal strength, charisma, or wisdom; though each of these will be given to us to help make us more fruitful.

The key to fruitfulness is for us to have our lives joined to the one, true, healthy vine—Jesus. As our lives are joined to his, as we "continue" in him and he in us, then fruitfulness happens naturally. As branches, we derive our health and productivity from the Vine. Want to live productively for God? Then have your life joined to Jesus! Invite him in to "continue" in you as you draw close to "continue" in him. Apart from him, unattached to him, we can do nothing!

PRAYER:

Holy God, draw my life closer to Jesus and help me "continue" in him. Mold me and make me to be more like him. Use me to bring you glory and to help others know about your grace in Jesus. Fashion your character in me and use me to bless others. Lord Jesus, as I pray in your name, please come and live in me—"continue" in me. You are welcome in my heart. I seek your presence and your power in all that I do. Amen.

CONTEXT: JOHN 15:1-17

RELATED REFERENCES: REVELATION 3:20; PHILIPPIANS 1:11; MATTHEW 13:23

Day: 278
REMAINING JOINED TO JESUS

JOHN 15:6-7

If you don't stay joined to me, you will be like a branch that has been thrown out and has dried up. All the dead branches like that are gathered up, thrown into the fire and burned. Stay joined together with me, and follow my teachings. If you do this, you can ask for anything you want, and it will be given to you."

REFLECTION:

Jesus is the Vine. A branch that does not remain connected to him is going to die. This is Jesus' very strong warning to stay connected to him. A person who is his follower must "continue" in Jesus or else he or she will die spiritually just like the branch of a plant is going to die if it is separated from its source of life. Dead branches are more than discarded and left to die; they are thrown into the fire and completely burned up. There is no such thing as a follower of Jesus who does not "continue" and stay attached to Jesus.

On the other hand, if someone does "continue" in Jesus and obeys his teaching, then Jesus has a fantastic promise for that person. One of the key blessings of being joined to Jesus is knowing that he promises to take our requests, concerns, and burdens to God for us. We can be confident that God hears our hearts and knows our needs. And as our lives are molded by our relationship with Jesus, we begin to ask God for things that bless his kingdom. If we "continue" in Jesus—if we remain joined to him—we can be confident that we are heard and understood by God because of Jesus.

PRAYER:

In the name of Jesus, I come to you Father, confident that you will hear my prayer and act for my best eternal good. Bless me as I want my life to be constantly joined to Jesus so that his life governs my own. In Jesus' name. Amen.

CONTEXT: JOHN 15:1-17

RELATED REFERENCES: GALATIANS 2:19-20; HEBREWS 4:14-16; COLOSSIANS 3:1-4

Day: 279
TRUE FOLLOWERS

JOHN 15:8

*"Show that you are my followers by producing much fruit. This will bring
honor to my Father."*

REFLECTION:

True followers become like their teacher (Luke 6:40). That means their lives
are fruitful. They take on the character attributes of Jesus (Gal. 5:22-23) as they
are transformed to be more like him (2 Cor. 3:18). They also care for people like
Jesus does by living sacrificially for the redemption of others (Phil. 2:5-11).
Their Christianity isn't all talk, but it is demonstrated in both word and deed
(1 John 3:18). They let the fruit of their lives bring glory to God through the
things they do and the way they live (Matthew 5:16).

PRAYER:

*Holy and righteous God, my heavenly Father, please fashion me into a true follower—one
of your children who brings you glory because of the quality of my character and because
of my commitment to bring others to know your grace. Help me to live like Jesus.
In Jesus' name I pray. Amen.*

CONTEXT: JOHN 15:1-17

RELATED REFERENCES: MATTHEW 3:7-10; MATTHEW 7:15-20; JOHN 4:34-38

Day: 280

REMAIN IN MY LOVE: OBEY WHAT I SAY

JOHN 15:9-10

"I have loved you as the Father has loved me. Now continue in my love. I have obeyed my Father's commands, and he continues to love me. In the same way, if you obey my commands, I will continue to love you."

REFLECTION:

When a little child is disciplined for playing in the road or walking on railroad tracks, they see the discipline as painful, unnecessary, and limiting. They don't want limitations. However, if they could understand the danger and parents' desire to protect their children from harm, they would see that discipline as loving. A parent calls on a child to obey because obedience protects and blesses that child.

Likewise, when Jesus asks us to obey, let's not see it as something onerous, burdensome, and limiting. Instead, let's see Jesus' commands, and our obedience to those commands, as a form of protection from a loving Savior trying to safeguard, bless, and care for his younger beloved brothers and sisters. When we obey Jesus, we remain under the protection of his love rather than the danger caused by our own rebellion!

PRAYER:

Almighty God, your ways are not my ways. Your understanding is way beyond my understanding. So I trust that when you call me to obey, you do so because of your protective love. Please know that I will do my best to obey both you and your Son in order to show you my love in return. In Jesus' name I pray. Amen.

CONTEXT: JOHN 15:1-17

RELATED REFERENCES: ROMANS 16:19-20; COLOSSIANS 2:6-7; HEBREWS 5:7-9

Day: 281

WHERE LOVE IS SHARED, JOY OVERFLOWS

JOHN 15:11-14

"I have told you these things so that you can have the true happiness that I have. I want you to be completely happy. This is what I command you: Love each other as I have loved you. The greatest love people can show is to die for their friends. You are my friends if you do what I tell you to do."

REFLECTION:

What a wonderful blessing it is to be loved! We know God loves us with an everlasting love. He has called us into a family of love. He blesses us each out of his love for us. But Jesus, of course, is God's greatest example of love. When this love fills your heart and rescues you from sin and death, there must be joy!

PRAYER:

Almighty and loving Father, God of all peoples, help me learn to be a more sacrificial and loving toward others. Keep my heart pure and my faith passionate.
In Jesus' name I pray. Amen.

CONTEXT: JOHN 15:1-17

RELATED REFERENCES: PHILIPPIANS 2:5-11; 1 JOHN 3:14-17; PHILIPPIANS 4:1

Day: 282

No Longer Servants

John 15:15-17

"I no longer call you servants, because servants don't know what their master is doing. But now I call you friends, because I have told you everything that my Father told me. You did not choose me. I chose you. And I gave you this work: to go and produce fruit—fruit that will last. Then the Father will give you anything you ask for in my name. This is my command: Love each other."

Reflection:

What is lasting fruit? In this context, Jesus wants his followers to know that lasting fruit is loving others. It is the theme that he repeatedly emphasizes in his last words with his followers (John chapters 13-17).

While many things seem important to us, they will vanish, decay, or die. Love, however, remains—it "continues," it abides, and it lasts. Death cannot separate us from God's love (Rom. 8:32-39). Love is stronger than death (SoS 8:6). So Jesus beckons his followers to this deeper relationship built on love and the Father's choice. Jesus' followers are no longer his servants, but his friends. As his friends, they know what is on the Father's heart and they are committed to displaying the Father's priorities in their own lives. That means that they will produce fruit; they will love each other!

Prayer:

Father in heaven, fill my heart with your love through your Holy Spirit that dwells in me. Motivate me to share that love with your children and those who don't yet know you. Give me the courage to love others sacrificially like you have loved me. Help me produce fruit that will "continue" through all of life. In Jesus' name I pray. Amen.

Context: John 15:1-17

Related References: John 13:33-35; 1 John 4:7-8; 1 Corinthians 13:8-13

Day: 283

HOSTILITY FROM THE WORLD

JOHN 15:18-20

"If the world hates you, remember that they hated me first. If you belonged to the world, the world would love you as it loves its own people. But I have chosen you to be different from those in the world. So you don't belong to the world, and that is why the world hates you. Remember the lesson I told you: Servants are not greater than their master. If people treated me badly, they will treat you badly too. And if they obeyed my teaching, they will obey yours too."

REFLECTION:

Hate! We don't like that word, do we? Especially when we are the target of hate. Yet our hero Jesus was unjustly murdered because of jealousy, hatred, misunderstanding, and rivalry.

We will follow in Jesus steps—we'll be hated by the world, too. Some will follow Jesus to martyrdom because the world hates Jesus and his followers.

Our hardships and difficulties do not invalidate Jesus' call. In some ways, they validate it more. Jesus said, "I have chosen you." We belong to him. We don't belong to the world so the world is going hate us—we don't belong to the world and the world loves only its own people.

These truths are reminders that there is a spiritual battle for every human heart. Satan will do all he can to silence the voices of those who bring God's salvation. Just like Jesus, we too may face very real hostility from the world, but because of Jesus, we have ultimate victory over the world (John 16:33).

PRAYER:

Father, please make me more aware of your servants who are facing persecution and hardship today. Give me courage to stand for your truth and live your ethics even if those values cost me ridicule or rejection. Please, God, let your glory be praised by my life, whether I find myself in hardship and persecution or in good times and acceptance. In Jesus' name I pray. Amen.

CONTEXT: JOHN 15:18-27

RELATED REFERENCES: JOHN 7:2-7; 1 JOHN 2:15-17; 1 JOHN 3:11-13

Day: 284

HATING THE FATHER

JOHN 15:21-25

"They will do to you whatever they did to me, because you belong to me. They don't know the one who sent me. If I had not come and spoken to the people of the world, they would not be guilty of sin. But now I have spoken to them. So they have no excuse for their sin. Whoever hates me also hates my Father. I did things among the people of the world that no one else has ever done. If I had not done those things, they would not be guilty of sin. But they have seen what I did, and still they hate me and my Father. But this happened to make clear the full meaning of what is written in their law: 'They hated me for no reason.'"

REFLECTION:

When Jesus' followers face rejection, persecution, hardship, and hatred because of their faith, they need to know that they are not alone. Jesus faced these things. Other Christians before them have faced these things. The rejection that Jesus' followers feel is not the rejection of the follower, but the rejection of the Father, the eternal God.

Jesus came to show people God and yet many still rejected him. Despite the incredible miracles he performed, the kind of life he lived, and the teaching he shared—things that no person had ever done before—they still rejected him. So we shouldn't be surprised if we are rejected for reasons we cannot understand. If they didn't have reason to hate and reject Jesus, we're probably not going to find a rational reason for them to hate and reject us. Our challenge is to remain faithful, just like the Lord Jesus, even in the face of ridicule, persecution, opposition, and death even though we cannot find a reason for people to want to do such horrible things to us.

PRAYER:

Give me courage, dear Father, so that I will always live passionately and faithfully for you and your Kingdom. Give me strength to never compromise my faith, my integrity, or my morals when facing hardship, scrutiny, or mistreatment. In Jesus' name I pray. Amen.

CONTEXT: JOHN 15:18-27

RELATED REFERENCES: HEBREWS 12:1-4; LUKE 10:16; 2 TIMOTHY 3:10-14

Day: 285

WHY WE TRUST THEIR MESSAGE

JOHN 15:26-27

"I will send you the Helper from the Father. The Helper is the Spirit of truth who comes from the Father. When he comes, he will tell about me. And you will tell people about me too, because you have been with me from the beginning."

REFLECTION:

The apostles of Jesus are trustworthy witnesses to the will of Jesus for several reasons. Jesus mentions two of those reasons here. First, Jesus sent them the Helper, the Holy Spirit, to ensure that they would know and could share God's truth. Second, they had been with Jesus from the beginning, hearing his words and observing his life.

Jesus had chosen these followers to be with him. He made sure that others would be left to start his church and teach his truth by selecting them and then sending them the Spirit to continue his work and teaching through them.

For us today, two truths should grab our attention. First, as Jesus knows he is about to be disgraced, mutilated, and murdered, he keeps working to lovingly prepare his closest followers to carry on without him. Second, he emphasizes why these early first followers, the apostles, are authoritative witnesses—they have the Helper, God's Holy Spirit, to reveal the truth, and they were eyewitnesses themselves.

Why is the rest of the New Testament so important to Christians? Because it is the message Jesus wanted his followers to give his church. So let's open our hearts to the New Testament message as the Lord's chosen messengers reveal Jesus and his will to us.

PRAYER:

Holy and righteous Father, thank you for leaving reliable and inspired witnesses to Jesus' life. I thank you for their stories of Jesus and their desire to bless future generations of your people. Make me more passionate to know your will revealed through their accounts of the life and teaching of Jesus and in the rest of the New Testament. In Jesus' name I pray. Amen.

CONTEXT: JOHN 15:18-27

RELATED REFERENCES: ACTS 2:41-47; MATTHEW 28:18-20; EPHESIANS 2:19-20

Day: 286
So You Won't Fall Away

John 16:1-4

"I have told you all this so that you won't lose your faith when you face troubles. People will tell you to leave their synagogues and never come back. In fact, the time will come when they will think that killing you would be doing service for God. They will do this because they have not known the Father, and they have not known me. I have told you all this now to prepare you. So when the time comes for these things to happen, you will remember that I warned you. I did not tell you these things at the beginning, because I was with you then."

Reflection:

Jesus doesn't pull any punches with his followers. What happens to the Master will also likely happen to many of his followers. They need to know that Jesus predicted this so they won't be overly surprised or discouraged when it eventually happens. Today, many proclaim a Gospel of only good and sweet things. If bad things befall you, it is because you weren't faithful enough, or didn't pray the right kind of prayers, or had secret sin in your life. We must reject such simplistic ideas. Our hero was massacred by an angry mob on a cross after being scourged and beaten. Many of his early followers were killed for their allegiance to him. Through the years, thousands upon thousands of Jesus' followers have been murdered because of their faith in him. This hatred and murder of Jesus' followers continues to this very day. We shouldn't be surprised: Jesus promised this would be the case right before his own death. Instead, we should find inspiration for our own periods of persecution from this long line of faithful witnesses who loved the Lord even more than their own lives (Rev. 12:11).

Prayer:

Father, please bless those who are being persecuted and mistreated because of their faith in Jesus. Give them courage to stand up to the mistreatment. Be present with them through your Spirit; guide their words and give them strength. Use your people to help reduce their suffering. In Jesus' name I pray. Amen.

Context: John 16:1-15

RELATED REFERENCES: LUKE 12:8-12; 2 TIMOTHY 3:10-12; JOHN 15:21

Day: 287

DON'T BE SAD, BETTER THINGS AHEAD

JOHN 16:5-7

"Now I am going back to the one who sent me. And none of you asks me, 'Where are you going?' But you are filled with sadness because I have told you all this. Let me assure you, it is better for you that I go away. I say this because when I go away I will send the Helper to you. But if I did not go, the Helper would not come."

REFLECTION:

I can't imagine how the followers felt or what they understood when Jesus talked about going away. Jesus did all he could to help his followers be prepared for his departure even though he was facing his own rejection, torture, and death. Jesus clearly loved his followers to the end of his earthly life! In this farewell time of teaching and prayer (John 13-17) Jesus repeatedly tells these followers that they will not be left alone. The Holy Spirit, the Helper from God, will come to them. Jesus will send the Spirit to them and they will do amazing things in Jesus' name. Jesus won't be gone, just present in a different yet very personal way.

PRAYER:

Father, thank you for your abiding presence in my life through the Holy Spirit. I am so thankful that Jesus' presence wasn't just confined to his earthly ministry, but that he has come to live inside my heart through the Helper. Please know that the Spirit is welcome in my heart to mend, purify, convict, correct, empower, remind, grow, and motivate me. In Jesus' name. Amen.

CONTEXT: JOHN 16:1-15

RELATED REFERENCES: JOHN 13:33 - 35; JOHN 14:1-14; JOHN 14:28

Day: 288

SIN, RIGHTEOUSNESS, JUDGMENT AND SALVATION

JOHN 16:8-11

"When the Helper comes, he will show the people of the world how wrong they are about sin, about being right with God, and about judgment. He will prove that they are guilty of sin, because they don't believe in me. He will show them how wrong they are about how to be right with God. The Helper will do this, because I am going to the Father. You will not see me then. And he will show them how wrong their judgment is, because their leader has already been condemned."

REFLECTION:

Jesus' promise to his followers was powerfully illustrated on the day of Pentecost after his resurrection (Acts 2). Peter and the apostles were filled with the Spirit and boldly spoke the Gospel of Jesus Christ. People were convicted in their hearts and believed that Jesus was Lord and Christ and were baptized (Acts 2:36-39). They were forgiven of their sins, received the gift of the Holy Spirit, and began a new life of righteousness (Acts 2:38-47). On that day, the Spirit brought conviction of sin and judgment to those who heard the message of Jesus. The Spirit showed the people the way of righteousness through Jesus Christ the Lord. The Spirit helped lead them to salvation. The Spirit still does the same today. Let's ask that God empower us and our words through his Holy Spirit so the lost around us can know the truth of Jesus!

PRAYER:

Holy and righteous Father, as your child, I know that your Holy Spirit lives in me. I ask, dear Father, that you empower my influence and my words by your Spirit so that they will be appropriate and powerful as I try to lead my friends to your salvation in Jesus, in whose name I pray. Amen.

CONTEXT: JOHN 16:1-15

RELATED REFERENCES: 1 CORINTHIANS 2:6-10; ACTS 2:32-33, 36-39; JOHN 5:24-30

Day: 289
The Truth of Jesus

John 16:12-15

"I have so much more to tell you, but it is too much for you to accept now. But when the Spirit of truth comes, he will lead you into all truth. He will not speak his own words. He will speak only what he hears and will tell you what will happen in the future. The Spirit of truth will bring glory to me by telling you what he receives from me. All that the Father has is mine. That is why I said that the Spirit will tell you what he receives from me."

Reflection:

Why do we trust the Gospel message that we have received? First, the Helper led, reminded, guided, and revealed the things of Jesus to his apostles as they shared the story of Jesus. This ensures their accuracy. Second, we have the Holy Spirit—the anointing or Helper from heaven—inside of us helping us to discern the truth of the message about Jesus that helps us know that their message is true (1 John 2:20-27).

Prayer:

Give me wisdom, dear Heavenly Father, to know falsehood when I see it. I want to know Jesus and to honor the truth about him in my heart, my head, and my life. Help me to know the truth of Jesus and the freedom it brings. Touch my heart by Jesus' words and example and call me to minister in his name. Make my life one of integrity and grace that reflects your Son's glory. In Jesus' name I pray. Amen.

Context: John 16:1-15

Related References: Galatians 1:3-5; 1 John 2:18-25; Ephesians 1:13

Day: 290

The Dark Night before Dawn

JOHN 16:16-22

"After a short time you won't see me. Then after another short time you will see me again."
Some of the followers said to each other, "What does he mean when he says, 'After a short
time you won't see me. Then after another short time you will see me again'? And what
does he mean when he says, 'Because I am going to the Father'?" They also asked, "What
does he mean by 'a short time'? We don't understand what he is saying." Jesus saw that
the followers wanted to ask him about this. So he said to them, "Are you asking each other
what I meant when I said, 'After a short time you won't see me. Then after another short
time you will see me again'? The truth is, you will cry and be sad, but the world will be
happy. You will be sad, but then your sadness will change to happiness. When a woman
gives birth to a baby, she has pain, because her time has come. But when her baby is born,
she forgets the pain. She forgets because she is so happy that a child has been born into the
world. It is the same with you. Now you are sad, but I will see you again, and you will be
happy. You will have a joy that no one can take away."

REFLECTION:

Jesus knows that darkness will descend on himself and those he loves. He has
tried to prepare them. They cannot imagine what the next four days will entail.
In just a few days, they will go from excruciating agony to inexpressible joy. So
often we face the dark night. We need to remember that the Holy Spirit, the
Helper, lives in us and is our assurance of a dawn of joy, blessing, and triumph
(2 Cor. 1:21-22; 5:5; Eph. 1:13-14).

PRAYER:

Give me courage, O Lord my Father and God, to trust in my darkest moments that you are
the Father of the Dawn and the gracious God who raises triumph out of defeat and joy
out of sorrow. Please bless the following people who now face darkness in their lives ....
Strengthen them through the Helper, your Holy Spirit, and bring them the dawn of joy in
your grace. In Jesus' name I pray. Amen.

CONTEXT: JOHN 16:16-33

RELATED REFERENCES: PSALM 30:5B & ISAIAH 66:14; JOHN 20:19-22; LUKE 24:35-43

Day: 291
Go Directly to the Father

John 16:23-27

"In that day you will not have to ask me about anything. And I assure you, my Father will give you anything you ask him for in my name. You have never asked for anything in this way before. But ask in my name, and you will receive. And you will have the fullest joy possible. I have told you these things, using words that hide the meaning. But the time will come when I will not use words like that to tell you things. I will speak to you in plain words about the Father. Then you will be able to ask the Father for things in my name. I'm not saying that I will have to ask the Father for you. The Father himself loves you because you have loved me. And he loves you because you have believed that I came from God."

Reflection:

We pray in Jesus' name. Why? Because Jesus is our mediator and the Holy Spirit is our intercessor. They give us the right to go directly to God with the burdens of our hearts, the struggles of our lives, and the weakness of our faith. We go boldly as God's beloved children, with Jesus, our older brother, as our advocate. We go confidently, knowing that the Helper makes our words and our unspeakable feelings known to God according to his will. Because of Jesus' work for us at the Father's side, and because of his gift to us of the Holy Spirit, we can speak directly to the Creator of the Universe and know we are heard. Not only that, but we are assured that God will respond because he loves us. Incredible!

Prayer:

Father, God of all creation and LORD of the universe and history, thank you for hearing my prayers, knowing my heart, and bidding me come to you as your child. I know that you provided this grace to me at the cost of Jesus' leaving heaven and coming to earth to die for me. I pray that my life will be a fitting tribute and praise for all that you have done for me. In Jesus' name I pray. Amen.

Context: John 16:16-33

Related References: Ephesians 2:16-18; Romans 8:26-27; 1 Timothy 2:5

Day: 292
THE GREAT CIRCLE OF GRACE
JOHN 16:28-30

"I came from the Father into the world. Now I am leaving the world and going back to the Father." Then his followers said, "You are already speaking plainly to us. You are not using words that hide the meaning. We can see now that you know all things. You answer our questions even before we ask them. This makes us believe that you came from God."

REFLECTION:

The story of Jesus is the great circle of grace. He began with the Father in heaven before time. He created all that there is and yet chose to come to his created world on earth and live among us as one of us. He let us crucify him in humiliation and shame. Yet he rose from death and returned to heaven. Jesus then poured out the Holy Spirit and brought salvation to all who responded to God's grace. Jesus' followers now live with a face toward the future, knowing that he has prepared us a place with him in heaven. It is the great circle of grace, brought to us by the love and sacrifice of Jesus.

PRAYER:

Thank you, dear God, for the great circle of your grace—the sending of Jesus from heaven to bring me home to you. Thank you, Jesus, for making such a journey and sharing such a burden. Please accept my life as an offering of thanks and praise for your grace and mercy. Amen.

CONTEXT: JOHN 16:16-33

RELATED REFERENCES: JOHN 1:1-3, 10-18; PHILIPPIANS 2:5-11; 1 PETER 3:18

Day: 293

SCATTERED AND ALONE

JOHN 16:31-32

Jesus said, "So now you believe? Listen to me. A time is coming when you will be scattered, each to his own home. In fact, that time is already here. You will leave me, and I will be alone. But I am never really alone, because the Father is with me.

REFLECTION:

The followers think they believe. They think they are courageous and loyal. Yet they will all scatter and leave Jesus alone when he is arrested. He will face the horrors of the Cross by himself. Yes, God will go with him. But on the Cross, Jesus will even feel abandoned by God as he bears the weight of the world's sin alone, forsaken, mocked, ridiculed and tortured.

Why did he do it? Why did he go to the Cross alone? Why did he withhold his power and allow himself to be killed?

He did it to save you. He did it to save me. He did it to save the lost world.

So how can we not rejoice and give God thanks for his matchless grace?

How can we not love our brothers and sisters for whom Christ died?

So how can we keep from sharing such costly grace with those who do not know it?

PRAYER:

O glorious Father, you are full of compassion and yet still the one, true, holy God. Please give us—your people, your Church, Jesus' followers—courage to proclaim your grace in ways that communicate it clearly. The unspeakable horrors of Jesus' betrayal night and crucifixion day humble us, dear Father. They make us realize that we, too, can fail and be unfaithful at crucial times. They also reminds us of your incredible love for us as well as for those who have never heard of your grace. Lead us to love others who do not know this grace as their own. In Jesus' name I pray. Amen.

CONTEXT: JOHN 16:16-33

RELATED REFERENCES: JOHN 3:16-17; 1 JOHN 2:1-2; LUKE 24:45-48

Day: 294

I HAVE OVERCOME THE WORLD

JOHN 16:33

"I have told you these things so that you can have peace in me. In this world you will have troubles. But be brave! I have defeated the world!"

REFLECTION:

The power of the world, the realm controlled by Satan, was defeated when Jesus accepted his Father's will to go to the Cross. He broke and defeated the power of sin and death. He brought life and immortality to light. He ensured that death would not have the final say.

In the middle of sorrows and trials, we can take heart and have peace because of Jesus' victory over the dark powers of the world. We can face them courageously, not because our challenges are easy, but because the hard things of this life are temporary and are preparing us for an eternal glory. Our peace is not found in the absence of strife or troubles in our lives, but in Jesus and what he has done to make our future sure!

PRAYER:

Be near, O God, in the middle of my trials and hardships. Stir my heart with your Spirit to remember your promises, your faithfulness, and your triumph over Satan and death through Jesus. Give me the peace of Jesus, in whose name I pray. Amen.

CONTEXT: JOHN 16:16-33

RELATED REFERENCES: PHILIPPIANS 4:4-9; 1 JOHN 2:15-17; 2 TIMOTHY 1:9-10

Day: 295

THE ESSENCE OF LIFE

JOHN 17:1-3

After Jesus said these things, he looked toward heaven and prayed, "Father, the time has come. Give glory to your Son so that the Son can give glory to you. You gave the Son power over all people so that he could give eternal life to all those you have given to him. And this is eternal life: that people can know you, the only true God, and that they can know Jesus Christ, the one you sent."

REFLECTION:

Jesus came to give us life. His goal wasn't just to prolong our life here, nor was it to just increase the quality of life here. His goal was to give us life that would endure—that would last longer than the mountains, oceans, earth, sky, and all other created things.

What is the secret to this life? To know God and to know his Son, Jesus Christ, is this secret to lasting life. This is more than just knowing facts about God and Jesus; it is a relationship and reliance on them in everyday life. It is seeking after God and finding him. It is learning to trust Jesus as our Lord with every fiber of our being.

PRAYER:

Holy and righteous God, my heavenly Father, please lead me to a deeper relationship with you. I want to know more about you. I also want to know you—your passion, your holiness, your might, your wisdom, and your grace. Please reveal more of yourself to me in my daily walk with you. In Jesus' name I pray. Amen.

CONTEXT: JOHN 17:1-12

RELATED REFERENCES: JOHN 5:24-26; JOHN 10:7-10; 1 CORINTHIANS 13:13

Day: 296
THE GLORY OF OBEDIENCE

JOHN 17:4-5

"I finished the work you gave me to do. I brought you glory on earth. And now, Father, give me glory with you. Give me the glory I had with you before the world was made."

REFLECTION:

Jesus did everything God had given him to do. Imagine, finishing your task at such a young age! But isn't that what Jesus did?

So often we don't look on obedience as a way to give God glory. Powerful praise songs in worship seem like a much more exciting way to give God glory. Leading someone to Christ is another example of giving God glory. Attributing some great accomplish to him is giving God glory.

However, let's not forget that in the simple and hard, everyday and heroic, intentional acts of obedience we offer to God, we are bringing him glory! Obedience is worship incarnate—worship coming to life in our daily lives. So rather than looking on obedience as a hard and sometimes harsh thing, let's look on it as the embodiment of our praise in daily worship (Romans 12:1-2).

PRAYER:

Father, thank you for sending Jesus to be my example. I know that he was obedient from the heart to all your desires and commands. I sometimes falter and fail in my obedience. Please forgive me. Open my heart to understand that you are brought glory when I obey you. In Jesus' name I pray. Amen.

CONTEXT: JOHN 17:1-12

RELATED REFERENCES: JOHN 4:31-34; JOHN 14:15, 21, 23; JOHN 19:25-29

Day: 297

THE FINISHED WORK OF GOD

JOHN 17:6-8

"You gave me some people from the world. I have shown them what you are like. They belonged to you, and you gave them to me. They have obeyed your teaching. Now they know that everything I have came from you. I told them the words you gave me, and they accepted them. They realized the fact that I came from you and believed that you sent me."

REFLECTION:

The work of God is to believe in his Son, the one whom God sent to earth (John 6:27-29). Jesus has helped bring his followers to that faith as much as possible before the Crucifixion and the Resurrection. He has given them God's words. He has shared with them God's love. He has offered them forgiveness. He has shown them his example. Now he must give his life and his Spirit so he can send them out with authority to share his story.

Jesus entrusted all that he did and all that he was to a group of human beings. They changed the world. So can we. We have the same Savior. We have the same Spirit. We have the opportunity. The real question is, "Do we have the same faith?"

PRAYER:

Holy and righteous God, my loving Father, please use me to be part of your plan to touch the world with your grace and salvation. In Jesus' name I pray. Amen.

CONTEXT: JOHN 17:1-12

RELATED REFERENCES: MATTHEW 28:18-20; JOHN 20:19-23; ACTS 4:8-13

Day: 298
THEY ARE MY GLORY!

JOHN 17:9-10
"I pray for them now. I am not praying for the people in the world. But I am praying for these people you gave me, because they are yours. All I have is yours, and all you have is mine. And my glory is seen in them."

REFLECTION:
Think of all the things the followers of Jesus did wrong. Recall all the things they misunderstood. Remember the many times they blew the opportunity to do the right thing or say the right word. During Jesus' earthly ministry, his followers often came up lacking. Yet Jesus did not give up on them. He still loved them. He even continued to invest himself in them.

What did these very fallible human followers do with Jesus' trust and unflagging confidence that they would be his glory? They changed the world! They helped create an enduring movement that exists today. They brought Jesus' message and Jesus' salvation to millions of people through their ongoing legacy of faith, courage, and obedience. They are his glory. And as we live for the Lord, so are we.

PRAYER:
Father, please forgive my lack of confidence in what Jesus can do through me. I know that the Lord's plans for me are greater than anything I could imagine. Help me not to get too despondent with my own failures. Renew my trust that Jesus will maximize my efforts to bring him glory. I ask this in the name of the one I want to honor, Jesus Christ my Lord. Amen.

CONTEXT: JOHN 17:1-12

RELATED REFERENCES: COLOSSIANS 3:1-4; EPHESIANS 3:20-21; 1 THESSALONIANS 2:18-20

Day: 299
DEPARTING PRAYER

JOHN 17:11

"Now I am coming to you. I will not stay in the world, but these followers of mine are still in the world. Holy Father, keep them safe by the power of your name—the name you gave me. Then they will be one, just as you and I are one."

REFLECTION:

Jesus' departing prayer was for his followers. He wants God to keep them and care for them. He wants them to find God's peace among themselves. He wants them to be unified—as closely "in sync" as he and his Father are "in sync" and as closely one as he and his Father are one.

I can't imagine any other prayer that has been more ignored than Jesus' prayer for his followers' unity. Let's make a commitment to be more united—in our personal relationships, in our congregations, and in our contact with other people of God all over the world. Let's not forget one of the Lord's last desires for his people ... and for us!

PRAYER:

Father, forgive us—and especially forgive me—for our selfishness, pigheadedness, and arrogance. But please, dear God, don't just forgive us, but use your Spirit to change us and unite us. Bring us to truth through the Helper and use us to minister to the lost world and bring more people to your Son. In Jesus' name. Amen.

CONTEXT: JOHN 17:1-12

RELATED REFERENCES: EPHESIANS 4:1-6; COLOSSIANS 3:15; EPHESIANS 4:11-16

Day: 300

THE GREAT PROTECTOR

JOHN 17:12

*"While I was with them, I kept them safe by the power of your name—
the name you gave me. I protected them. And only one of them was lost—
the one who was sure to be lost. This was to show the truth of what
the Scriptures said would happen."*

REFLECTION:

Jesus came to save, to bless, to redeem, and to protect. The whole focus of Jesus' last moments with his followers was protection. He wanted to protect them spiritually from discouragement, so he told them about what was going to happen with him and promised to send the Holy Spirit as the Helper to be with them. He wanted to protect them physically, so he takes control of his own arrest and makes sure that his followers are not involved with the torturous night and day that follow (John 18:8-9). All of this means that he must bear his impending death, his mockery of a trial, his brutal scourging, his belittling beating, and his agonizing trip to Calvary alone.

Why did he do it this way? Because of his love for his own and his desire to protect them. And that, dear friend, is just a sample of how much he cares for you, too!

PRAYER:

Father, even in my struggles, please help me to find Jesus. I know he is there, comforting me and strengthening me through the Holy Spirit and joining me when I meet with other Christians. Please give me courage that does not flag in the face of opposition, ridicule, or pain. Help me see my Lord Jesus and never doubt his desire to bring me safely home to you. I pray this in Jesus' name. Amen.

CONTEXT: JOHN 17:1-12

RELATED REFERENCES: JOHN 18:3-9; LUKE 13:34; ROMANS 8:35-39

Day: 301
OUR SOURCE OF JOY

JOHN 17:13

"I am coming to you now. But I pray these things while I am still in the world. I say all this so that these followers can have the true happiness that I have. I want them to be completely happy."

REFLECTION:

Jesus is our source of real, unending joy! The apostle Paul said it this way, "Always be happy in the Lord. I will say it again. Be happy. Let all people see that you are gentle and kind. The Lord is coming soon" (Philippians 4:4-5).

From his birth to his resurrection and to his coming again to take us home to God, the Lord Jesus is our source of joy. He has shown us God's great love for us. He has taught us how to live victoriously in a hostile world. He has promised to never forsake us or leave us. He has ensured that death cannot sever us from his love. He has promised that he will return and bring us home with him. Jesus is our source of joy. Like the prophet Nehemiah reminded us so long ago, "Today is a special day to the Lord. Don't be sad! Why? Because the joy of the Lord will make you strong" (Ne. 8:10).

PRAYER:

Father God, sovereign master of all Creation, thank you for giving me the one true source of joy that cannot be extinguished or exhausted. Your gift of Jesus has brought me hope, salvation, and JOY even when I face life's most painful moments. I pray in the name of Jesus, my source of joy. Amen.

CONTEXT: JOHN 17:13-26

RELATED REFERENCES: LUKE 2:8-12; JOHN 16:20; MATTHEW 28:1-10

Day: 302

YOU DO NOT BELONG

JOHN 17:14-15

"I have given them your teaching. And the world has hated them, because they don't belong to the world, just as I don't belong to the world. I am not asking you to take them out of the world. But I am asking that you keep them safe from the Evil One."

REFLECTION:

God loves the world. He sent his Son to redeem the world through his death. But, the world does not love God. The world, its processes and powers, rejected his Son. Since we have become Christians, we are no longer part of the world opposed to God and his work. We should not be surprised when the world does not accept us. We should not be shocked when the world opposes and hates us. Jesus longs to protect us, but he does ask us to live in the place of risk; he calls us to join him in helping save people caught by the processes and powers of this current world. We are called to live on the boundary of darkness and light; we are to shine our light to help those trapped in deep darkness find their way to the One True Light, Jesus. As we do this, we know that Jesus is our advocate at the Father's side, asking that we be kept safe from the evil one.

PRAYER:

Grant me courage and compassion, dear Father, as I live in the place of danger and grace—that place of salvation where light penetrates the darkness and lost men and women are rescued from the decay and despotism of the world and its dark prince. Keep my heart focused on the Light and my strength renewed when I face the powers of darkness and the hate this world might offer. Please, dear Father, guard my heart from cynicism and hate, so that I can be one of your many tools of redemption. In Jesus' name I ask this. Amen.

CONTEXT: JOHN 17:13-26

RELATED REFERENCES: COLOSSIANS 1:11-14; MATTHEW 24:4-13; JOHN 15:18-21

Day: 303
MADE PURE AND HOLY

JOHN 17:16-17
""They don't belong to the world, just as I don't belong to the world. Make them ready for your service through your truth. Your teaching is truth."

REFLECTION:

God's Word is truth. God's teaching is truth. His goal in giving us his teaching, his truth, is not to limit us or restrict us, but to make us pure and holy. Here, however, Jesus reminds us of another reason for God's teaching: it makes us ready for service to him. Paul told Timothy, "All Scripture is given by God. And all Scripture is useful for teaching and for showing people the things that are wrong in their lives. It is useful for correcting faults and teaching how to live right. Using the Scriptures, the person who serves God will be ready and will have everything he needs to do every good work" (2 Tim. 3:16-17).

We live in the center of God's intention when we open our hearts to his teaching and apply that teaching to our lives through obedience. God's Spirit is at work to transform us into people who are pure and holy—people who are more like Jesus. In addition, God's teaching makes us ready for every good work as we seek to serve him. Let's be more committed to seeking God's teaching in the Bible so we can serve him and minister to the world in better ways.

PRAYER:

Holy God, my loving Father, mold me to be more what you want me to be as I open my heart to your truth and ask that your Spirit transform my will, my actions, and my character. Help me with my discipline so that I can study your teaching and fill my life with your will. In Jesus' name I pray. Amen.

CONTEXT: JOHN 17:13-26

RELATED REFERENCES: HEBREWS 4:12-13; 1 CORINTHIANS 6:9-11;
1 CORINTHIANS 1:30

SENT!

JOHN 17:18-19

"I have sent them into the world, just as you sent me into the world. I am making myself completely ready to serve you. I do this for them, so that they also might be fully qualified for your service."

REFLECTION:

Jesus was sent from God to us so we could return to God as his beloved children. Now Jesus sends his followers (including us) into the world to make a difference in the lives of those we meet. Jesus now gives himself totally to God so that our mission and our future and our lives will be useful to the Father as well. Our mission is God-led, God-inspired, God-powered, and God-willed. We belong to him and our mission is to serve others for him.

PRAYER:

Father, take control of my heart, my life, and my will. Use me and my influence and my relationships to touch the world with your truth and grace. Jesus, thank you for not only dying for me to save me from sin, but also for saving me and serving me so that I can serve and honor the Father. In your name I pray. Amen.

CONTEXT: JOHN 17:13-26

RELATED REFERENCES: JOHN 20:19-21; MATTHEW 6:24-27; MATTHEW 28:18-20

Day: 305

He Prayed for You and Me

John 17:20-21

"I pray not only for these followers but also for those who will believe in me because of their teaching. Father, I pray that all who believe in me can be one. You are in me and I am in you. I pray that they can also be one in us. Then the world will believe that you sent me."

Reflection:

Jesus didn't just pray for his immediate followers who were with him when he prayed. He also prayed for those who would believe on Jesus because of their teaching. I don't know if you realize what he is praying so let me spell it out. He is praying for you and me! He was seeing down the long road of history and the needs of his people in future generations—all the people who would believe on him because of the teaching of these first followers.

As Jesus looked beyond the first generation of believers, his prayer for them and for us is that we would be unified. His prayer for unity wasn't just so that his followers could have peace with one another. He prayed for unity so that the world could see that unity and be led to believe that God sent Jesus to be the Savior of the world. So let's get together by coming to Jesus and seeking his life, his love, his will, and his Spirit to help us be what he has called us to be.

Prayer:

Holy and almighty God, please break down the walls that separate your people and keep us apart. Forgive us for our arrogance and selfishness. Bring us to unity as we seek to serve the world as your Son did. As we focus more on Jesus, please conform us more to your will. In Jesus' name I pray. Amen.

Context: John 17:13-26

RELATED REFERENCES: JOHN 16:4-15; 1 TIMOTHY 2:1-2; MATTHEW 28:20

Day: 306

THE POWER OF ONE

JOHN 17:22-23

"I have given them the glory that you gave me. I gave them this glory so that they can be one, just as you and I are one. I will be in them, and you will be in me. So they will be completely one. Then the world will know that you sent me and that you loved them just as you loved me."

REFLECTION:

The world is divided. Unity is simply not found on a grand scale in our fractured, divided, and segmented world. We divide on race, politics, social issues, nationality, opinions, and religion. Only when people come together, across the boundaries that normally divide humans, do other people begin to take notice.

Our perfection, our unity, our becoming One, is found in Christ. Only in him do we find the barriers brought down and all are made into one family. Only in him do we find things that normally divide us becoming the very witness to God's powerful love.

To help illustrate this, I want to encourage you to draw a triangle on a sheet of paper. Make sure that one point of the triangle is pointed up. At the top of that point print the word, Jesus. On the left point of the triangle write your name. On the right point of the triangle write the words, "other believers." Now notice a simple, but profound truth. As you and "other believers" move closer to Jesus, you will find yourselves closer to each other! Jesus came to reconcile and reunite. So let's live and love as one; one with Jesus and one with each other. And we will do this by more passionately pursuing being one with Jesus!

PRAYER:

Today, dear Father, I pray again that you make your people one in Spirit and purpose, in doctrine and in service. Help us to pursue Jesus more passionately so that we can be drawn closer together. In Jesus' name. Amen.

CONTEXT: JOHN 17:13-26

RELATED REFERENCES: GALATIANS 3:26-28; EPHESIANS 2:14-18; REVELATION 7:9-10

Day: 307
ENDURING GLORY

JOHN 17:24

"Father, I want these people you have given me to be with me in every place I am. I want them to see my glory—the glory you gave me because you loved me before the world was made."

REFLECTION:

So often, we try to find glory for ourselves while we are here on earth. In our brief span of years, we try all sorts of ways to gain glory in the eyes of others. True glory, however, only comes from the Lord!

Jesus longs to share his eternal glory with us. He had this with God before coming to earth. He has it now as he sits at the Father's side. Jesus longs to share his glory with us. He longs to have us by his side and to gaze at him in all his heavenly glory along with the glory of his angels. Let's look forward to this future with anticipation as we wait for the day we will see Jesus, face to face, in all of his glory.

PRAYER:

O Lord God, my glorious heavenly Father, I long for the day that I can see you and your Son in all of your glory. I know my limited imagination cannot even begin to grasp the beauty, majesty, and brilliance of your glory. Please stir my passion and steel my will to live for that day of glory with purity and holiness. In Jesus' name I pray. Amen.

CONTEXT: JOHN 17:13-26

RELATED REFERENCES: 1 JOHN 3:1-3; ROMANS 8:18-25; 1 CORINTHIANS 15:43

Day: 308
JESUS REVEALS THE FATHER

JOHN 17:25-26

"Father, you are the one who always does what is right. The world does not know you, but I know you, and these followers of mine know that you sent me. I showed them what you are like, and I will show them again. Then they will have the same love that you have for me, and I will live in them."

REFLECTION:

Jesus is the one who reveals God to us. He shows us what God is like because he is God and has come from God. If we want to know what God is like, all we have to do is look at Jesus. If we want to know how God cares for people, we can look at how Jesus ministered to them. If we want to know God's will for our lives, we can listen to Jesus' words and know they reveal God's truth. Jesus reveals the nature of God in his actions and his words. And, Jesus continues to reveal God to us. He is the one through whom the fullest revelation of God comes. Let's look to Jesus if we really want to know God.

PRAYER:

Father God, thank you for revealing yourself to me in Jesus. I truly believe that Jesus reveals your heart, your character, your compassion, your holiness, and many more of your qualities. Now I ask, dear Father, that you reveal yourself to me as I seek to know you more fully through your Son's ministry here on earth through the Gospel of John. Please make yourself more fully known to me and through me. I ask this in Jesus' name. Amen.

CONTEXT: JOHN 17:13-26

RELATED REFERENCES: JOHN 1:14-18; 1 JOHN 1:1-4; TITUS 2:11-14

Day: 309

BETRAYED IN THE PLACE OF FRIENDS

JOHN 18:1-3

When Jesus finished praying, he left with his followers and went across the Kidron Valley. He went into a garden there, his followers still with him. Judas, the one responsible for handing Jesus over, knew where this place was. He knew because Jesus often met there with his followers. So Judas led a group of soldiers to the garden, along with some guards from the leading priests and the Pharisees. They were carrying torches, lanterns, and weapons.

REFLECTION:

Judas knew where to find Jesus. Jesus had taken his followers to this place many times for prayer and to enjoy time alone with his Father and his followers.

To our horror, Satan often uses people near to God's children to wound and betray them in places where they should feel safe. That makes the wounds they receive all the more grievous and the methods of betrayal all the more harsh and garish. The very acts of betrayal seem to make the once holy places defiled.

We must recognize, however, that the place and the people where we are betrayed are not the problem. Satan is! If Jesus was betrayed by one close to him, we should not expect things to be all that different for us. However, we must not let the potential for betrayal keep us from God's people or God's places! If Satan can keep us from Jesus' followers and the place of prayer and fellowship, then he has us just where he wants us. Don't let the unfaithfulness of others drive you from the people of God!

PRAYER:

Father, give me strength and courage to never let the ruthless and duplicitous actions of others drive me from your people or the places I need to go for strength, encouragement, and support. Jesus, please come to me and minister to my broken spirit in times like these. Amen.

CONTEXT: JOHN 18:1-11

RELATED REFERENCES: MATTHEW 10:16-22; JOHN 15:21; 1 JOHN 3:13

IN CONTROL

JOHN 18:4-6

Jesus already knew everything that would happen to him. So he went out and asked them, "Who are you looking for?" They answered, "Jesus from Nazareth." He said, "I am Jesus." (Judas, the one responsible for handing Jesus over, was standing there with them.) When Jesus said, "I am Jesus," the men moved back and fell to the ground.

REFLECTION:

John helps us see that Jesus' rejection and crucifixion was not some terrible accident that occurred because he couldn't prevent it. Jesus is in control. He protects his followers. He makes others fall back in fear. He will die on the Cross only because he allows it to happen in order to follow his Father's will and to bring salvation to us. The Cross, along with its shameful agony and ridicule, is made all the more precious for us because Jesus had the ability to stop it from happening, but instead, submitted his will to the will of God and to the needs of sinners, like you and me.

PRAYER:

How can I thank you, dear God, for loving me so much? How can I ever show my appreciation, Lord Jesus, for the price you willingly paid for my sin? Thank you for knowing the cruelty that lay ahead of you and yet bearing it for it me. To you, Lord Jesus, belong all glory, honor, and majesty. Amen.

CONTEXT: JOHN 18:1-11

RELATED REFERENCES: JOHN 13:1-4; HEBREWS 12:2; JOHN 19:9-11

Day: 311

LET THESE OTHERS GO!

JOHN 18:7-9

He asked them again, "Who are you looking for?"
They said, "Jesus from Nazareth." Jesus said, "I told you that I am Jesus. So if you are looking for me, let these other men go free." This was to show the truth of what Jesus said earlier: "I have not lost anyone you gave me."

REFLECTION:

Imagine being in the target of hatred, jealousy, and murderous intent yet still protecting those closest to you. Jesus' protection of his followers during his arrest, trial, and crucifixion is a great reminder of his love for us. In fact, in the protection of the followers, we can see our own eternal protection. Jesus is willing to pay the horrible price of the Cross to ensure our protection from sin and death. He says to Satan, "Let these others go!" Then he pays the price for our sin and we are set free!

PRAYER:

Gracious God, I praise you for Jesus' sacrificial love for his followers and also for me. My words are inadequate to say how I feel. Jesus, my appreciation for your wounds that protected and healed me is deeper than words. I trust that the Holy Spirit will communicate the emotions that are beyond my ability to express so that you will receive my praise with the depth and the passion with which I offer it to you this day. Amen.

CONTEXT: JOHN 18:1-11

RELATED REFERENCES: JOHN 17:12; ROMANS 8:38; LUKE 21:12-19

Day: 312
THE CLASH OF WILLS

JOHN 18:10-11

Simon Peter had a sword, which he pulled out. He struck the servant of the high priest and cut off his right ear. (The servant's name was Malchus.) Jesus said to Peter, "Put your sword back in its place! I must drink from the cup the Father has given me."

REFLECTION:

Peter thought that the biggest battle would be between the forces of Jesus and the forces of religious and political authority. As he had promised Jesus when Jesus washed his feet, he was ready to fight to the death for the Lord (John 13:36-38). He was wrong. The biggest battle was one of the will.

Jesus had the authority to call down angels from heaven to slay his enemies. He did not ask for their help, but instead offered himself up as a sacrifice to be our help. The battle was between Peter's earthbound vision of a worldly kingdom and Jesus' passion to glorify God by obeying his Father's will.

So often, we try to battle Satan with worldly wisdom and worldly weapons. Our biggest battle at times isn't with Satan, but our own will. Do we choose to obey? Do we obey when we don't understand or it doesn't make sense? Is our apparent victory less important than our obedience to God? Jesus chose the will of God. Will we?

PRAYER:

Holy and gracious God, my Abba Father, I surrender my will to you to obey and honor you as you command. I offer my body as a living sacrifice to you. Use me as you so chose and mold my heart to be like that of Jesus, in whose name I pray. Amen.

CONTEXT: JOHN 18:1-11

RELATED REFERENCES: MATTHEW 16:16-25; JOHN 13:36-37; JOHN 12:27-28

Day: 313

WHO IS IN CHARGE HERE?

JOHN 18:12-14

Then the soldiers with their commander and the Jewish guards arrested Jesus. They tied him and brought him to Annas, the father-in-law of Caiaphas. Caiaphas was the high priest that year. He was also the one who had told the other Jewish leaders that it would be better if one man died for all the people.

REFLECTION:

Who really is in charge of what happens here?

Jesus will be put to death by the Roman executioners authorized by Pontius Pilate at the request of the Jewish religious hierarchy.

But let's ask the question again. Who is in charge here?

Jesus is bound, but they cannot restrain him. His obedience to the will of the Father is all that keeps him bound. Meanwhile, soldiers, Temple guards, leaders, priests, and others who appear to be in power are really powerless to restrain, much less, defeat Jesus.

Jesus lays down his life according to the Father's plan and will. Jesus lays down his life to be the atoning sacrifice for our sins, and for the sins of the world. Jesus lays down his life or they could not crucify him. Everything is reversed. Jesus is bound, but free to obey the will of God. The leaders are free, but bound by their hatred to follow the plan of God. The events of the Cross are the great reminder that God can use the worst of situations to bring about the greatest of results to his glory.

PRAYER:

Almighty God, please give me the courage to live for you no matter the cost. Help me trust that your reward and your power make the sufferings and struggles of this life pale in comparison to the glory that awaits me. Thank you for your Son, who pioneered this trail to glory before me. May my life reflect his faith in you and may it not waver even in the face of threat, suffering, or pain. In Jesus' name I pray. Amen.

CONTEXT: JOHN 18:12-27

RELATED REFERENCES: ROMANS 8:17-18; JOHN 11:45-52; 1 JOHN 2:1-2

Day: 314

THE FIRST DENIAL

JOHN 18:15-18

Simon Peter and another one of Jesus' followers went with Jesus. This follower knew the high priest. So he went with Jesus into the yard of the high priest's house. But Peter waited outside near the door. The follower who knew the high priest came back outside and spoke to the gatekeeper. Then he brought Peter inside. The girl at the gate said to Peter, "Are you also one of the followers of that man?" Peter answered, "No, I am not!" It was cold, so the servants and guards had built a fire. They were standing around it, warming themselves, and Peter was standing with them.

REFLECTION:

Jesus protected his followers from harm. Peter, on the other hand, is confused. Hours earlier, he had proclaimed his love and had predicted his faithfulness to Jesus even in the face of death. He had proved that faithfulness by drawing a sword to help defend his Lord. Now, however, he wavers in his loyalty when the prospects are not a glorious victory in battle.

Confusion and disappointment with what we think should be God's methods and God's plans often lead us to moments of withered loyalty, too. Let's remember the lesson of Peter; just because things are not going the way we think they should go doesn't mean that God has abandoned us. God does bring the victory, but oftentimes it comes at a different time and through a different doorway than we presume.

PRAYER:

My Lord God, forgive me for those times when my loyalty wavered and withered under the onslaught of unexpected trials. So often, dear Father, I get an idea of how I think things should go. I expect you to follow my path, rather than for me to be faithful as I follow your path. Forgive my arrogance, my impatience, and my Peter-like confusion. Thank you, dear Father, for the sure knowledge that you do restore those of us who waver and that you do make us stronger even when our weakness has caused that failure. In Jesus' name. Amen.

CONTEXT: JOHN 18:12-27

RELATED REFERENCES: LUKE 22:21-32; PROVERBS 16:25; PROVERBS 3:1-7

Day: 315

NO PRIVATE MATTER

JOHN 18:19-21

The high priest asked Jesus questions about his followers and what he taught them. Jesus answered, "I have always spoken openly to all people. I always taught in the synagogues and in the Temple area. All the Jews come together there. I never said anything in secret. So why do you question me? Ask the people who heard my teaching. They know what I said."

REFLECTION:

Jesus taught openly. He preached to the masses in the countryside. He spoke openly in the Temple courts when he was in Jerusalem. He did not found a secret society built on deception or private meetings. In contrast, Jesus was illegally tried at night away from the people.

Jesus is the Light. He taught and healed in the open, available for people to accept or reject him. In much the same way, the Christian life is not meant to be hidden or kept tucked away. While our goal is never to be obnoxious or pushy about our faith, we also must realize that our Christian life is intended to be demonstrated openly before others, so they can accept or reject it based on its integrity, character, and good deeds as seen in us.

PRAYER:

O LORD God, please help the light of Jesus shine through me. May my life be one that brings you glory and may my attitude show that every good thing I have comes from you. In Jesus' name I pray. Amen.

CONTEXT: JOHN 18:12-27

RELATED REFERENCES: JOHN 3:16-21; JOHN 8:12; MATTHEW 5:13-16

Day: 316

A SLAP IN THE FACE OF GOD

JOHN 18:22-23

When Jesus said this, one of the guards standing there hit him. The guard said, "You should not talk to the high priest like that!" Jesus answered, "If I said something wrong, tell everyone here what was wrong. But if what I said is right, then why do you hit me?"

REFLECTION:

The Temple guard didn't know it at the time, but he was not only slapping a greater High Priest in the face than the one he was protecting, he was also slapping God in the face. Jesus suffered many indignities in his trial and crucifixion. However, the greater tragedy is that those who inflicted these horrible cruelties never had any idea that they were abusing the Son of God, the Messiah that God had sent to redeem them. Their hatred and jealousy blinded them to the truth and perverted their system of justice to ensure that they could put Jesus to death.

PRAYER:

Father, thank you for your forgiveness. Thank you for your patience. Thank you for long-suffering kindness. Thank you for your overwhelming grace. I see these demonstrated in Jesus' willingness to submit to humiliation, abuse, and torture so that the very ones who hurt him could one day come to know you as their Father and find your saving grace. I know that this same grace is given to me. I praise you and thank you in Jesus' name. Amen.

CONTEXT: JOHN 18:12-27

RELATED REFERENCES: LUKE 11:29-32; HEBREWS 4:11-16; LUKE 10:16

Day: 317
THE SECOND DENIAL

JOHN 18:24-25

So Annas sent Jesus to Caiaphas the high priest. He was still tied. Simon Peter was standing at the fire, keeping himself warm. The other people said to Peter, "Aren't you one of the followers of that man?" Peter denied it. He said, "No, I am not."

REFLECTION:

I don't know if you are like me when I read this passage. I feel like I'm watching a slow moving train wreck! It's awful. Jesus' closest followers have fled away into hiding. The few that are in the vicinity of what is happening are quiet in the crowd or boldly denouncing their association with him. And Jesus is all alone to face the horrendous events and suffering that happen around him.

"Are you one of the followers ...?" The question is directed to Peter, but in a sense, it is also meant for us. A follower is one who accompanies a master in order to become like him (Luke 6:40). Clearly, Peter hasn't gotten the concept yet. He might be willing to be like Jesus in his power—performing miracles and amazing the people. However, this "Cross thing" that holds Jesus' attention is not understandable to Peter. So he fails, again. Not just once, but now a second time he denies his Lord—the very Lord he is seeking to emulate. History will later show that Peter did become like his Master and was faithful even to death. But not this time. Peter denies his connection to Jesus a second time.

Aren't we glad that Jesus didn't give up on Peter when he failed again! Aren't we glad that Jesus doesn't give up on us either!

PRAYER:

Dear Heavenly Father, forgive me for my failure and my sin. I do not like my sinfulness and I want to be more than I am. Please fashion me into a vessel fit for useful and faithful service to you and to your kingdom. I truly believe that you can make me more than I am. I trust, dear Lord, that you can use my failure and my sin to grow me into a more holy and useful person for you. In Jesus' name, and because of his saving grace, I pray. Amen.

CONTEXT: JOHN 18:12-27

RELATED REFERENCES: MATTHEW 18:21-22; PSALM 103:8-12; COLOSSIANS 1:13-14

Day: 318

THE THIRD DENIAL

JOHN 18:26-27

One of the servants of the high priest was there. He was a relative of the man whose ear Peter had cut off. The servant said, "I think I saw you with him in the garden!" But again Peter said, "No, I was not with him!" As soon as he said this, a rooster crowed.

REFLECTION:

Three strikes and you're out. That's true in baseball. That's also true under the law in many places. Thankfully it is not true with God's grace.

Three strikes and you're broken, but not too broken to be restored. Jesus will confront Peter about his three-fold failure. However, each time Jesus will affirm his value and call him back to useful service. Sin—failure in our most important commitment, our commitment to God—is horrible. It brings all sorts of problems into our lives. However, sin does not have the final word in our lives: God's grace does.

Jesus died for sinners—that, my friend is you and me! Our sin does not disqualify us from being used by God if we will repent and let holy God remake us into someone fit to serve! So don't give up if you have struck out repeatedly in your walk of faith. Jesus reclaimed Peter and he can reclaim you!

PRAYER:

Holy God and Father, please don't let my sin steal my faith away from your transforming power and grace. I believe that you can remake me and empower me beyond my failures and my moments of unfaithfulness. Grow me and mature me so that those moments occur less and less frequently. Raise me up to be your loyal, useful, righteous, and faithful servant. In Jesus' name I pray. Amen.

CONTEXT: JOHN 18:12-27

RELATED REFERENCES: ROMANS 5:6-11; JAMES 5:19-20; ACTS 2:14, 36-41

Day: 319

NOT WANTING TO BE DEFILED

JOHN 18:28-32

Then the guards took Jesus from Caiaphas' house to the Roman governor's palace. It was early in the morning. The Jews there would not go inside the palace. They did not want to make themselves unclean, because they wanted to eat the Passover meal. So Pilate went outside to them and asked, "What do you say this man has done wrong?" They answered, "He is a bad man. That is why we brought him to you." Pilate said to them, "You take him yourselves and judge him by your own law." The Jewish leaders answered, "But your law does not allow us to punish anyone by killing them." (This was to show the truth of what Jesus said about how he would die.)

REFLECTION:

Semantics and blind spots often get in the way of seeing things clearly! These are two of the biggest problems religious people of every age have had. Rather than pursuing righteousness from the heart, we have a tendency to try to justify ourselves using legalistic maneuvering. Notice how Jesus' opponents do this before Pilate: they were illegally asking for Jesus to be killed, but wanted to be righteous by the letter of their law. The great irony is that they were worried about the Passover Feast, and yet their evil actions fulfill God's plan that Jesus would be the Passover Lamb, sacrificed for his people's sins.

While we can see the blind spots and the legalistic semantics of Jesus' opponents, can we see our own? A world of evil lurks in the hearts of men and women who seek to justify their religious actions rather than asking for God to reveal and eradicate every evil thought and desire from their hearts.

PRAYER:

God forgive me! I recognize that at times my own heart is so very deceitful. I want to be pure. I don't want try to justify myself by legalistic maneuvering. Cleanse me by your Spirit and transform me to be more like Jesus. Help me see my blind spots so that I can wholly serve you with a pure heart. In Jesus' name I pray. Amen.

CONTEXT: JOHN 18:28-40

RELATED REFERENCES: 16:11-15; LUKE 10:25-29; MARK 8:31

Day: 320
NOT OF THIS WORLD

JOHN 18:33-36

Then Pilate went back inside the palace. He called for Jesus and asked him, "Are you the king of the Jews?" Jesus said, "Is that your own question, or did other people tell you about me?" Pilate said, "I'm not a Jew! It was your own people and their leading priests who brought you before me. What have you done wrong?" Jesus said, "My kingdom does not belong to this world. If it did, my servants would fight so that I would not be handed over to the Jewish leaders. No, my kingdom is not an earthly one."

REFLECTION:

The crux of the major issue for Jesus' life is found in one statement: "But my Kingdom is not of this world." Jesus lived by a sense of heavenly timing. Jesus lived to honor his Father in heaven by doing his Father's will and fulfilling his Father's work. He taught values that were upside down to the way the world worked. Why? Because his Kingdom was a heavenly Kingdom. Because his goal was to bring heaven's glory to life in earthly people. Jesus was no threat to Pilate, the Emperor, or Herod because he had no desire to take their palaces or places; he wanted their hearts to be changed and their lives to reflect the will of heaven.

Jesus is not a threat to you either. He wants your heart—not so that he can conquer you, but so that he can give you life and make you ready for a home with him. Is Jesus your king? Is Jesus' Kingdom your passion?

PRAYER:

Holy and loving God, my Abba Father, thank you for blessing me with citizenship in your Kingdom. Reign over my heart and use me for your glory for "Thine is the Kingdom, and the power, and the glory, forever!" In Jesus' name. Amen.

CONTEXT: JOHN 18:28-40

RELATED REFERENCES: PHILIPPIANS 3:20-21; HEBREWS 12:18-29; MATTHEW 6:7-13

Day: 321
THE KING OF TRUTH

JOHN 18:37

Pilate said, "So you are a king." Jesus answered, "You are right to say that I am a king. I was born for this: to tell people about the truth. That is why I came into the world. And everyone who belongs to the truth listens to me."

REFLECTION:

Jesus came as king. He did not come as a king in robes of royalty, nor with a fine palace and a royal court. Instead, Jesus came as the King of Truth in simplicity and with a band of everyday folks called apostles. His mission was not to conquer the political landscape, but for God's truth to win the hearts of the people—all people, not just the Jewish or religious people.

Truth, however, is dangerous. Every pretender to royalty is threatened by one who is genuinely qualified. They fear the truth. So the true King was murdered so that all the pretenders could feel secure. Only problem was that once the truth was out there, no political power and no royal pretender could keep the truth from triumph.

Where is Pilate's power today? And where is Herod's thirst for royal recognition? And where is Caesar's rule? And where is the Roman Empire?

All are gone, with nothing left but old stones and a few sentences in the history books to tell about their passage across the stage of time. On the other hand, one King still reigns over the hearts of millions of men and women from all races. This King is Jesus, the King of Truth, Son of God, Christ our Lord!

PRAYER:

Father, thank you for the blessing of an everlasting Kingdom and a triumphant King, your Son and my Savior, Jesus. May his truth and his Kingdom come to complete triumph in my life. I offer my thanks to you in Jesus' name. Amen.

CONTEXT: JOHN 18:28-40

RELATED REFERENCES: MATTHEW 2:1-12; LUKE 1:26-33; JOHN 19:14-15,

Day: 322

THE QUESTION OF IRONY AND GRACE

JOHN 18:38

Pilate said, "What is truth?" Then he went out to the Jewish leaders again and said to them, "I can find nothing against this man."

REFLECTION:

Pilate answered his own question: Jesus is not guilty of any crime. The whole proceedings are a great reminder of the travesty of justice and the loss of human decency and integrity. Jesus is delivered into the hands of those who hate him. The Messiah is convicted on trumped up charges in an illegal trial. Jesus is rejected by people crying out for his death while trying not to defile themselves and disqualify themselves from the Passover celebration. The true King is rejected by God's people as they cry out that they have no king but Caesar. People committed to righteousness put the Lord to death and set a murderous criminal free. Pilate's question directed to Jesus should have been directed to the crowd, "What is truth?"

When you are treated unfairly, please remember the Lord at this moment. Before you feel abandoned ... betrayed ... and unjustly punished, remember Jesus. Then understand that he went through what he faced so that you could know the truth and that truth could set you free! If you have Jesus, you have everything of lasting value and no one can take him away from you. That's the truth!

PRAYER:

Righteous and triumphant God, King of the nations, thank you for the triumph that is mine in Jesus. I know your truth is liberating. I know your truth is powerful. Please give me the courage to trust that Word and build my life upon it. In Jesus' name I pray. Amen.

CONTEXT: JOHN 18:28-40

RELATED REFERENCES: JOHN 8:31-32; ROMANS 8:38-39; JOHN 17:17-19

Day: 323
CHOOSING THE CRIMINAL OVER THE CHRIST
JOHN 18:39-40

"But it is one of your customs for me to free one prisoner to you at the time of the Passover. Do you want me to free this 'king of the Jews'?" They shouted back, "No, not him! Let Barabbas go free!" (Barabbas was a rebel.)

REFLECTION:

At first glance, we look at the choice made by the people on this dark day and wonder how they could do it. However, when we take a long look at ourselves, we are struck by the many times we have chosen other things over Christ in our lives. In fact, that is what sin is—choosing something we want over the will and the work of Jesus! So today, let's be humbled and reminded how fickle we can be. One day, we are shouting hosannas and hallelujahs to Jesus. A few days later, we are choosing something totally opposite to Jesus. Let's not trade the Lordship of Christ in our lives for anything else, for that would be...criminal!

PRAYER:

Give me an undivided heart, O God, and help me follow my Lord Jesus Christ with passion and perseverance. Open my eyes to the many things that would distract me from my commitment to Christ. In Jesus' name I pray. Amen.

CONTEXT: JOHN 18:28-40

RELATED REFERENCES: MATTHEW 7:21-23; MATTHEW 6:19-24; JAMES 4:8

Day: 324
SCOURGED!

JOHN 19:1
Then Pilate ordered that Jesus be taken away and whipped.

REFLECTION:

Pilate believed Jesus was innocent, but had him whipped! The word for "whipped" here means "scourged." This was a political move for Pilate. It was torture for Jesus. Having your back beaten and chunks of skin ripped out with each splat of the lash with bits of metal, glass, and gravel was horrific punishment. Pilate thought it would appease the blood-lust of the mob. The goal of a scourging was leave a man near death, but not dead.

Pilate appears to have thought something like this: "Surely seeing Jesus this near death will be enough to appease this crazed mob?" It was not. Instead, scourging Jesus only the set the stage for worse tortures that would be inflicted upon him.

So often, we read about people who have been touched by a disaster or a catastrophe. Because we don't know these people, the reality of their suffering doesn't really register. However, Jesus knows their suffering and their pain! They are not just another faceless name on another casualty list to Jesus—they are very real people Jesus knows personally! And when we are that faceless unknown sufferer, we can be assured that our hardships and anguish matter to the One whom Pilate had flogged!

PRAYER:

Holy God, thank you that you know me. Thank you that you care personally for me and my pain, suffering, struggles, temptations, tragedies, hurts, illnesses, anxieties, wounds, and weariness. In a world where I often feel like a number, I thank you that I am always intimately and personally loved by you. I offer you my thanks in the name of the one who loved each person he met with a personal touch, Jesus. Amen.

CONTEXT: JOHN 19:1-15

RELATED REFERENCES: ISAIAH 53:4-6; LUKE 12:6-8; HEBREWS 10:32-36

Day: 325

CROWN OF MOCKERY

JOHN 19:2-3

The soldiers made a crown from thorny branches and put it on his head. Then they put a purple robe around him. They kept coming up to him and saying, "Hail to the king of the Jews!" And they hit him in the face.

REFLECTION:

"If you can't beat him, mock him." That might have been the slogan of the religious leaders who hated Jesus. A long night of mockery and torture is well underway. The people Jesus came to save are repeatedly, one group after another, rejecting him and sending him to his death on a cross.

This is not some token sort of pain. Scourging, beatings, long sharp thorns, and being hit with fists is only part of the journey of pain Jesus will face. The saddest part about this to me isn't Jesus' pain—although that is horrific enough. The saddest part to me is that Jesus is the rightful King come from heaven and they reject him unmercifully.

I wonder how many times God has presented me with a blessing or an opportunity which I've not only missed, but also criticized and ridiculed. Jesus is God's blessing to the people. So Jesus' mistreatment by those who were the most religious should humble those of us who consider ourselves to be spiritually committed today.

PRAYER:

Father, open my eyes and my heart so that I never reject your opportunities and blessings. I don't want my heart hard to your gracious work in the world and neither do I want to be harsh with those with whom I disagree or don't understand. Give me wisdom to pursue your will and to turn from pettiness and evil. In Jesus' name I pray. Amen.

CONTEXT: JOHN 19:1-15

RELATED REFERENCES: JAMES 1:12; REVELATION 3:10; MATTHEW 2:1-12

Day: 326
NOT GUILTY...AGAIN

JOHN 19:4

Again Pilate came out and said to the Jewish leaders, "Look! I am bringing Jesus out to you. I want you to know that I find nothing I can charge him with."

REFLECTION:

Pilate knows the truth, but can't bring himself to live by it! Jesus is innocent. He says it again and again. Only problem is, he won't live up to what he knows is true. For Christians, Pilate is a hideous and weak ruler, catering to the will of the mob rather than his conscience. Yet before we rake Pilate over the coals, let's be honest with ourselves about all the times we have not lived up to what we knew was right, honest, true, or honorable because we didn't want to go against the will of the crowd around us. Peer pressure isn't just a problem for teenagers. Peer pressure is Satan's tool to get us to abandon our commitment to righteousness and faithfulness. Even those in power become powerless when the acceptance of the crowd is more important than the truth of God.

PRAYER:

Forgive me, dear LORD my heavenly Father! I still struggle with knowing how to be courteous to those who oppose me while not caving in to the pressures around me to conform to worldly standards rather than holy standards. Please give me courage, wisdom, and a proper sense of timing to live with integrity and grace wherever your path for me may lead. Deliver me from making my decisions and determining my values based on the pressure of my culture and the acceptance of my peers. In Jesus' name. Amen.

CONTEXT: JOHN 19:1-15

RELATED REFERENCES: 1 PETER 3:13-17; LUKE 12:8-12; LUKE 6:22

Day: 327

I Find Him Not Guilty

JOHN 19:5-6

Then Jesus came out wearing the crown of thorns and the purple robe. Pilate said to the Jews, "Here is the man!" When the leading priests and the Jewish guards saw Jesus they shouted, "Kill him on a cross! Kill him on a cross!" But Pilate answered, "You take him and nail him to a cross yourselves. I find nothing I can charge him with."

REFLECTION:

"Not guilty!" That's the true verdict on Jesus. However, he assumes our guilt and sin on the Cross so that we can be freed from it. He dies as a sacrifice for our sins and the sins of the whole world so that everyone who truly comes to him can be declared "not guilty" before God. Praise God for his incredible grace and praise Jesus for his incredible sacrifice—the innocent Son of God sacrificed for the guilty people of the world!

PRAYER:

Father, I praise you and your Son for the incredible gifts of forgiveness and freedom from sin that are mine through Jesus bearing my sins on the Cross. May my life show that I appreciate these incredible gifts and that I take sin seriously enough to stay away from it. In Jesus' name I pray. Amen.

CONTEXT: JOHN 19:1-15

RELATED REFERENCES: 2 CORINTHIANS 5:17, 19, 21; COLOSSIANS 1:19-23; 1 JOHN 2:1-2

SON OF GOD

JOHN 19:7

The Jewish leaders answered, "We have a law that says he must die,
because he said he is the Son of God."

REFLECTION:

Some scholarly critics say Jesus never really claimed to be "Son of God." Jesus' opponents clearly felt he made that claim and accepted that title. A careful reading of the Gospels—Matthew, Mark, Luke, John—reveals that he did in several ways. Jesus often referred to God as his Father. He accepted the title "Son of God" without correction when others gave it to him, unless they were demon possessed. He answered yes to the question, "Are you the Son of God?" during his trial.

The Gospel of John wants us to make a decision about Jesus as Son of God. Is he a self-deluded crazy man or is he really God's Son. Those are our two choices and our lives should be built on our answer. If we don't choose the latter, then we assume the former. What's your choice? Who do you believe Jesus really is?

PRAYER:

Lord Jesus, I believe that you are the Son of God, that you left heaven to deliver me from sin and death, and that one day you will return to earth to take me home to your glory. Thank you! Amen.

CONTEXT: JOHN 19:1-15

RELATED REFERENCES: MATHEW 26:62-68; MARK 1:1; ROMANS 1:1-4

Day: 329

FRIGHTENED OR FEARLESS?

JOHN 19:8-9

When Pilate heard this, he was more afraid. So he went back inside the palace and asked Jesus, "Where are you from?" But Jesus did not answer him.

REFLECTION:

Pilate is trying to find a way out of dealing with Jesus. He knows Jesus is innocent, but can't appease the crowd. What if Jesus is who he says he is? How can he convict an innocent man? How can he keep his constituents happy?

Pilate loses his integrity unless he releases Jesus. Yet he can't release Jesus without infuriating the crowd. Jesus will not answer him because he refuses to be a pawn in Pilate's political game. He will follow the will of his Father and no one will deter his commitment to righteousness.

Facing a choice about Jesus' identity, Pilate the ruler shows fear, gives up his integrity, and becomes a prisoner to the fickle will of the mob. In the face of death, Jesus shows courage, displays integrity, and demonstrates the freedom to be who he is no matter the will of the crowd. The stark differences in their choices and character remind us of the importance of the choices we make about Jesus and the will of God.

In our lives we will be given many opportunities to do important things. We need to approach each of those decisions remembering that we will only choose to do them if we can be an influence for Jesus. If we choose to take a job or seize an opportunity that calls on us to sacrifice our commitment to Christ and to Kingdom living, then we are no better than Pilate.

PRAYER:

Righteous and holy God, what can I say to convey my thanks and appreciation of the terrible price paid for my sin? Thank you! Even more, please purify me and strengthen me. Open my eyes to help me make decisions that will not compromise my faith and my love for Jesus, my Savior, in whose name I pray. Amen.

CONTEXT: JOHN 19:1-15

RELATED REFERENCES: JOHN 10:14-18; 1 JOHN 2:1-2; MATTHEW 8:5-13

Day: 330

THE TRUTH ABOUT SIN

JOHN 19:10-11

Pilate said, "You refuse to speak to me? Remember, I have the power to make you free or to kill you on a cross." Jesus answered, "The only power you have over me is the power given to you by God. So the one who handed me over to you is guilty of a greater sin."

REFLECTION:

Sin clouds our thinking. Sin tempts us to overestimate our abilities. Then, sin ensnares us in its deceitful and deadly web of death. However, Jesus reminds us here that not all sin is the same.

Some folks have suggested that one sin is not greater than another because all sin separates us from God. While the latter part of that statement is true, the first isn't. While Pilate's weakness and pandering to the crowd is definitely sin, Jesus emphasizes that the sin of his own leaders was the greater sin. Sin matters to God—all sin and every sin matters to God! However, some sin involves influencing others to sin. Some sin—especially that of parents, Bible teachers, and leaders—gets replicated and passed on as a sin problem to coming genera-tions. Some sin involves our own bodies, the very temple of God through his Holy Spirit. Some sin involves others in our rebellion against God and influences them away from God's goodness.

So let's not be glib about sin. Rather, let's focus on doing what is right, saying what is true, and keeping our commitments to the God of all grace.

PRAYER:

O LORD, God of the heavens and of the earth, you are a great wonderful God, full of holiness and grace. Forgive me of my sin; I regret my rebellion. I ask you for your forgive-ness. I need the power of your Holy Spirit to both cleanse me and strengthen me as I seek to live for you. In Jesus' name. Amen.

CONTEXT: JOHN 19:1-15

RELATED REFERENCES: 1 JOHN 1:5-2:2; 1 CORINTHIANS 6:18-20; MATTHEW 18:5-6

Day: 331

WHAT HAPPENS WHEN YOU'RE PLEASING THE WRONG AUDIENCE

JOHN 19:12

After this, Pilate tried to let Jesus go free. But the Jewish leaders shouted, "Anyone who makes himself a king is against Caesar. So if you let this man go free, that means you are not Caesar's friend."

REFLECTION:

Who is Pilate trying to please, God or the masses? Who are the masses trying to please, themselves or God? Who are you trying to please, yourself, your peers, or your Savior?

Answering that last question is just as crucial for you as it was for the masses and for Pilate nearly two thousand years ago as Jesus stood before them. Who you are trying to please will either consecrate you or corrupt you!

PRAYER:

O Father in heaven, I have no idea how many days you have left for me to live. However, I do know that from today forward, I choose to live to please you and reflect your character and grace in my life. My heart's desire is to consciously make that same choice each day. Please guard my heart from evil, arrogance, selfishness, pride, deceit, lust, or any other corrupting force Satan might use to gain a stronghold in my life.
In Jesus' name I pray. Amen.

CONTEXT: JOHN 19:1-15

RELATED REFERENCES: DEUTERONOMY 24:14-15; EXODUS 20:2-3; 1 TIMOTHY 2:1-5

Day: 332
WE HAVE NO KING!?

JOHN 19:13-15

When Pilate heard this, he brought Jesus out to the place called "The Stone Pavement." (In Aramaic the name is "Gabbatha.") Pilate sat down on the judge's seat there. It was now almost noon on Preparation day of Passover week. Pilate said to the Jews, "Here is your king!" They shouted, "Take him away! Take him away! Kill him on a cross!" Pilate asked them, "Do you want me to kill your king on a cross?" The leading priests answered, "The only king we have is Caesar!"

REFLECTION:

God was Israel's true King. This was true even in these centuries when a human king sat on Israel's throne. So often back then, Israel chose to go with their human king and abandon their heavenly King. Once again, the leaders of God's people pull away from their heavenly King and pledge their loyalty to a secular king. Their actions are a warning of how easily we can be dissuaded from giving our complete loyalty to the only true Lord and King, Jesus.

PRAYER:

Almighty God, my precious and righteous Father, please keep my heart pure in its allegiance to you. I don't want to ever let anything or anyone lead me away from my loyalty to you. Forgive me for the past times when I've let other things distract my attention and distort my loyalty. Thank you, in Jesus' name. Amen.

CONTEXT: JOHN 19:1-15

RELATED REFERENCES: PSALM 2:1-8; PSALM 45:6-7; LUKE 1:32

Day: 333

BETWEEN TWO THIEVES

JOHN 19:16-18

So Pilate handed Jesus over to them to be killed on a cross. The soldiers took Jesus. He carried his own cross to a place called "The Place of the Skull." (In Aramaic the name of this place is "Golgotha.") There they nailed Jesus to the cross. They also nailed two other men to crosses. They put them on each side of Jesus with him in the middle.

REFLECTION:

Jesus came to earth to live among us and to pay the ransom price to buy us out of sin and death. So where should we expect to find him in his death? In between two sinners offering forgiveness and grace.

Jesus entered our world in humility as a baby placed in a manger. Jesus died in humiliation placed on a cross between two thieves. In between the two events, Jesus ministered, served, blessed, taught, and called all sorts of different people so that we could know that he wants to save, serve, and bless all of us.

No matter where you have been or what you have done, God wants you to know that Jesus' grace is close to you. If he was willing to die a humiliating death between two other men who were sentenced to death for their crimes, why wouldn't he be willing save you no matter where you are now or where you have been in the past. The Cross is our great assurance that Jesus came to save us!

PRAYER:

Father, thank you for showing me that you love everyone, even a sinner like me. I know that Jesus was perfect in every way; but in his death, between two sinners and before an angry mob, I can see that his love triumphs over this moment of horror and every sinful horror in my life. Thank you for your gracious love. Help me as I try to display that same love for those around me. In Jesus' name. Amen.

CONTEXT: JOHN 19:16-27

RELATED REFERENCES: 1 PETER 3:18; 2 CORINTHIANS 5:21; 1 JOHN 4:7-12

Day: 334
THAT MANY PEOPLE...

JOHN 19:19-22

Pilate told them to write a sign and put it on the cross. The sign said, "Jesus of Nazareth, the King of the Jews." The sign was written in Aramaic, in Latin, and in Greek. Many of the Jews read this sign, because the place where Jesus was nailed to the cross was near the city. The leading Jewish priests said to Pilate, "Don't write, 'The King of the Jews.' But write, 'This man said, I am the King of the Jews.'" Pilate answered, "I will not change what I have written."

REFLECTION:

The sign declaring Jesus to be the King of the Jews was written in Hebrew (language of faith and promise), Latin (language of the empire), and Greek (language of trade) so that many people could read it. It was originally written to ridicule Jesus, but it declared the real truth about him. So the Cross became a place where people understand God's truth, believe it, and then find life in the King it proclaims. Jesus wasn't just the Savior for the Jews, but for all people. So while dying outside the city like a "piece of criminal scum" was horrible, God used it to be the place where many people could see that his love could reach them and save them wherever they were.

PRAYER:

Loving Father, every time I think of the cost of the Cross, I am humbled that you would love me so much. Motivate me by this grace to share your love with others so that they, too, can find life in Jesus, in whose name I pray. Amen.

CONTEXT: JOHN 19:16-27

RELATED REFERENCES: JOHN 3:16-17; JOHN 12:32-33; 1 JOHN 2:1-2

Day: 335

THE GAMBLE

JOHN 19:23-24

After the soldiers nailed Jesus to the cross, they took his clothes and divided them into four parts. Each soldier got one part. They also took his tunic. It was all one piece of cloth woven from top to bottom. So the soldiers said to each other, "We should not tear this into parts. Let's throw lots to see who will get it." This happened to make clear the full meaning of what the Scriptures say, "They divided my clothes among them, and they threw lots for what I was wearing." So the soldiers did this.

REFLECTION:

There was a whole lot more gambling going on at the Cross than just the gamble for Jesus' seamless robe. Some gambled that their understanding was correct enough to put another man to death even though he did amazing things. Some gambled that Jesus was just another Jewish criminal being executed, never imagining they were putting nails in the hand of God himself. Others gambled that their mockery was justified and that they had a worthy target of their abusive words.

No one should look at the Cross and then reject it without realizing the awful gamble being made. If Jesus is the Son of God, then everything is completely different ... new ... clean ... holy because of what he did! He cannot be taken lightly. We dare not trifle with God's sacrificial love by just playing at being a Jesus follower. As Isaac Watts said it in the old hymn, *When I Survey the Wondrous Cross*, "Love so amazing, so divine, Demands my life, my soul, my all."

PRAYER:

I am simply amazed and stunned at your bold "risk" of love in Jesus. We, your human creatures, have often rejected your greatest gifts of love. How could you keep loving us so much, Father, that you would offer, and dare I say it, gamble for our souls with such a costly gift? I do not understand it, but I do believe it and I offer you my life, my love and my all because of it. In Jesus name I thank you and pledge my allegiance to you. Amen.

CONTEXT: JOHN 19:16-27

RELATED REFERENCES: JOHN 5:24; JOHN 14:6; JOHN 20:30-31

Day: 336
FAMILY AT THE FOOT OF THE CROSS
JOHN 19:25-27

Jesus' mother stood near his cross. Her sister was also standing there with Mary the wife of Clopas, and Mary Magdalene. Jesus saw his mother. He also saw the follower he loved very much standing there. He said to his mother, "Dear woman, here is your son." Then he said to the follower, "Here is your mother." So after that, this follower took Jesus' mother to live in his home.

REFLECTION:

We find our family at the foot of the Cross. Jesus' death brings us all together, destroying any and every barrier that would keep us from coming home and being family with each other. Jesus reminds us of this when he entrusts his mother to his beloved follower—whom we know as John. The Cross is where we commit to care for each other as family. Those who are family in the blood of Christ find their allegiance to each other trumps any other human allegiance. We make our family with those whose lives find their identity at the foot of the Cross of Jesus.

PRAYER:

Holy and righteous Father, make our church your real family as we look with each other at the Cross and what it should mean to us. Please make us more concerned with each other and more unified in our purpose as we all draw more closely to your Son Jesus, in whose name I pray. Amen.

CONTEXT: JOHN 19:16-27

RELATED REFERENCES: 1 JOHN 1:1-4; LUKE 8:21; ROMANS 8:15

FINISHED!

JOHN 19:28-30

Later, Jesus knew that everything had been done. To make the Scriptures come true he said, "I am thirsty." There was a jar full of sour wine there, so the soldiers soaked a sponge in it. They put the sponge on a branch of a hyssop plant and lifted it to Jesus' mouth. When he tasted the wine, he said, "It is finished." Then he bowed his head and died.

REFLECTION:

Jesus lived just a little over three decades. When he died, he declared his work "finished." I'm not sure that I can even say that about the work of one day at the end of the day, much less say it at the end of my life. I have a cartoon someone gave me that read, "I believe that God gives us all a certain amount of work we are to get done in our lifetime. At the rate I'm going, I figure I'm going to live another 110 years!"

Jesus' secret to completing his life's work was really pretty simple: he sought to please God with what he did rather than trying to make everyone else happy. Jesus accomplished what God sent him to do. How about us—you and me? With all we are trying to do, are we really focused on the main thing or are we being diminished by trying to do too many things? Let's live so that when our end is near, we can say, "It is finished!"

PRAYER:

Holy God and loving Father, help me to better know your will for me today so that I can accomplish the most important things and not just be involved running around trying to do many things. Please reveal to me more clearly the work you have for me to do; and then, dear Father, please give the courage and power through your Holy Spirit, the Helper Jesus promised to me, to do it. I want my work to be finished when my time has come to leave this earth and go home to you. In Jesus' name I pray. Amen.

CONTEXT: JOHN 19:28-42

RELATED REFERENCES: JOHN 4:34; JOHN 9:1-5; JOHN 13:1-5

Day: 338

BLINDED BY THE WRONG

JOHN 19:31

This day was Preparation day. The next day was a special Sabbath day. The Jewish leaders did not want the bodies to stay on the cross on the Sabbath day. So they asked Pilate to order that the legs of the men be broken. And they asked that the bodies be taken down from the crosses.

REFLECTION:

Have you ever caught yourself doing something awful and wrong just so you could carry out your sense of religious ritual? I fear that many of us have!

I can remember the time I came upon a car full of young Christian women who had run out of gas on the way to church. Hundreds had passed them, but none had offered to stop and help them. Ironically, they were all going to teach children's Bible classes, and most likely, some who passed by them were irritated that their child's teacher was late for class.

How about the service staff at places Christians eat on Sunday? Did you know that Sunday is the day most servers hate to work because "church people's" tips are low and they tend to be rude and more demanding and demeaning that non-church folks?

While comparing those two things with the request to speed up death for criminals by breaking their legs is a stretch, these events do remind us that we have huge blind spots about the confession of our faith and our living it. Jesus was adamant that we live our faith better than we talk it. How are you doing on that score? What one thing can you do to live the Gospel more fully today and the days ahead?

PRAYER:

Forgive me, dear Heavenly Father, for being a better religious talker than I am a Christ-like servant. Convict my heart of what I need to do and give me a soft and courageous heart to do it with boldness and grace. In Jesus' name I pray. Amen.

CONTEXT: JOHN 19:28-42

RELATED REFERENCES: MATTHEW 23:1-4; MATTHEW 7:21-27; MATTHEW 28:18-20

Day: 339
WATER AND BLOOD

JOHN 19:32-34

So the soldiers came and broke the legs of the two men on the crosses beside Jesus. But when the soldiers came close to Jesus, they saw that he was already dead. So they did not break his legs. But one of the soldiers stuck his spear into Jesus' side. Immediately blood and water came out.

REFLECTION:

"Blood and water came out." Jesus was dead when the soldier stabbed him with the spear. That's what the blood and water that flowed out of his side meant to the Romans. No need to break his legs. For Christians, the blood and water mean other things as well.

"Blood and water." The follower whom Jesus loved—and who wrote the Gospel of John—saw this come out of Jesus' side at the crucifixion. This blood and water are great reminders that Jesus was a real person who died a real death in a real body. He was part of our mortal existence. He did this for us.

"Blood and water." John reminded Christians that the blood, the water, and the Spirit are the great witnesses to Jesus (1 John 5:6-10). Jesus is God's Son because he has God's Spirit without limit—he both received the Spirit and he pours out his Spirit on those who become Christians. Jesus is God's Son because he submitted to baptism by John to fulfill all righteousness. Jesus is God's Son because he submitted to the Father's will on the Cross.

"Blood and water." We too become witnesses of Jesus' love when we share in baptism and the Lord's Supper. We participate in and share with Jesus in his death for us. We are caught up in the great story of redemption, forgiveness, sacrifice, love, and triumph.

PRAYER:

Almighty God, thank you for inviting me to be a witness to your great act of deliverance on the Cross by giving me baptism and the Lord's Supper as gifts to share in the Cross. Thank you for Jesus' sacrificial love that took him to the Cross to die for my sins. In Jesus' name I pray. Amen.

CONTEXT: JOHN 19:28-42

RELATED REFERENCES: 1 JOHN 5:6-9; 1 JOHN 4:9-10; ROMANS 4:20-25

Day: 340

A WITNESS SO WE CAN BELIEVE

JOHN 19:35-37

(The one who saw this happen has told about it. He told about it so that you also can believe. The things he says are true. He knows that he tells the truth.) These things happened to give full meaning to the Scriptures that said, "None of his bones will be broken" and "People will look at the one they stabbed."

REFLECTION:

Our faith is built on the eyewitness accounts of those who saw Jesus daily and told his story at great personal cost. Our faith is built on the trustworthiness of God, who is faithful to fulfill his promises. Our faith is built on the love of Jesus to die for our sins. Our faith is built on the promise of Scriptures that were fulfilled in Jesus' life and ministry.

We don't believe out of blind hope or because of a broken psyche desperately in need of some magical fix. While the human condition is sick beyond human repair, our faith in a heavenly solution is rooted in God, who became flesh and walked in our world and died our kind of death to give us his kind of life.

The changes in ordinary men and women who watched that life are part of the chorus of testimony on which we build our faith. Believing in Jesus as the Son of God may be a leap of faith, but it is not a blind leap! It is a leap based on the testimony of witnesses who had seen his life and found their lives changed and enriched in the process.

PRAYER:

Father, I know that even my faith is a gift of your grace. I thank you that this faith is not something I have had to do on my own. I thank you for a heritage of faith found in the long line of people who have shared the story of Jesus with me. I thank you that this heritage goes all the way back to men and women who ate, talked, and witnessed the life and death of Jesus. Even more, I thank you that this story doesn't end in their witness to his death, but in his resurrection. I thank you for the faith handed down to me. I pray that I may share it and pass it on to others. In Jesus' name. Amen.

CONTEXT: JOHN 19:28-42

RELATED REFERENCES: LUKE 1:1-4; ACTS 1:1-7; MATTHEW 10:18

Day: 341

FEAR LOSES OUT TO LOVE

JOHN 19:38

Later, a man named Joseph from Arimathea asked Pilate for the body of Jesus. (Joseph was a follower of Jesus, but he did not tell anyone, because he was afraid of the Jewish leaders.) Pilate said Joseph could take Jesus' body, so he came and took it away.

REFLECTION:

Fear has incredible power over us. Fear can paralyze us into inaction. Fear can make us uncertain about what steps to take. Fear can make us pull away from a friendship. Fear has incredible power to destroy our integrity and our fortitude. However, fear loses out ultimately to love. Love has a power over us to move us and motivate in ways that fear cannot. Joseph had strong reasons to fear being identified with Jesus in his death, but this time love won out over his fear.

Are you not sure if your faith can stand up to the fear of rejection? Are you not certain you can face ridicule and ostracism because you are a follower of Christ? Working on your courage is not nearly as important as seeking to know Jesus in your life. After all, that's why John wrote this gospel—so all of us who are like Joseph would come to love Jesus for what he did for us and be emboldened by that love to do what courage cannot do and fear cannot stop. Learn to love Jesus for what he did for you ... for what he is doing with you ... and what he will do in you! And when you doubt or worry, look at Jesus on the Cross giving himself to bring you to God. When you see his love and you respond with love for him, you will find fear on the retreat.

PRAYER:

O Father, God of the heavens and King over all, please help me know Jesus more passionately through your Word and in my daily life. Fill my heart with love for him by the power of the Holy Spirit. I pray this in the name of Jesus. Amen.

CONTEXT: JOHN 19:28-42

RELATED REFERENCES: JOHN 20:30-31; 1 JOHN 5:11-13; 2 PETER 1:2-4

Day: 342
AT THE WORST TIME POSSIBLE
JOHN 19:39-40

Nicodemus went with Joseph. He was the man who had come to Jesus before and talked to him at night. He brought about 100 pounds of spices—a mixture of myrrh and aloes. These two men took Jesus' body and wrapped it in pieces of linen cloth with the spices. (This is how the Jews bury people.)

REFLECTION:

Jesus had promised that the Cross on which he would be "lifted up" would be the power that would draw all sorts of people to him in faith (John 12:32). For Nicodemus, the Cross was the deciding moment, just as Jesus had told him (John 3:14-15).

The Cross was the worst possible time for Nicodemus to identify with Jesus. After all, Jesus was a criminal in the eyes of Roman and Jewish authorities, a false messiah rejected by the Jews, and a dead body that could only make Nicodemus unclean. Yet Nicodemus steps forward and helps do the loving work of burial preparation—something only a family member normally did. It was also political suicide. It rendered Nicodemus unclean for the Passover ritual that began that evening. It identified him as one of Jesus' followers when he could possibly be put into prison, or worse. Yet the Cross has such power! Power enough to melt the heart and build the courage of one man who had everything to lose. Yet Nicodemus stepped out of the shadows of his life into the Light of Jesus. The Cross has great power when we really understand what happened there for us.

PRAYER:

Father, thank you for the touching story of Nicodemus who came with questions to Jesus at night and found his answers at the Cross. Please teach me those same answers and give me that same dedication to the crucified Lord. In Jesus' name I pray. Amen.

CONTEXT: JOHN 19:28-42

RELATED REFERENCES: JOHN 3:15; JOHN 7:45-52; JOHN 8:28

LAID TO REST

JOHN 19:41-42

In the place where Jesus was killed on the cross, there was a garden. In the garden there was a new tomb. No one had ever been buried there before. The men put Jesus in that tomb because it was near, and the Jews were preparing to start the Sabbath day.

REFLECTION:

There are few things harder than leaving a loved one at the grave in which they will be buried. Walking away leaves such a sense of finality and loss. Can you imagine the heartbreak of Joseph and Nicodemus as they leave Jesus' body at this place of death? How many shattered dreams and hopes did they place in that tomb with the one they hoped was Israel's Savior?

Gather it into your heart; Jesus died and was placed in a borrowed tomb! Jesus, who was God come in human flesh, is claimed by the mortality that will claim each of us. What unbelievable love for God to share our mortal plight in such a personal way! Yet he did. And John's telling of the story—especially for those who shared Jesus' first century culture—is so simple and real and down to earth. Think of the key words and phrases that go with Jesus' death: nails, wood, gambled, clothes, thirsty, mother, son, legs, spear, blood, water, spices, linen cloth, and tomb. God came to our world in every way. How can we ever thank him enough?

PRAYER:

Thank you, dear God, that you would have Jesus not only die for my sins, but that he would also share my human existence. The very thought of all this boggles my mind and fills my heart with wonder, awe, and appreciation. In Jesus' name. Amen.

CONTEXT: JOHN 19:28-42

RELATED REFERENCES: 1 CORINTHIANS 15:3-8; COLOSSIANS 2:12; ROMANS 6:4

Day: 344

SUNDAY SHAKE UP

JOHN 20:1-2

Early on Sunday morning, while it was still dark, Mary Magdalene went to the tomb. She saw that the large stone was moved away from the entrance. So she ran to Simon Peter and the other follower (the one Jesus loved very much). She said, "They have taken the Lord out of the tomb, and we don't know where they put him."

REFLECTION:

Ever have one of those Sunday's when you didn't feel like doing the "church thing" and facing the challenges of getting everyone ready? Most of us have! In fact, some of my hardest mornings have come on Sunday.

This was true of Jesus' earliest and most faithful followers, too. They came very early in the morning to fulfill a very loving commitment; they came to anoint Jesus' dead body with spices. There are no words to describe how hard this must have been for them—their spirits were crushed and their dreams were dashed by the death of Jesus. Yet like so many of us and our bad-start Sundays, God turned their hard morning into something precious and joyful and they experienced it first because of their loving faithfulness to Jesus.

Their Sunday started with hopelessness and a hard task. But, we know how it ended. Jesus was raised! Hopes were restored. Joy came back to grief-filled hearts. So on your bad-start Sunday mornings, remember Mary, Peter, and the follower whom Jesus loved. Remind yourself how their bad Sunday turned into a day of great joy that no believer will ever forget!

PRAYER:

Father, thank you for the hard times. I confess that I don't like them, but I see where you have used those tough times to bring blessing, hope, and triumph from my heartache and defeat. Thank you for not only raising Jesus from the dead, but for raising my heart to a place of hope and joy. Help me remember that bad-start Sunday mornings are just the place that Jesus chooses to appear and make his glory known. In Jesus name, and because of Jesus' victory, I pray with joy. Amen.

CONTEXT: JOHN 20:1-18

RELATED REFERENCES: JAMES 1:2-4; ROMANS 8:28-30; REVELATION 1:9-17

Day: 345

CONFUSION TO CONVICTION

JOHN 20:3-8

So Peter and the other follower started going to the tomb. They were both running, but the other follower ran faster than Peter and reached the tomb first. He bent down and looked in. He saw the pieces of linen cloth lying there, but he did not go in. Then Simon Peter finally reached the tomb and went in. He saw the pieces of linen lying there. He also saw the cloth that had been around Jesus' head. It was folded up and laid in a different place from the pieces of linen. Then the other follower went in—the one who had reached the tomb first. He saw what had happened and believed.

REFLECTION:

So often we need the support of a friend to do that next necessary thing. That's a big reason why the church got together on Sunday in the early church. They remembered that first great Sunday and how important it is to stick together and remain faithful to Jesus.

On this Sunday, Peter and the follower whom Jesus loved (presumably John) alternated taking the next needed step in this story. Peter takes off for the tomb, followed by John. John outruns Peter, but doesn't go in the tomb. Peter goes into the tomb and sees. John goes in and sees, then believes.

We need each other. Not just for the times of joyous praise, but also for times of weakness, confusion, and distress. Sometimes, maybe even often times, we can't take the next step on our own and we need the help of a brother or sister in Christ. Please, don't try to do the Christian life as solo flight. We need each other to make it to the risen Lord with faith and to live vibrantly for him!

PRAYER:

Holy God, my heavenly Father, thank you for the friends I have who have faithfully encouraged me and nudged me further down the walk of faith and have often taken that next step to help me get to Jesus. Help me be that friend to others so that they, too, can encounter the risen Savior and believe. In Jesus' name I pray. Amen.

CONTEXT: JOHN 20:1-18

RELATED REFERENCES: MATTHEW 18:20; ECCLESIASTES 4:9-12; PROVERBS 27:17

Day: 346

THEY WENT HOME?

JOHN 20:9-10

(These followers did not yet understand from the Scriptures that Jesus must rise from death.) Then the followers went back home.

REFLECTION:

John and Peter have made the most amazing discovery in the history of the universe and what do they do? They go home! They go home? Why didn't they go out into the streets of Jerusalem and shout the news? Why didn't they tell everyone within earshot that Jesus was alive again? I'm not sure, but there is something powerful and centering about what they did: "they went home" to try to make sense of it all.

Our faith must be lived and shared at home. We must try to make sure it works there, is demonstrated there, and is shared there. Faith must work with the people who know us, know our hearts, and know our disappointments. The Gospel always starts where we are and radiates out. So in the face of great things that we may not always fully understand, let's go back home and start from there!

PRAYER:

Lord God Almighty, please help my influence and my character at home to be a blessing to my family. Help them see the power of the resurrected Lord in what I do, what I say, and how I treat them. Give me the influence and the integrity to inspire faith among those I love. In Jesus' name I pray. Amen.

CONTEXT: JOHN 20:1-18

RELATED REFERENCES: DEUTERONOMY 6:4-9; MARK 5:19; MATTHEW 8:13

Day: 347
MY LORD!

JOHN 20:11-13

But Mary stood outside the tomb, crying. While she was crying, she bent down and looked inside the tomb. She saw two angels dressed in white sitting where Jesus' body had been. One was sitting where the head had been; the other was sitting where the feet had been. The angels asked Mary, "Woman, why are you crying?" Mary answered, "They took away the body of my Lord, and I don't know where they put him."

REFLECTION:

"Some people have taken away the body of my Lord." Ponder that sentence a moment. Try to imagine how Mary would have said it. So much painful emotion crystallized into one short sentence. But notice how the sentence ends: "my Lord!"

What would make you surrender your faith in Jesus as Lord? One of the things I have always appreciated about Mary Magdalene is her determination to hang on to Jesus in the middle of her sorrow, confusion, and loss. Jesus may be dead, but to her, Jesus is still her Lord.

Often we qualify our faith in Jesus' lordship based upon our outward circumstances. If things aren't going well, we question why he is ignoring us and our prayers. When disaster strikes, some struggle to still believe in the Lord. Let's remember Mary at this moment of confusion. She has nothing left to gain from Jesus. She is clearly not expecting him to be raised from the dead—she is bringing spices to anoint a dead body! Yet Mary did not let go of the central truth of her life: Jesus was her Lord. Let's follow her example and hang on tenaciously to the conviction that Jesus is Lord even when—and maybe especially when—we don't understand what is happening in our lives.

PRAYER:

Father, I do believe that your Jesus, my Savior, is Lord. Strengthen me by the power of your Spirit so that I never relinquish that conviction no matter what the circumstances of my life may suggest. In Jesus' glorious name I pray. Amen.

CONTEXT: JOHN 20:1-18

RELATED REFERENCES: PHILIPPIANS 2:5-11; ROMANS 10:9-13; ACTS 2:36-39

MARY!

JOHN 20:14-16

When Mary said this, she turned around and saw Jesus standing there. But she did not know that it was Jesus. He asked her, "Woman, why are you crying? Who are you looking for?" She thought that this was the man who takes care of the garden. So she said to him, "Did you take him away, sir? Tell me where you put him. I will go and get him." Jesus said to her, "Mary." She turned toward him and said in Aramaic, "Rabboni." (This means "Teacher.")

REFLECTION:

Jesus had said,"The sheep listen to the voice of the Shepherd. The shepherd calls his own sheep, using their names..." (John 10:3). Indeed, they do. While Mary did not recognize Jesus at first, as soon as he said her name, she knew!

Jesus promised that one of these days he will say each of our names and we will rise to meet him and go home to live with him forever (John 5:28-29; 1 Thes. 4:13-18). Our assurance of this future is rooted in what happened here to Mary—her Lord died, was buried, was raised and has given each of us the promise of life with him forever.

PRAYER:

Almighty God, how can I thank you for such a wonderful hope! Thank you for Mary, whose faith held firm through her sorrow, despair, and confusion. Thank you for her experience, which helps me anticipate the day when Jesus will say my name and I will see him face to face. In the glorious name of my Lord and Savior, Jesus Christ, I pray. Amen.

CONTEXT: JOHN 20:1-18

RELATED REFERENCES: JOHN 5:24-25; 1 THESSALONIANS 4:13-18; MATTHEW 11:2-5

Day: 349

DON'T CLING, GO TELL

JOHN 20:17-18

Jesus said to her, "You don't need to hold on to me! I have not yet gone back up to the Father. But go to my followers and tell them this: 'I am going back to my Father and your Father. I am going back to my God and your God.'" Mary Magdalene went to the followers and told them, "I saw the Lord!" And she told them what he had said to her.

REFLECTION:

One of the biggest tasks we have as Jesus' followers is to not hold on too tightly to Jesus—by that, I mean we are not to cocoon ourselves in our churches and in the presence of Jesus-related stuff—at the expense of going to tell others about him. We have a message of hope and a never-ending life to share with others who are trapped in hopelessness, despair, and death. As followers, we are not to spend the majority of our time in holy pep rallies, but we are to enter the world, touching its hurt and offering it hope in Jesus. Jesus accompanies us when we go share that message and go serve those who are broken just as much as he does when we meet together as his people. So let's get out there and give others his message in word and deed.

PRAYER:

Father, forgive me for being part of a watered down faith that spends so much time on sharing Jesus with itself and avoids entering the world to serve as Jesus served and to show that Jesus is alive today by our actions. Help me share Jesus' message with those around me—not arrogantly or self-righteously, but with genuine concern and through authentic service. In Jesus' name, and for Jesus sake, I pray. Amen.

CONTEXT: JOHN 20:1-18

RELATED REFERENCES: MATTHEW 18:20; MATTHEW 25:31-40; MATTHEW 28:18-20

Day: 350

FROM FEAR TO JOY!

JOHN 20:19-20

The day was Sunday, and that same evening the followers were together. They had the doors locked because they were afraid of the Jewish leaders. Suddenly, Jesus was standing there among them. He said, "Peace be with you!" As soon as he said this, he showed them his hands and his side. When the followers saw the Lord, they were very happy.

REFLECTION:

What a roller coaster weekend it had been for Jesus' followers. He was arrested, tried, and executed. They had eaten the Last Supper with him and then abandoned him in his hour of need. They had been marked as wanted men—associates of a crucified criminal rebel, they had huddled in a locked room in fear for their lives. They heard rumors that Jesus was alive, but couldn't quite grasp it with solid faith because it was outside their experience or even hope. Then suddenly, he was among them.

They heard his voice and were both comforted and thrilled with his familiar greeting, "Shalom!" They saw the marks on his body of his crucifixion and yet there he was among them. Suddenly, joy rushed in and forced out every other emotion. The Lord is alive! I see him with my eyes! He lives! And because he lives, so can we!

PRAYER:

O God, my Father, thank you for the assurance of life I have as your child. Thank you for my Savior and Lord, who also claims me as my older brother. I look forward so much to the day when I will see him, and you dear Father, face to face. Until that day, please know that I will build my life on the power of my risen Lord, Jesus, in whose name I pray. Amen.

CONTEXT: JOHN 20:19-31

RELATED REFERENCES: HEBREWS 2:11-15; 1 JOHN 3:1-2; 1 PETER 1:8-9

Day: 351

PEACE FROM PASSION

JOHN 20:21

Then Jesus said again, "Peace be with you. It was the Father who sent me, and I am now sending you in the same way."

REFLECTION:

So often in our times, peace is defined as a selfish retreat from the world. Jesus calls us to find our peace, real peace, in him—a peace rooted in his defeat of death and his presence in us through his Holy Spirit. That peace should restore our passion to do the work of Jesus and to be sent by him into the world to bless it with his grace.

PRAYER:

Father, please restore my passion to touch the lost and broken around me with the grace of Jesus. Give me the peace of your dear Son so that I, too, can be sent to bless a fractured world. In Jesus' name I pray. Amen.

CONTEXT: JOHN 20:19-31

RELATED REFERENCES: MATTHEW 28:18-20; ACTS 1:4-8; COLOSSIANS 1:28-29

Day: 352

THE SPIRIT'S POWER TO FORGIVE

JOHN 20:22-23

Then he breathed on them and said, "Receive the Holy Spirit. If you forgive the sins of anyone, their sins are forgiven. If there is anyone whose sins you don't forgive, their sins are not forgiven."

REFLECTION:

Jesus ties personal forgiveness of others to our own forgiveness in the Lord's Prayer. Here, he reminds us that the Holy Spirit was crucial in giving the gift of forgiveness in the church setting. Clearly part of the work of the Spirit in this context is discernment and authority to forgive as God's community. However, the Spirit, who forms Christ in us and brings to maturity spiritual fruit in us, is crucial in our power to forgive. So our prayer probably should be that the Lord continue to fill us, to guide us, to lead us, and to transform us by his Spirit so that we can truly be his agents of redemption, reconciliation, and grace.

PRAYER:

Father in heaven, glorious and mighty, please forgive my sins as I am forgiving the sins of those who have wronged me. In Jesus' name. Amen.

CONTEXT: JOHN 20:19-31

RELATED REFERENCES: MATTHEW 18:21-22; EPHESIANS 4:29-32; MATTHEW 6:14-15

Day: 353

SOMEONE TO DOUBT FOR US?

JOHN 20:24-25

Thomas (called Didymus) was one of the twelve, but he was not with the other followers when Jesus came. They told him, "We saw the Lord." Thomas said, "That's hard to believe. I will have to see the nail holes in his hands, put my finger where the nails were, and put my hand into his side. Only then will I believe it."

REFLECTION:

Some churches don't want you to ask honest questions. That's sad. For most us, after we are Christians awhile, we kind of get trained to know which questions to ask and which ones to let go.

This is where new Christians can be so refreshing. They ask bold and honest questions. They're not afraid to seek the Lord and find his answers. Thomas is our designated doubter. His doubts and questions enable our doubts to be expressed and to receive an answer from the Lord himself. Let's be careful not to squash honest and seeking questions. Of course our goal isn't the question, but an authentic faith in the Lord who is the answer to our questions!

PRAYER:

Father, stir my heart to continue to seek after you. I want to know more about you and I also want to be more aware of your presence in my life. I want my character to be more completely conformed to your will. Father, you know that my doubts and questions are my seeking you and not a desire for some random tidbit of knowledge. Give me the Spirit of revelation to know you more completely so that I might be transformed by your will rather than being conformed to the culture around me. In Jesus' name I pray. Amen.

CONTEXT: JOHN 20:19-31

RELATED REFERENCES: MATTHEW 7:7-8; EPHESIANS 1:15-17; ROMANS 12:1-2

Day: 354

MY LORD AND MY GOD

JOHN 20:26-28

A week later the followers were in the house again, and Thomas was with them. The doors were locked, but Jesus came and stood among them. He said, "Peace be with you!" Then he said to Thomas, "Put your finger here. Look at my hands. Put your hand here in my side. Stop doubting and believe." Thomas said to Jesus, "My Lord and my God!"

REFLECTION:

What is our reaction to the resurrected Lord? Who are we to understand Jesus to be? What is his role in our lives? Thomas gives us the words and the attitude, "My Lord and my God!" Now it is our turn to make them true in our own lives!

PRAYER:

Lord God Almighty, come in human flesh as Jesus, I praise you for your love, mercy, power, and grace. I bow down before you and offer you my life, my future, and my time to your glory. Amen.

CONTEXT: JOHN 20:19-31

RELATED REFERENCES: TITUS 2:11-14; JOHN 1:1-3; JOHN 5:17-21

Day: 355

WE'RE BLESSED!

JOHN 20:29

Jesus said to him, "You believe because you see me. There are great blessings for the people who believe without seeing me!"

REFLECTION:

One of the things I love about the Gospel of John is that we get to see Jesus specifically thinking about us—those of us who believe *after* the first generation of followers. We believe, but without having seen. We must trust the testimony of those who did. We have to look at their changed lives after Jesus' resurrection as our starting point.

Today, we can take great comfort that Jesus looked beyond the horizon of the first generation of believers. He saw those of us who would later believe without having seen him alive both before and after his crucifixion. As the Savior looks down through the generations of believers to us, his blessing still holds true: "Those people that believe without seeing me will be truly blessed."

PRAYER:

Thank you, Lord Jesus, for thinking of our generation and our challenge to believe in your resurrection. Thank you for offering us your blessing. We thank you for the ways you minister to us at God's right hand as our exalted Lord. May we, your Church, more fully demonstrate your character and your compassion as we live as your presence in the world. Amen.

CONTEXT: JOHN 20:19-31

RELATED REFERENCES: JOHN 17:20-21; 1 PETER 1:3-9; MATTHEW 18:15-20

FOR LIFE!

JOHN 20:30-31

Jesus did many other miraculous signs that his followers saw, which are not written in this book. But these are written so that you can believe that Jesus is the Christ, the Son of God. Then, by believing, you can have life through his name.

REFLECTION:

Clearly, a biography of Jesus would be more full and complete. John was guided by the Spirit. He wrote to produce faith and so he chose his material carefully. His Gospel is very different from Matthew, Mark, and Luke who all use a similar outline, John gives us a deeper glimpse at a few of Jesus' conversations. He focuses in depth on his interactions with a few people. He doesn't give us many miracles, but instead concentrates on a few signs. Why?

John wrote to help us believe in Jesus as the Christ (Messiah) and the Son of God. He knew that if we were to find life, it would be in Jesus! Sometime soon, sit down with the Gospel of John and read the whole Gospel at one sitting. As you do, ask God to enrich and deepen your faith in Jesus and your relationship with Jesus. I do think you will find all of your life blessed in the process!

PRAYER:

Father, I do believe that Jesus is your Son, Israel's Messiah, and my Lord. Draw me closer to him, both in terms of his abiding presence within me and also in terms of my service to others in his name. Through your Spirit, conform me more closely to the character and nature of your Son. By the authority and in the name of Jesus I pray. Amen.

CONTEXT: JOHN 20:19-31

RELATED REFERENCES: JOHN 3:16-17; ROMANS 10:9-13; ACTS 2:36-41

Day: 357

BY THE FAMILIAR SEA

JOHN 21:1

Later, Jesus showed himself again to his followers by Lake Galilee.
This is how it happened:

REFLECTION:

Jesus appears to his followers again, this time in a very familiar place—the Sea of Galilee. For several of the apostles, this was the place they had fished, lived, collected taxes, and built their lives. This was also the place Jesus had found them and captured their hearts. In many ways, at this very familiar place, Jesus would rekindle their sense of mission and ministry just like he had at first.

Do you have a place where the Lord has been very real to you in the past? A familiar place where you have met him in quiet time or he has touched you in some way? If not, I hope you will work to find such a place. If so, I would encourage you to go back to that place from time to time and let him renew, restore, and recall you to your life's mission and ministry!

PRAYER:

Holy and righteous God, my heavenly Father, stir in me a holy passion to serve and honor you. I cannot manufacture that passion on my own, but I need the power of your Spirit and a deeper sense of your continuing presence in my life. Give me spiritual discernment so I can more clearly see the direction you are calling me to serve you. In Jesus' name.
Amen.

CONTEXT: JOHN 21:1-14

RELATED REFERENCES: MARK 1:35-39; 1 PETER 2:9-10; COLOSSIANS 1:28-29

WHAT TO DO?

JOHN 21:2-3

Some of the followers were together—Simon Peter, Thomas (called Didymus), Nathanael from Cana in Galilee, the two sons of Zebedee, and two other followers. Simon Peter said, "I am going out to fish." The other followers said, "We will go with you." So all of them went out and got into the boat. They fished that night but caught nothing.

REFLECTION:

What do you do when you don't know what to do? The followers weren't really sure what they were supposed to do with the resurrected Jesus. This response was to be expected; after all, none of them had ever had a friend rise from the dead and Jesus hadn't told them about their ongoing mission.

Two things, however, are crucial in their response. First, they hung together. They knew they were bound together by something, and Someone, very significant. So they didn't let go of each other. Second, they stayed in Galilee near the Sea —a familiar place and also the place Jesus told them to go after his resurrection.

In other words, when all else fails, and you're not sure what to do, stick with other believers and obey the Lord's clear instructions. Doesn't sound very fancy, but it was the key for the followers meeting Jesus and being called to the next level of mission with him.

PRAYER:

Father, I confess that I often want things to be spectacular, exciting, and inspiring. Yet I know that so often my sense of your presence and my most effective ministry occurs when I go do the next right thing I'm supposed to do, especially if that next thing involves being with your people. Give me a heart of obedience and a passion to be with your people as I listen for your call in my life. In Jesus' name I pray. Amen.

CONTEXT: JOHN 21:1-14

RELATED REFERENCES: JOHN 14:15-23; JOHN 6:61-69; JOHN 8:31-32

Day: 359

THE GIFT AT DAWN

JOHN 21:4-7

Early the next morning Jesus stood on the shore. But the followers did not know it was Jesus. Then he said to them, "Friends, have you caught any fish?" They answered, "No." He said, "Throw your net into the water on the right side of your boat. You will find some fish there." So they did this. They caught so many fish that they could not pull the net back into the boat. The follower Jesus loved very much said to Peter, "That man is the Lord!" When Peter heard him say it was the Lord, he wrapped his coat around himself. (He had taken his clothes off to work.) Then he jumped into the water.

REFLECTION:

For the followers of Jesus this day, dawn was the end of a hard and discouraging night. A night of work and no fish! Dawn broke and they knew the night had been a waste. They were going to shore empty handed, embarrassed, tired, and hungry.

Then Jesus gave them a great surprise gift: an enormous catch of fish and a breakfast on the beach with their risen Lord. Peter was a fisherman. Jesus had called Peter with a large catch of fish. Jesus will call Peter to ministry again with a large catch of fish. But most significant at this point in the story, a fisherman gets one of his biggest catches of fish ever, but leaves it behind as nothing for the sheer joy of being in the presence of his risen Lord. Peter left it all behind to be with Jesus! What is holding you back?

PRAYER:

Father, I know that you want to be God of all of my life. You want me to recognize that all I have is from you and given to me by you to do your work in the world. I confess to you, dear Father, that there are some things that I hold on to tightly. I don't offer to you for your work as freely as I should. Help me to surrender all that I have and all that I am to you, so that you can more fully use me to do your work in the world through me. In Jesus' name I pray. Amen.

CONTEXT: JOHN 21:1-14

RELATED REFERENCES: LUKE 5:1-11; MARK 8:34; MATTHEW 8:18-22

Day: 360

PETER AND THE OTHERS

JOHN 21:8-11

The other followers went to shore in the boat. They pulled the net full of fish. They were not very far from shore, only about 100 yards. When they stepped out of the boat and onto the shore, they saw a fire of hot coals. There were fish on the fire and some bread there too. Then Jesus said, "Bring some of the fish that you caught." Simon Peter got into the boat and pulled the net to the shore. It was full of big fish—153 of them! But even with that many fish, the net did not tear.

REFLECTION:

I'm one of the other followers, aren't you? In the Kingdom of God, work gets done because there are two types of servants. Some servants of God are superstars—they are bold, extravagant, and talented. They do what many of us would like to do, yet they do it to serve the King of Glory. Some servants are also like the other followers in this story—they do the tedious, hard, difficult jobs that get taken for granted while the superstars get all the notice.

Jesus confronted the "superstar" (Peter) in this story and gently humbled him as he challenged him to direct his leadership to be more pastoral, more encouraging and less self-aggrandizing. But, it takes both types in the Kingdom for great work to get done. We need passionate and bold "out front" people and we need hardworking "behind the scenes" people if the lost of the world are going to be brought safely home. Whichever kind of person you tend to be, please know you are needed, wanted, and vital for the work of the Kingdom!

PRAYER:

Father, I offer myself, my talents, my gifts, my treasure, my time, and my future to you. Please use me to your glory and the benefit of your Kingdom. Take my personality and my interests and use them effectively. Take my job and my hobbies and use them as tools to influence others. I want to be used by you in work that matters to others eternally. In Jesus name. Amen.

CONTEXT: JOHN 21:1-14

RELATED REFERENCES: 1 PETER 4:10-11; EPHESIANS 4:4-7, 11-13; ROMANS 12:6-8

Day: 361
JESUS SERVED THEM

JOHN 21:12-14

Jesus said to them, "Come and eat." None of the followers would ask him, "Who are you?" They knew he was the Lord. Jesus walked over to get the bread and gave it to them. He also gave them the fish. This was now the third time Jesus showed himself to his followers after he was raised from death.

REFLECTION:

Here is the resurrected Lord, the King of Glory, and he is preparing breakfast for his followers. How fitting! Jesus didn't come to be served, but to serve. His leadership was courageous and bold, but always filled with compassion and practical service.

This is our hero, and in his moment of glory, he is the servant to those who failed him. Bosses may get a lot out of workers, but servant leaders put a lot into workers so that the work gets done and the workers are blessed. No one has to question their leadership, because those who follow servant leaders are sure of it!

PRAYER:

Father, if your Son and my Lord could serve those that disappointed him, then so can I. If Jesus can serve when he is powerful and glorious, then so should I. So, dear Father, use me as a servant and convict me when I am not. In Jesus' name I pray. Amen.

CONTEXT: JOHN 21:1-14

RELATED REFERENCES: MARK 10:41-45; LUKE 22:24-27; JOHN 13:1-5

Day: 362

THE THIRD TIME

JOHN 21:15-17

When they finished eating, Jesus said to Simon Peter, "Simon, son of John, do you love me more than these other men love me?" Peter answered, "Yes, Lord, you know that I love you." Then Jesus said to him, "Take care of my lambs." Again Jesus said to him, "Simon, son of John, do you love me?" Peter answered, "Yes, Lord, you know that I love you." Then Jesus said, "Take care of my sheep." A third time Jesus said, "Simon, son of John, do you love me?" Peter was sad because Jesus asked him three times, "Do you love me?" He said, "Lord, you know everything. You know that I love you!" Jesus said to him, "Take care of my sheep."

REFLECTION:

Do you think Peter heard the rooster crow again when Jesus asked him the question the third time? Three times he denied his Lord by a charcoal fire. Three times beside another charcoal fire his Lord asks Peter about the genuineness of his love.

Jesus was creative and sensitive, but he was also determined—Peter had to face his failure. So Jesus confronts him three times. Peter had claimed that his dedication was stronger than the rest. Jesus asks him if he still claims to love his Lord more than the rest. Peter claimed that he would never deny his Lord, but he did so three times. Jesus' loving confrontation of Peter wasn't about shaming Peter, but about reclaiming him. Peter had to face his failure, so Jesus asked him three times. Jesus also reaffirms Peter's call to ministry three times.

Have you failed the Lord? Don't despair. He can and will use you if you will be open about your failure and let him "re-call" you to ministry and service.

PRAYER:

Father, forgive me for my failures, sin, and moments of unfaithfulness. Restore me to your service, renew me in my passion for holiness, and rekindle me with your Spirit. I want to honor and serve you always. In Jesus' name. Amen.

CONTEXT: JOHN 21:15-25

RELATED REFERENCES: PSALM 51:1-3, 7-13; PSALM 32:1-4; JAMES 5:16

Day: 363
FOLLOW ME

JOHN 21:18-19

"The truth is, when you were young, you tied your own belt and went where you wanted. But when you are old, you will put out your hands, and someone else will tie your belt. They will lead you where you don't want to go." (Jesus said this to show how Peter would die to give glory to God.) Then he said to Peter, "Follow me!"

REFLECTION:

There was a time when Peter thought he was ready for anything. He wasn't. Jesus told him so. Peter argued with Jesus. Jesus was right, of course. By the time his breakfast was over at the charcoal fire, Peter had been humbled by his own failure and called back to pastoral ministry.

Peter now realizes that the course of his being Jesus' follower begins with humility. He is ready to follow, even if his path will lead to his own death and Jesus lets Peter know that it won't be pleasant. He will be bound and taken somewhere he doesn't want to go. Yet Jesus still says to Peter, "Follow me!"

You and I don't know exactly what the future holds or how our time on earth will end. However, Jesus calls us to follow him and trust him, even if it means a Cross. Let's follow!

PRAYER:

Give me courage and strength, O God, so that I can follow Jesus no matter what challenges, difficulties, or hardships come my way. Please, never ever let me outlive my love for your Son or for you. In Jesus' name I pray. Amen.

CONTEXT: JOHN 21:15-25

RELATED REFERENCES: LUKE 9:21-27; LUKE 14:27; 1 PETER 4:12-19

Day: 364

WHAT ABOUT...?

JOHN 21:20-22

Peter turned and saw the follower Jesus loved very much walking behind them. (This was the follower who had leaned against Jesus at the supper and said, "Lord, who is it that will hand you over?") When Peter saw him behind them he asked Jesus, "Lord, what about him?" Jesus answered, "Maybe I want him to live until I come. That should not matter to you. You follow me!" So a story spread among the followers of Jesus. They were saying that this follower would not die. But Jesus did not say he would not die. He only said, "Maybe I want him to live until I come. That should not matter to you."

REFLECTION:

It is very hard not to compare! We want to compare our lot with others. We want to compare our future with others. We want to compare our faith, our church, our efforts ... to others.

Christianity isn't about comparing. The Lord doesn't grade on the curve. He calls us to follow him whole-heartedly through the course of our uniquely important and distinctive life. Comparing ourselves to others is the cause of envy, jealousy, strife, covetousness, resentment, and a host of other sins. Instead, we are to follow and serve. We are to help encourage others to do the same! Rather than getting involved in the comparison game with other Christians, Jesus simply says, "You follow me!"

PRAYER:

O God, the Almighty and gracious Father, thank you for judging me with grace, empowering me with your Spirit, and calling me to a wonderfully unique life in your service. Forgive me for the times I've been envious of other believers. Forgive me for comparing my faith with others, whose hearts I could not know. Focus me upon your will and lead me to you so that the glory that others see in me is attributed to your grace and presence in my life. In Jesus' name I pray. Amen.

CONTEXT: JOHN 21:15-25

RELATED REFERENCES: JAMES 3:13-18; GALATIANS 6:2-5; ROMANS 14:4

Day: 365

TOO BIG FOR THE WORLD

JOHN 21:24-25

That follower is the one who is telling these things. He is the one who has now written them all down. We know that what he says is true. There are many other things that Jesus did. If every one of them were written down, I think the whole world would not be big enough for all the books that would be written.

REFLECTION:

Jesus' greatness is too big for the world to contain. Why? Because Jesus did many great deeds when he was here. And he continues to do those great deeds for the people of the world. But even though the world could not contain the book that recorded all the good things that Jesus did, Jesus did walk on our planet, look up at our stars, and face our mortal frailties.

Why did Jesus do this? Three reasons were especially important to John as he shared his story of Jesus with us. First, Jesus loves us, as does his Father. God wanted to show us that love up close and in person. God is not distant, but near. Second, we needed Jesus' love, grace, example, message, and truth. There were certain things that only Jesus could teach us. Jesus is not just an example of how God would live on our planet. He is also the perfect example of how a human being should live on our planet. Third, the Father wanted Jesus to come and reveal himself to us. So as we come to the end of this Gospel, let's never forget that we are loved, that we need Jesus, and that Jesus did what he did to honor the Father. Those are good things for us to commit to do in our lives—love others, seek Jesus, and honor God. God bless you as you seek to know and to follow the Lord Jesus in the days ahead.

PRAYER:

Father, as I finish John's story of the life of Jesus, I know that you have moved me closer to you through a deeper knowledge of and walk with your Son. I look forward to the Spirit's transforming work in me in the days ahead, and trust that you will continue that work in me until you call me home. In Jesus' name. Amen.

CONTEXT: JOHN 21:15-25

RELATED REFERENCES: PHILIPPIANS 1:6; PHILIPPIANS 2:13; 2 CORINTHIANS 3:17-18